# Partnering for Content Literacy: PRC2 in Action

# Partnering for Content Literacy: PRC2 in Action

## Developing Academic Language for All Learners

**Donna Ogle**

*National-Louis University*

Boston   Columbus   Indianapolis   New York   San Francisco   Upper Saddle River
Amsterdam   Cape Town   Dubai   London   Madrid   Milan   Munich   Paris   Montreal   Toronto
Delhi   Mexico City   Sao Paulo   Sydney   Hong Kong   Seoul   Singapore   Taipei   Tokyo

**Editor-in-Chief:** *Aurora Martínez Ramos*
**Editorial Assistant:** *Amy Foley*
**Managing Editor:** *Barbara Strickland*
**Marketing Manager:** *Amanda Stedke*
**Production Editor:** *Annette Joseph*
**Editorial Production Service:** *Nesbitt Graphics, Inc.*
**Manufacturing Buyer:** *Megan Cochran*
**Electronic Composition:** *Nesbitt Graphics, Inc.*
**Interior Design:** *Nesbitt Graphics, Inc.*
**Cover Designer:** *Jenny Hart*

**Library of Congress Cataloging-in-Publication Data**
Partnering for content literacy : PRC2 in action : developing academic language for all learners / [edited by] Donna Ogle.
    p. cm.
Includes bibliographical references and index.
    ISBN 978-0-13-245874-0
1. Content area reading—United States. 2. Academic language—United States. 3. Advancing Literacy for Learning (Project) I. Ogle, Donna.
    LB1050.455.P37 2011
    372.47'6—dc22

                                                    2009053912

10  9  8  7  6  5  4  3  2  1   RRD-VA  14  13  12  11  10

**www.pearsonpd.com**

ISBN-10: 0-13-245874-8
ISBN-13: 978-0-13-245874-0

*To Bud and Amy*

*and*

*the Chicago teachers and students
who share in this work*

# About the Author

**Donna Ogle** is Professor of Reading and Language at National-Louis University (NLU) in Chicago, Illinois, and is active in research and professional development projects. She is currently senior consultant to the Chicago Striving Readers Project; Co-Director of the Reading Leadership Institute; and Co-Director of the Literacy Partners Project, a collaboration among the Chicago Public Schools, NLU, and the Chicago Community Trust.

Donna also serves as a literacy consultant internationally, including with Critical Thinking International and Grupo SM in Latin America. She is on the editorial review boards of *Lectura y Vida*, *The Reading Teacher*, and the *Journal of Adolescent and Adult Literacy*. Donna is a past president of the International Reading Association and an elected member of the Reading Hall of Fame. She also conducts research on visual literacy and content comprehension, having developed both the K-W-L and PRC2 (Partner Reading and Content, Too) frameworks. She is the author of many books, book chapters, professional articles, and curriculum materials.

# Contents

**3** Developing Academic Talk: Providing Guidance and Structure 37

*Amy Correa*

**4** Change Across Time: A Look at One Sixth-Grade Classroom 47

*Adam Geisler*

**5** Developing PRC2 in a Primary Classroom 65

*Avni Patel*

## 6 Assessing Students' Interests, Knowledge, and Concepts 91

*Christine Kamp Seidman*

## 7 Teacher Ongoing Assessment 113

*Debbie Gurvitz*

## 12 Activities to Reinforce Vocabulary Learning 233

*Carol Schmitz*

## 13 Academic Talk: Supporting English Learners 261

*Jeannette Hamman*

# Preface

If you want to learn how to successfully develop your students' interests in and strategies for reading and learning from informational texts, this book can be your guide. The chapters have been written by a team of teachers, literacy leaders, and university project members as a result of three years of working together developing our approach to content area reading in the project titled Advancing Literacy for Learning (ALL). The team included teacher leaders who speak English as a second language and several who have lived in other cultures. All of us were and are interested in the challenges of language learning.

The book is very practical; each chapter reflects our years of work in classrooms testing and refining our ideas. Literacy leaders explain the tools that we have developed to assess and guide student learning. Teachers describe in detail how they thought through ways to change their curriculum and use of time so that they could focus more attention on the actual reading, discussion, and development of academic vocabulary as part of content units in social studies and science. This book is not designed to explain the teaching of the content itself; rather, it focuses on ways to build students' abilities to read and comprehend the variety of informational texts that support content learning.

The original concerns that brought us together focused on the challenges and struggles English learners face when they transition from bilingual classrooms to general education classrooms in third and fourth grade. Teachers worried that their students floundered when confronted with difficult textbooks and the need to use academic vocabulary and language. The teachers and literacy leaders wanted to develop ways to ensure that these students could be successful in learning; they knew that some students tend to drop out when the academic challenges seem too great and wanted to prevent this from happening. Although our focus was on the English learners, we soon learned that many students in the middle grades benefited from the same instructional strategies we were developing. As we kept working together, we also gained the interest of some primary teachers, and they extended our work to the lower grades.

What has evolved is a practical and powerful set of assessments and instructional practices focused on partners reading short books and articles together in a process we have named Partner Reading and Content, Too (PRC2). The importance of organizing classroom routines so that students can work with partners was one of our first challenges. In this book, teachers have been very generous in sharing explicitly how they manage their classroom routines, use centers and guided reading groups, create games and activities to focus students' attention on the distinctive features of informational texts, and build academic vocabulary through direct instruction about how words work and the creation of engaging games and activities for students to reinforce their learning. Using assessments to determine students' reading skills and to monitor their learning is foundational to this work. The specific assessments we have developed and ways to modify them for your own students are also included. If you want ideas about how to create a rich program in informational reading, you have come to a good resource.

In Chapter 1, Donna Ogle sets the context for the book: the importance of teachers and school personnel working together with foundations, university personnel, and parents as partners is explained using the development of Project ALL as an example. In Chapters 2 and 3, Amy Correa, Co-Director of Project ALL, describes the central component of our approach to content reading and learning, PRC2, and our focus on discussion as a tool for learning.

Chapters 4 and 5, written by classroom teachers, explain how those teachers rethought their instruction so that they could incorporate PRC2 into their curriculums. In Chapter 4, Adam Geisler describes his journey as a sixth-grade teacher of social studies and the routines he carefully developed over two years that work with his diverse group of students. In Chapter 5, Avni Patel explains how she extended PRC2 into her primary classroom and made several adjustments, including modifying the name to Reading and Thinking with My Buddy. She addresses the major issues she faced when trying to introduce informational reading and discussion to her students and includes mini-lessons she developed in response to student needs.

Good instruction requires good assessments. In Chapter 6, Christine Seidman explains the specific tools we developed to monitor student learning. These include a Table of Contents Assessment to determine students' understanding of basic disciplinary structures, a Concept Web in which students associate key terms with concepts, a Visual Interest Inventory, and vocabulary assessments (Rate Your Knowledge and Morphology). In Chapter 7, Debbie Gurvitz introduces the Classroom Fluency Snapshot as a way to initially match partners based on their reading development and then as a monitoring tool to help both students and teachers track improvements in students' fluency.

In Chapters 8 and 9, Kristina Utley provides explicit guidelines for how she uses PRC2 and academic-vocabulary activities in her classroom. Chapter 8 focuses on how she adapts the partner reading time for her guided reading groups. For anyone wanting to know how to create productive center activities, Chapter 9 is a gold mine. Kristina shares the specific directions for each center, including the content. She also discusses the importance of having specific goals and sharing the outcomes of center activities with students via rubrics.

Renee Mackin explains the importance of slowing down and ensuring that students know the vocabulary needed to navigate the features of informational texts. She realized that many of her students needed time to explore and learn the value of the specific features of these books. Chapter 10 includes the series of activities Renee developed that introduce students to the features and their uses: the table of contents, index, glossary, and illustrations and captions. These are all included, along with a scavenger hunt and a test to check for mastery.

Chapters 11 and 12 concentrate on developing students' interest in vocabulary and their attention to important academic terms. Although most authorities are clear on the importance of building academic vocabulary, many teachers have a hard time making it a regular part of their instruction. Both Margaret McGregor and Carol Schmitz, Literacy Lead Teachers, have worked closely with teachers to develop activities that make vocabulary learning meaningful and the reinforcement activities fun. The resources they have located to support teachers' growing interests in words and their origins are also important in moving attention to vocabulary to a central place in academic instruction.

The final chapter is written by one of our international teacher leaders, Jeannette Hamman, who grew up Irish in England and taught in Wales for a year (and had to learn Welsh). Her interest in language is clear and so is her sensitivity to her mostly Spanish-speaking students. The book closes with this chapter as a reminder that an essential ingredient in a successful classroom and school is that teachers listen to their students and enjoy helping them develop their language abilities. This has been a major conclusion of our work in Project ALL and is an abiding commitment we take from this partnership.

The DVD that accompanies this book is an important component of the message we are sharing. It includes a video of students engaged in PRC2 in urban classrooms, as well as an example of a content unit we developed to support teachers in orchestrating the many components of academic content reading and learning. Our hope is that the unit can be a model you can adapt to your own content and students. Finally, Margaret McGregor has let us include the templates for the vocabulary activities she has developed. She provides clear directions for how to use an Excel spreadsheet to create these engaging reinforcement activities. We hope you will take full advantage of all the resources included in both the text and the DVD.

# Acknowledgments

This book is the outgrowth of Project ALL, a collaboration among the Chicago Public Schools Office of Literacy, the Chicago Community Trust, and the Reading Department of National-Louis University supported by the Searle Funds of the Chicago Community Trust. Without the generous support of these partners, we would not have been granted the time to meet and learn together and to develop the frameworks and activities included in the book.

We owe deep gratitude to the teacher leaders and classroom teachers who invited us into their classrooms and were willing participants in our explorations. In the first year, it was at Carson, Waters, Jordan, and Bateman schools that we found willing teacher collaborators and students who provided us with incredible support and insights. Then the Literacy Lead Teachers at Yates and Casals joined us and we extended our work to classrooms in those schools. In all schools, the principals were important to our efforts and we are grateful for their support.

As editor of this collection of chapters representing the powerful insights of Project ALL participants, I want to especially recognize the team that made my learning so enjoyable over the life of Project ALL. I always looked forward to our Friday gatherings and was never disappointed. It has been one of the highlights of my professional career to have a team this focused and dedicated to improving the school experiences of our urban students. I thank especially Amy Correa, a Chicago Office of Literacy leader, who came to National-Louis University on loan from the Chicago Public Schools to co-direct Project ALL and has been the driving force behind our work. Her experiences as a dual-language teacher and Spanish-first speaker as well as her perceptive leadership abilities have been essential in shaping our partnership. My deep gratitude goes to Peggy Gyftakos, Carol Schmitz, Andalib Kilgati, Jimmi Cannon, Javier Arriola, and Maria Gustafson, our initial team; then to Stephanie Mulder, Renee Mackin, Kris Utley, Jen Hamman, and Margaret

McGregor, who joined our work and added so much as we continued our refinements. Debbie Gurvitz and Chris Seidman, from National-Louis University, were invaluable members of this team, too, providing much-appreciated attention to the assessments and ongoing data collection.

I also wish to thank the editors at Pearson; Mary Sanger at Nesbitt Graphics; and the reviewers, Gail Fazio, Rutgers University, and Ellen Fogelberg, Evanston School District 65, for their insightful comments and suggestions.

# Partnering for Content Literacy: PRC2 in Action

# Developing Reading and Learning with Informational Texts

2

Chapter
One
Developing
Reading and
Learning with
Informational
Texts

*P*artnering for Content Literacy was carefully chosen as the title for this book. Without strong partnerships at many levels, the development of the rich approach to content area reading described in these chapters would not have been possible. Elementary reading instruction in this country is deeply grounded in the use of fiction; expanding teachers' commitments to building a strong informational reading program is challenging. The team of literacy leaders from urban schools involved in this project invested heavily of their professional expertise, influence, and time in addressing the multiple layers of challenge as they worked in their buildings. These challenges included engaging classroom teachers in experimenting with new ways of teaching, demonstrating and modeling in classrooms, locating quality informational texts in social studies and science, developing assessments, creating a unit framework and instructional lessons to build understanding of informational texts, and helping students develop oral discussion of content while engaged with a partner and then with the whole class. The more attention we focused on the array of skills and strategies elementary students need to be successful in learning from informational text materials, the more the complexity of content reading and learning became apparent. As we worked together we developed a primary adaptation called Reading and Thinking with My Buddy, created supports for academic discussions, used technology to create activities to reinforce academic vocabulary learning, created videotapes in classrooms, and created new structures and organizational tools that work with partner and small-group content instruction. Partnering together was essential for all these accomplishments.

Our use of the term *partnering* includes several important types of partnership. At the heart of this concept is the strategy we have developed called Partner Reading and Content, Too (PRC2). This strategy has evolved as part of our commitment to supporting English learners (ELs) as they face the challenges of becoming part of the academic community in elementary schools, especially the challenge of succeeding in reading and learning in the content areas. The following themes, included under the umbrella of partnering, are described in this section:

- Partnering of literacy instruction with content reading
- Partnering of teachers
- Partnering of students
- Partnering of teachers and students
- Partnering materials
- Partnering with parents and community members

# Essential Partnerships

A rich and ongoing instructional program that integrates academic literacy with content learning involves all of the partnerships listed above. Each takes time and thoughtful commitment to develop and involves the school's instructional team. What students learn in one grade needs to be continued as they move along in the succeeding grades so that teachers' efforts aren't lost and the continuity of strategic reading is maintained and deepened each year the children are in school.

## Partnering of Literacy Instruction with Content Reading

Many students need explicit instruction in reading and learning from materials they are expected to use for social studies, math, science, and other academic courses. Teachers who teach students to use and comprehend informational texts that are part of the curriculum enhance students' motivation to learn reading and writing strategies and provide them needed tools to be successful learners. Combining the teaching of reading and writing strategies with the focus on content learning maximizes the students' abilities to attain both objectives. The significant differences between fiction and informational texts in the density of ideas and in the structure and use of visual information mean that all students need and deserve instruction in how to manage these different genres.

One of the most productive ways for this partnering of content and processes or strategies to be effective is through implementation of carefully planned integrated instructional units. In these units, teachers can identify particular types of informational reading and then help students become aware of the particular features and demands of these texts and teach students to read and learn from them. The unit structure permits teachers to include a variety of text materials so that students can explore their commonalities as well as learn to appreciate the range of ways the materials can be presented. As students read more text and discuss ideas, their academic vocabulary also expands. A unit can extend over enough time that students can hear, see, and engage in productive learning experiences with the same content and vocabulary, thus deepening and solidifying their learning.

## Partnering of Teachers and Other Professionals

Forming partnerships between teachers so that all teachers work together ensures that students will benefit from more intensive attention to their learning.

4

Chapter
One
Developing
Reading and
Learning with
Informational
Texts

Reading teachers, bilingual teachers, and special education teachers all work together with the classroom teacher and the content area teacher (if the school is departmentalized) in planning and implementing appropriate differentiated instruction for students. With the current awareness of the limitations of "pull-out" programs (Allington & Cunningham, 2006), it is clear that the more all teachers can be part of a functioning instructional team, the more likely it is that the needs of all students will be met. Keeping students together in regular education settings also ensures that the students will feel honored and recognized as contributing members of the regular education program. Students all want to be part of the mainstream in schools. The more teachers work together in creating differentiated instruction and coaching to address students' specific needs, the more likely it is that this inclusive learning can be achieved. As our work has developed, the response to intervention (RTI) mandate has also evolved, and we have been able to work closely with school intervention teams to provide an instructional framework for regular classroom intervention for students that permits close observation and monitoring of each student's progress.

In this area of teacher partnering, it is particularly important to have bilingual and language teachers as part of the team. Research supports the importance of having ELs in settings where they hear English regularly spoken by native speakers who can model the English language for them. Learning with English speakers also increases the motivation of ELs to use English and receive feedback from their peers.

The work we are engaged in represents another important level of partnering: among the university, the Chicago Public Schools, and the Chicago Community Trust (CCT). Significant educational change requires time, energy, and resources. With the commitment and support from the CCT, the literacy faculty at National-Louis University has entered a long-term partnership with the Chicago Public Schools to engage together in addressing the literacy needs of urban students. The faculty members bring knowledge and experience working closely with students as they develop literacy; the school teachers and administrators bring their understanding of the classrooms, students, and communities, as well as specific needs for which they want collaborative problem-solving. These partnerships take energy and time to create, and from them emerge new formats and strategies for teaching, like those shared in this book.

## Partnering of Students

Partnering students with others in the classroom promotes their learning. One of the biggest needs is for teachers to provide more time for students to engage in productive conversations with each other. Most classroom talk is dominated by teachers who use their platform to engage in explanations; teachers then quiz students to check for their understanding. Mehan (1979) identified this recurrent pattern as the Initiation-Response-Evaluation (I-R-E) model of classroom talk. This model does not encourage students to engage in processing ideas, making connections, and deepening their thinking. When students can relax and listen to each other, when they can express their own ideas, and when they can ask questions, they are most likely to push their thinking (Beck, McKeown, Hamilton, & Kucan, 1997; Goldenberg, 1992–93; Ogle & Beers, 2009; Valdes, Bunch, Snow, & Lee, 2005). In addition, as one student explained, "When I read with my partner he can help me with words, since I don't know English so well; then sometimes I can also help him when we read and talk about the ideas."

Several frameworks for students to work together as partners have evolved over the last decade. Think-Pair-Share (T-P-S) and Turn and Talk are two basic ways teachers periodically stop their own presentations and give students permission to engage in brief dialogues with another classmate. More extensive use of partner and small-group dialogue is encouraged in *Reciprocal Teaching* (Palincsar & Brown, 1986) and in *Questioning the Author* (Beck et al., 1997). Ogle and Beers (2009) also have outlined good partner models for students to use as they read and discuss together. Within both general education and bilingual/second-language instruction (Anthony, 2008), there are strong recommendations that students be given opportunities to talk with a partner about lesson content. Some routines suggest partnering a strong reader or learner with a weaker learner or an EL; others, like PRC2, suggest pairing students with similar learning and language abilities and development.

## Partnering of Teachers and Students

The goal of teaching is for students to become independent learners by building their knowledge each year, mastering more learning strategies, and understanding more about how to monitor their learning and achievement. Teachers who involve students in setting goals and collecting information about their progress help students become much more active partners in their education. The work presented in this book is built on the assumption that honoring and respecting students involves setting clear expectations and providing opportunities for students to begin each unit by identifying what they already know and what they need to learn. When teachers involve students in planning and goal-setting, they build a partnership for learning. Students deserve teachers

6

Chapter
One
Developing
Reading and
Learning with
Informational
Texts

who are interested in creating learning environments for their students and who scaffold so that all students can be successful in pursuing individual goals within a group structure. The more teachers provide clear explanations and model the kinds of learning strategies students need to use and then give them regular opportunities to monitor and evaluate their own progress, the more students gain confidence and control over their learning and the more they feel empowered and engaged.

Students deserve to know what teachers and schools expect of them and what good work looks like. Students also deserve to learn from teachers how to produce quality work. Simple activities like having students keep notebooks in which they list their use of learning strategies, note what they learn each day, and identify key vocabulary they are learning can transform classrooms into shared learning partnerships. Teachers can also help create clear and shared learning by putting content and language objectives on the board or in students' unit guides. Teachers who send their unit objectives home to families add another important dimension to the partnership so that parents can also support students' growing independence as learners.

## Partnering Materials

Partnering materials from a variety of sources help teachers differentiate learning experiences for students. As teachers develop learning activities for the range of students in any classroom with their different skills, interests, and needs, it is important to have a variety of different sources available. Many commercial reading and content textbook programs provide a range of suggestions and materials within their own guides and resources. These are generally well worth exploring and making available. However, with the increasingly diverse range of abilities and backgrounds of our students, it is impossible for these commercial programs to meet the needs of all students in all schools. Therefore, finding the array of resources that will make learning most accessible to all students requires some added work on the part of teachers. In our work in urban schools, we have found the range of reading levels of the students very wide. That led us to collect what we call text sets of small supplementary books that as much as possible reflect the reading levels of the students in a classroom or grade. These supplemental books now are very attractive, have good content, and are generally laid out in ways that make the content accessible to students. These text sets became the foundation for development of content unit guides that include information about the books, the academic vocabulary, assessments to monitor students' learning, and instructional strategies to help students read informational texts. An example of a unit guide is included on the DVD that accompanies this book.

In collecting supplemental materials, we have learned that, in addition to print materials, it is valuable to have materials in auditory and visual formats as well. Many students need to hear and see concepts and ideas before they can read and write them. The Internet is a great resource with many instructional supports available; a teacher can easily introduce a new topic with a short video that permits students to form their own visual images more easily and to be more accurate in the process. For example, in our sixth-grade unit on Ancient Egypt, students are shown a video of life along the Nile in ancient Egypt; the landscape, the physical appearance of the inhabitants, and the architecture are all included. This makes subsequent reading the students will do much more accessible; students can easily create their own mental pictures as they read, based on a short initial video presentation.

Vocabulary in content areas is always a central concern. Teachers can provide audio recordings and supplemental visual materials to give students more support for their vocabulary development. In addition, computer-based programs and specific teacher-made reinforcement activities make vocabulary practice interesting for students. We have also realized that most teachers lack good collections of dictionaries (both monolingual and bilingual) at levels their students can use productively. Dictionaries and thesauruses in both print and electronic formats are important tools for students to have and to use. Lists of cognates and attention to morphology are also important for multilingual classrooms. These resources support the general education program and make it more meaningful and accessible for many learners from other linguistic and cultural backgrounds. When students engage in partner reading, they can also record their conversations so that they can become their own diagnostic evaluators.

The abundance of materials available to support classroom instruction means that teachers can, with some ingenuity and perseverance, find those resources that make learning possible for all students as they work with teachers, as they work with other students in small groups and in partnerships, or when they study independently.

## Partnering with Parents and Community Members

One of the most powerful ways to engage all students in the school learning enterprise is to open the doors of the classroom to parents and community members. This can be done in many ways (Ogle, 2007), from inviting them in

8

Chapter
One
Developing
Reading and
Learning with
Informational
Texts

as speakers and guides, to including them in their children's homework projects, to using them in the classroom as support personnel to read with children or to support their work on computers. Each time a new content unit is initiated, parents should be notified so that they can extend the learning at home by discussing the topic with their children, finding TV and video programs that can be shared, or participating in a variety of other ways.

The more students know that their parents are part of the school community, the more likely they are to engage fully in that community. This partnership means, too, that parents are more likely to ask questions of their children, engage in academic conversations at home, and provide more positive reinforcement to the children for the work they do. Many schools find it valuable to have Parent Learning Nights during which the content of the curriculum and the learning activities the school uses regularly are modeled and explained for parents. Parents may be part of small reading-response groups, may participate in creating a K-W-L (Know, Want to know, Learn) chart on a science unit, or may follow a guide for an Internet Web quest.

## Establishing the Need for This Work

Reading in the twenty-first century demands that students develop high levels of literacy, including academic, visual, and critical literacies. The recognition that teachers need to broaden their approach to reading instruction is evolving. New basal programs, state and national assessments, and publishers of materials for children have all provided much more focus on informational reading and responding than in the past. In addition, content area professional organizations have begun to focus their members' attention on the fact that students must be able to read and learn from print and visual materials if they are going to be successful in academic content learning.

One group for whom good teaching in content or academic literacy is clearly needed is English learners. With the No Child Left Behind (NCLB) yearly assessments and analysis by subgroups, the levels of literacy among our ELs have become clearly visible. Second-language learners continue to lag behind their monolingual classmates. The good news is that, in the last National Assessment of Educational Progress (NAEP) assessments, these ELs have shown small but positive growth, but second-language learners still lag behind. Good instruction can make a clear difference in their academic achievement.

Teachers recognize that ELs have particular challenges in academic content areas—social studies, science, and mathematics. Conversational language develops quite rapidly for ELs, within two to three years, but academic terms and ways of speaking and writing take much longer to develop. Cummins (2003) has indicated that seven to eight years may be needed for students to develop adequate "academic English" and they may never achieve the depth of English that native speakers possess. Several Ph.D. second-language educators we know have expressed frustration at their continued lack of full access to English. It is no wonder that with the increasing numbers of ELs in our schools, teachers are concerned about what they can do to most effectively accelerate their students' learning.

Insistent pleas from Chicago Literacy Lead Teachers (LLTs) who were part of a partner grant sponsored by the CCT that the biggest issues they faced in reading comprehension were related to the increasing numbers of ELs in their schools led to our project and this book. For three years, the Searle funds of the CCT has sponsored our project, Accelerating Literacy for Learning (ALL). The LLTs, or coaches, in six schools with high concentrations of ELs partnered with faculty and associated professionals (facilitators) from National-Louis University in developing rich instructional frameworks and strategic instruction to build students' content reading and learning. As director of the project, I received compensation so that I could be reassigned to the project half-time. I met with the LLTs and our facilitators weekly over two years and periodically since then as we continue to extend our work.

# Theoretical Foundations

Our work builds on years of research in learning, content literacy development, and English language acquisition.

## How Children Learn

Learning is a constructive process that begins with students' curiosity and activation of their prior knowledge. Bransford, Brown, and Cocking (1999), in summarizing the research on learning, identify some key findings:

1.  Students come to school with their own conceptions about the world. It is important for teachers to learn as much as possible about their students' prior knowledge so that school learning can enhance or modify what students already know.

**10**

Chapter
One
Developing
Reading and
Learning with
Informational
Texts

2. Learning involves three levels of understanding: (a) a deep foundation in factual knowledge, (b) basic ideas within the context of a larger conceptual framework, and (c) the ability to organize knowledge in ways that makes retrieval and application easy.

3. Teachers should use a metacognitive orientation to instruction with the goal of helping students take control of their own learning. They do this by setting clear learning goals and monitoring students' progress in achieving them.

The same basic understandings are reflected in Guthrie's research (2003) on Concept-Oriented Reading Instruction (CORI). By embedding intermediate- and middle-grade students' reading instruction in interesting content in science, teachers were able to accelerate students' literacy development. Guthrie identifies this rich instructional grounding as "engaged learning"; his findings are a clear example of the Bransford, Brown, and Cocking (1999) synthesis applied to elementary reading instruction. The Seeds & Roots project at the University of California Berkeley has found similar results in its science reading project. Students learn more in the integrated units (Cervetti, Pearson, Barber, Hiebert, & Bravo, 2007).

These ideas echo suggestions from the field of second-language learning that regularly call for integrated units of instruction. The unit approach provides a wider, deeper, and more extensive time frame for learning. As Pearson, Cervetti, and Tilson (2008) explain, "Situating literacy instruction in subject areas such as science or social studies can create an engaging and authentic context for literacy learning and can invite meaningful involvement in reading and writing."

New content and strategies are not learned quickly; the process Pearson and Gallagher (1983) describe holds true: Teachers model and provide initial input; this focus needs to be applied by students under teacher guidance until students have a good understanding of what is required. Then teachers create settings in which students take over more of the control in small groups or partner situations. Finally, with supported and frequent-enough practice, students develop self-control and use of the content or strategy. Studies regularly confirm that the newer the material or strategy, the more supportive teaching and coaching are needed to ensure student ownership. Students need to understand and become engaged in the instructional focus, and then they need clear and explicit teacher explanation followed by scaffolded opportunities to practice and apply that content or process in increasingly independent settings. Anything worth teaching is worth teaching well, which requires the gradual release of responsibility over an extended time and with varied opportunities to learn, to practice, and to apply the ideas or strategies.

# Content Literacy

Beyond the primary grades and continuing throughout the rest of their lives, the majority of reading students do will be in informational and procedural texts. Yet, these materials are still the least frequently used by elementary reading teachers. Probably part of this is because of the stunning array of well-written and illustrated fiction available to teachers and children. However, outstanding informational books, magazines, and computer-based materials are also available for classroom and personal use.

An essential foundation for enjoying and learning from informational texts of all kinds is awareness of the ways these materials are structured and where the important information is presented (Ogle & Blachowicz, 2001). This means attending to external organization (table of contents, chapters, headings, and so on) and a variety of visual displays (charts, graphs, maps, timelines, diagrams, and pictures). Students also need to recognize how key vocabulary is identified and explained. These are all features that are distinct to informational texts; in fiction they are not important because students already carry a good sense of narrative structure in their heads, and visual features and vocabulary are much less central to the presentation of the content.

To be able to comprehend informational materials, students need visual literacy skills (Callow, 2008; Leu, Kinzer, Coiro, & Cammack, 2004). Yet many teachers have not focused students' attention on each of the types of visual displays found in elementary materials. For example, students must learn to examine pictures and drawings carefully and know a set of questions to ask so that their examination can be thoughtful (Wu, 2007). Students deserve instruction in how to read and interpret and then connect visual displays with the narrative material they are intended to support and explain.

Students are much better able to make sense of informational texts when they look for the underlying framework or structure of the material: sequence, main idea and details (descriptive), compare-contrast, problem-solution, and argument (thesis and supporting arguments). Young children need to learn to use the structures and graphic features of informational materials if they are going to be able to take full advantage of them, comprehend them, and respond to them aesthetically and critically. In contrast to fiction, informational texts carry a table of contents and headings and subheadings, which often provide a good preview of the way the material is structured and can help readers begin to organize their own search for information (Blachowicz & Ogle, 2008).

Academic literacy, the ability to read and respond to informational materials, also requires students to know and develop precise academic vocabulary

12

Chapter
One
Developing
Reading and
Learning with
Informational
Texts

(Marzano, 2004). Most informational materials include a high level of content-specific vocabulary to explain the content. It is possible that in one textbook chapter over a dozen new terms may need to be learned for the content to be understood. Teachers of content areas generally recognize the demands academic vocabulary places on students and try to provide supportive activities and reinforcements (Blachowicz, Fisher, Ogle, & Watts-Taffe, 2007). Of particular importance is students' ability to practice using the new terms in extended contexts both orally and in written pieces of texts they compose. However, it is not easy given the short time teachers have available for instruction.

## Academic Literacy for English Learners

The content literacy task for first- and second-language learners is similar in many ways. Both need to become familiar with the academic discourse of each content area they are studying, and both must learn the important vocabulary. Students need to develop ways of writing and speaking that are academic, and they need to learn to use the textbooks and resource materials in each content area. They generally need to move between text-based and activity-based learning and integrate a variety of modes of input. In fact, many of our urban teachers have made that an important connection for their students who come from dialect-speaking communities.

The research literature on ELs highlights many challenges, too. The widely used Sheltered Instruction Observation Protocol (SIOP) synthesizes the components of effective instruction into eight key areas (Echevarria, Vogt, & Short, 2008):

- Lesson Preparation
- Building Background
- Comprehensible Input
- Strategies for Learning
- Interaction
- Practice/Application
- Lesson Delivery
- Indicators of Review/Assessment

In our use of the SIOP with teachers who have students in their classrooms representing a wide range of ethnicities, the model is particularly strong. It provides a framework for analyzing instruction and for making modifications that support ELs. With our regular education teachers, it was particularly help-ful in raising two issues for consideration by the teachers. The first is the need for comprehensible input. Although this has been a major focus for second-language teachers (VanPatten, 2003), most monolingual regular classroom teachers have not paid much attention to their own communication skills and strategies in the classroom.

The second issue is the idea of including language objectives in addition to content objectives. Most teachers know that identifying the content stan-dard, or benchmark, is important for students to focus their lessons. Most do not know that identifying some key aspect of language that is needed for suc-cess with the content being studied is also important when working with ELs. Teachers who analyze the language needed for success with their content can do a great deal to make the learning tasks much clearer and to create scaffolds to academic discourse for their students.

In fact, many of our urban teachers have made an important connection for their students who come from dialect-speaking communities. They recog-nize that their students do not come from homes where extensive talk occurs; their students come from homes that are like those headed by mothers on wel-fare in the Hart and Risley study (1995) in which opportunities to hear and engage in extended language use are minimal. The need for environments for academic talk and extended opportunities to use content language is clear to them. This problem is highlighted by Anthony (2008), who argues for "output strategies for English-language learners." She suggests three areas through which teachers can increase language output:

- A supportive learning environment: Create "a setting that is safe" in which to produce and explore a new language (p. 474)

- Collaborative conversations or "true collaborative dialogues between the teacher and children in the group" (p. 475)

- Vocabulary instruction: "Robust instruction involves engaging students with word meanings and providing opportunities for children to actively deal with meanings of new vocabulary after they have been introduced." (p. 477)

These frameworks for classroom teaching are helpful with ELs. The research foundation for these instructional modifications are minimal. As August and Shanahan concluded in *Developing Literacy in Second-Language Learners* (2006), much more research is needed. We do know that more attention to aca-demic language and to the critical vocabulary in each academic area as well as more opportunities for students to be actively engaged in using the concepts and language are essential if we are going to strengthen classroom supports for ELs.

14

Chapter
One
Developing
Reading and
Learning with
Informational
Texts

# Developing the PRC2 Approach

As our project evolved, we agreed that we wanted to create a setting in which all students, but particularly ELs, would have more opportunity to successfully engage with the content and language of their academic subjects. We noted that most of the ELs were being asked to use textbooks and other print material well above their reading levels. These materials contained language that was too advanced for their reading level and also used vocabulary beyond their understanding. No links were being made to their first language, so even potentially useful cognates were not activated. Observations in our classrooms and confirmation from other research indicated that students have few opportunities to use language orally. Yet we know that for language to develop, this condition must change. Our work is intended as a support for the regular content instruction; it does not replace that instruction. Over the last three years, we have created an instructional framework for integrating reading in social studies and science units and activities that provide the following:

- Text sets with books at students' independent and instructional reading levels
- Content unit guides (see DVD)
- Pre- and post-assessments of content and academic vocabulary

Developing the PRC2 approach.

- A strategy for students to practice reading and thinking with a partner: PRC2

- A guide for student discussions

- Vocabulary notebooks

- Vocabulary reinforcement activities (see DVD)

- Teacher observation guide with which to make anecdotal records of students' reading and academic conversations

## Visualizing the Classrooms

Teachers who use these units and the strategies embedded within them create classrooms alive with learning. They transform a more traditional approach to lecturing and teacher-dominated lessons and seat work into a collaborative engaged learning community. When walking into one of the rooms, observers often have a hard time locating the teacher. Pairs of students are scattered throughout the classroom—at their desks, on the floor, at learning centers, or on carpeted reading areas. The teacher may be listening to and observing a few sets of partners as they do PRC2. In some classrooms, some students work at learning centers, while others work in small groups or read with their partners.

Visual evidence of student learning is all around the room. On one wall, a large K-W-L chart indicates what students knew at the beginning of the unit and the questions they wanted to have answered. The teacher has typed the questions and students have put sticky notes beside those they have found answers for. Above the chalkboard, students have made webs of words coming from the same roots: *uni*, *duo*, *tre*, and so on. One classroom has a list of English–Spanish cognates for key terms in the Human Body unit. Student work abounds: vocabulary notebooks, PRC2 folders and supplemental books students have brought to share, and pictures of key ideas connected to their learning.

## Transformation Process

These classrooms didn't just happen. Their transformations have come as part of an ongoing collaboration among teachers, administrators, and university faculty. It was the questions and urgency felt by the LLTs, coaches in the Chicago Project (now Chicago Literacy Instruction Project) schools, that brought Project ALL to life. During the first years of the partnership funded by the Searle Funds of CCT and the Chicago Public Schools, National-Louis University faculty worked with ten Chicago schools needing to increase their reading

16

Chapter
One
Developing
Reading and
Learning with
Informational
Texts

achievement. As we delved deeper into the literacy issues, several LLTs expressed their frustration that what they most needed help with was reaching their English learners. When we had an opportunity to apply for a second round of funding, we wrote a proposal that was funded for Project ALL and focused on developing content-reading strategies for ELs. It was the funding and support that has continued from the CCT and the Chicago Public Schools that has made the partnership between the university and the schools possible: the money for faculty to be devoted to the project, the money for the LLTs to participate in our regular professional development meetings, and the money to purchase student materials and develop assessments. For two years, the LLTs from six schools met weekly with university faculty, the project co-director who was a dual-language teacher on loan from the Chicago Public Schools, and a coordinator from the Office of Language and Culture of the Chicago Public Schools. During this intense collaboration, the PRC2 process, the assessments, and the instructional supports were developed. The collaboration continues now but in new forms and with support from other funders.

It has been a cross-school collaboration, too, as the literacy leaders have learned from and with one another. Each year more detail and structure have been added to the project instructional framework. The challenges the LLTs face in reaching students are what propel our work forward; each challenge leads to discussion within our group, which leads to experimentation with new ways to be more explicit or to add some dimension to the learning structure. For example, when one LLT noted that her student pairs didn't engage in much "real talk," it led her and then the group to create a bookmark of ways to respond to a partner: how to receive what the partner says, how to ask for clarification, how to challenge interpretation of a text, and how to make connections and add to the ideas (see Appendix 2.3). By working together we have all grown in our understanding of how difficult it is to change school practices.

*Partnering* and *collaboration* are terms we also apply to many aspects of our work. We are committed to the way content and processes of learning need to be woven together. This involves building literacy and oracy in content. It includes using content to develop oral language and vocabulary as well as bringing students and their experiences and interests together in engaging learning contexts. Academic content learning, content literacy, multiple literacies—the names may vary, but the foundation of this work is to unite processes and content in such a way to maximize their potential for students. In the following chapters by LLTs, teachers, and university faculty, we share the results of our collaboration.

# References

Allington, R., & Cunningham, P. M. (2006). *Schools that work* (3rd ed.). Boston: Allyn & Bacon.

Anthony, A. R. (2008). Output strategies for English-language learners: Theory to practice. *Reading Teacher, 61*(6) 472–482.

August, D., & Shanahan, T. (Eds.). (2006). *Developing literacy in second-language learners: Report of the national literacy panel on language minority children and youth*. Mahwah, NJ: Lawrence Erlbaum.

Beck, I., McKeown, M., Hamilton, R. L., & Kucan, L. (1997). *Questioning the author: An approach for enhancing students' engagement with text*. Newark, DE: International Reading Association.

Blachowicz, C., Fisher, P., Ogle, D., & Watts-Taffe, S. (2007). Vocabulary: Questions from the classroom. *Reading Research Quarterly, 41,* 524–539.

Blachowicz, C., & Ogle, D. (2008). *Reading comprehension: Strategies for independent learners*. New York: Guilford.

Bransford, J. D., Brown, A. L., & Cocking, R. R. (Eds.). (1999). *Brain, mind, experience and school*. Committee on Developments in the Science of Learning and Commission on Behavioral and Social Sciences and Education, National Research Council. Washington, DC: National Academy Press.

Callow, J. (2008). Show me: Principles for assessing students' visual literacy. *Reading Teacher, 61*(8), 616–626.

Cervetti, G. N., Pearson, P. D., Barber, J., Hiebert, E., & Bravo, M. (2007). Integrating literacy and science: The research we have, the research we need. In M. Pressley, A. K. Billman, K. Perry, K. Refitt, & J. Reynolds (Eds.), *Shaping literacy achievement* (pp. 157–174). New York: Guilford.

Cummins, J. (2003). Reading and the bilingual student: Fact and fiction. In G. G. Garcia (Ed.), *English learners: Reaching the highest level of English literacy* (pp. 2–33). Newark, DE: International Reading Association.

Echevarria, J., Vogt, M. E., & Short, D. J. (2008). *Making content comprehensible for English learners: The SIOP model*. Boston: Pearson.

Goldenberg, C. (1992–93). Instructional conversations: Promoting comprehension through discussion. *Reading Teacher, 46*(4), 316–326.

Guthrie, J. T. (2003). Concept-oriented reading instruction. In C. Snow & A. P. Sweet (Eds.), *Rethinking reading comprehension* (pp. 115–140). New York: Guilford.

Hart, B., & Risley, T. R. (1995). *Meaningful differences in the everyday experiences of young American children*. Baltimore: Brookes.

18

Chapter
One
Developing
Reading and
Learning with
Informational
Texts

Leu, D. J., Kinzer, C. K., Coiro, J., & Cammack, D. W. (2004). Toward a theory of new literacies emerging from the Internet and other informational and communication technologies. In R. B. Ruddell & N. Unrau (Eds.), *Theoretical models and processes of reading* (5th ed., pp. 1570–1613). Newark, DE: International Reading Association.

Marzano, R. (2004). *Building background knowledge for academic achievement.* Alexandria, VA: Association for Supervision and Curriculum Development.

Mehan, H. (1979). *Learning lessons.* Cambridge, MA: Harvard University Press.

Ogle, D. (2007). Coming together as readers (2nd ed.). Thousand Oaks, CA: Corwin Press.

Ogle, D., & Beers, J. W. (2009). *Engaging in the language arts: Exploring the power of language.* Boston: Allyn & Bacon.

Ogle, D., & Blachowicz, C. (2001). Beyond literature circles. In C. C. Block & M. Pressley (Eds.), *Comprehension instruction: Research-based best practices.* New York: Guilford.

Palincsar, A. M., & Brown, A. (1986). Interactive teaching to promote independent learning from text. *Reading Teacher, 39,* 771–777.

Pearson, P. D., Cervetti, G. N., & Tilson, J. L. (2008). Reading for understanding. In L. Darling-Hammond (Ed.), *Powerful learning: What we know about teaching for understanding* (pp. 71–111). San Francisco, CA: John Wiley.

Pearson, P. D., & Gallagher, M. (1983). The instruction of reading comprehension. *Contemporary Educational Psychology, 8,* 317–344.

Valdes, G., Bunch, G., Snow, C., & Lee, C., with Matos, L. (2005). Enhancing the development of students' language(s). In L. Darling-Hammond & J. Bransford (Eds.), *Preparing teachers for a changing world: What teachers should learn and be able to do* (pp. 126–168). San Francisco, CA: Jossey-Bass.

VanPatten, B. (2003). *From input to output: A teacher's guide to second language acquisition.* New York: McGraw-Hill.

Wu, X. (2007). All learners visual literacy curriculum. In M. Newman & C. Spirou (Eds.), *Picturing Chicago.* National Endowment for the Humanities. Chicago: National-Louis University.

# The PRC2 Framework

**?** How can I implement the PRC2 framework for content area reading?

In this chapter, **Amy Correa**, Co-Director of Project ALL, explains the basic procedures that have been developed by the Project ALL team so that teachers can implement PRC2 in their classrooms. A key to using PRC2 successfully is motivating all students to be willing to engage at a high level of academic learning through the personal and enjoyable contexts created for learning.

Amy is Co-Director of Project ALL and is one of the directors of the Literacy Partners, a collaboration among National-Louis University, the Chicago Public Schools, and the Chicago Community Trust. Amy began her career as a dual-language teacher in Chicago and then served as an area reading coach and as a Coordinator for the Office of Literacy of the Chicago Public Schools.

***What José's social studies teacher thinks:*** José just doesn't like doing any social studies homework.

***What José thinks:*** I don't like reading my social studies book. . . . It's boring. . . . I don't understand it anyway.

***What Susan's science teacher thinks:*** Susan is a good student during language arts time, she's always got her nose in a book, . . . but when it's time for science . . . she refuses to read.

***What Susan thinks:*** I hate reading science; it's boring and I can't read it as fast as my novels; besides, the rest of the kids will figure out that I don't read as well as they think I do.

Content reading isn't easy for all students. As content area teachers, we take for granted that if a student can read, he or she can read everything we assign as long as it is at grade level. Not so. In the past decade, we have learned much from teacher-educators such as Stephanie Harvey, Doug Buhle, and Cris Tovani about how content reading needs different types of reading strategies than fiction reading. Those teacher-educators have taken the research conducted by researchers such as Richard Allington, Richard Vacca, Donna Ogle, and P. D. Pearson to help teachers understand how to teach content reading. Chapter 1 of this book helps teachers understand *why* we should teach students how to read content; this chapter explains *how* we should teach students content reading in a way that is not only educationally sound but enjoyable to students as well.

## Developing an Instructional Framework

Working together in Project ALL we developed an instructional framework to help teachers adapt content instruction to the range of readers they have within their regular classrooms, paying special attention to adaptations for ELs and other struggling readers. We decided to work within the existing curriculums in both social studies and science and create added supports and scaffolds for students whose reading and vocabulary skills were not at grade level. We left the identification of content standards, objectives, and assessments to the classroom teachers. A central part of our early effort was building text sets, collections of short content-specific books on a variety of reading levels that support key units in social studies and science curriculums for each grade level from 4 through 8. We also knew that students needed to read and discuss content in these books and so explored ways to create meaningful partner reading and, finally, crafted what we now call Partner Reading and Content, Too (PRC2).

## Getting Started with PRC2

In PRC2, the students are partnered together prior to starting the program. Classroom Fluency Snapshots (see Chapter 7), interest inventories, and student personalities are used to partner students. After the Classroom Fluency Snapshots are administered, the teacher has a general understanding of the students' fluency levels. Once those levels are determined, students are matched with the appropriate reading-leveled text. A key purpose of PRC2 is to provide students with materials at their instructional or independent reading levels. Richard Allington's research shows that students need to be put at their differentiated levels (Allington, 2006).

The next step is purchasing a variety of leveled texts around one theme from a variety of publishers who produce high-quality informational texts that have all the elements of informational reading. The texts should include external text features (headings, subheadings, highlighted vocabulary, visual information with captions), internal text structures (sequence, comparison-contrast, cause-effect, problem-solution), and description and text resources (glossary, index, and online references). Once books have been purchased, establishing content-vocabulary instruction and practice for the whole class is essential. (See the text for the Native American Content Unit Guide on the DVD.)

Because a theme may include from four to fifteen different books, it is imperative to choose key vocabulary that hits key contents within the unit. Review the key vocabulary with the whole class. Sometimes we assume that students know pronunciations of words that are common in a discipline. However, many students, especially ELs, may find it helpful for teachers to pronounce the key vocabulary in the unit. For example, when doing a Native American unit, we soon discovered that students were mispronouncing the names of nations. Having the teacher pronounce the words and asking students to repeat the pronunciation several times for the first few days of the unit helped the students greatly; after all, *Iroquois*, *Sioux*, and *Cheyenne* don't sound the way they look.

You know the reading levels of your students, you have purchased appropriate materials, and you have identified and reviewed important content vocabulary; now, before students begin PRC2, you must model the process. We have used PRC2 extensively with grades 1 through 8. Keep in mind that, like reading, the PRC2 process is intricate and has many layers. It is important to model, model, and model this next part with students. Regardless of grade level, you must model this process in different ways. Using the gradual release of responsibility model of instruction developed by Pearson and Gallagher (1983), the teacher moves through the process while students watch. Some teachers model the process with a colleague, while others use the DVD. The teacher is the doer and students are the observers. Once students have seen a good model of the process, the teacher models while students help. Teachers have modeled the process by having the whole class be a united partner and the teacher the other partner. Teachers who have modeled the process in the past will ask a former student to model it for current students. Other teachers teach it to a pair of students until they have mastered the process and then ask the students to model for the rest of the class. This way, students are able to try the process with support from the teacher. The teacher moves around the classroom and listens to the partners. Teachers need to see which students require more support in doing the PRC2 process correctly. Teachers support students by providing immediate feedback on the implementation of the PRC2 process. Finally, with this support, teachers can allow partners to move through the process independently.

# Getting Organized with PRC2 Materials

This chapter is organized according to the PRC2 Student Guide (Appendix 2.1). As they begin a unit of study, students spend the first day getting ready to read together. Ideally, for each unit of study, students have two or three books available at their independent or instructional reading level (if the teacher will be giving support to the partners) that they can choose from. However, they can start off with just one book. Students sit together, bringing with them their PRC2 folder, which includes the PRC2 Student Guide sheet (Appendix 2.1), the PRC2 Questions sheet (Appendix 2.2 or 2.4), the bookmark (Appendix 2.3), the WOW! Look at All I've Read! sheet (Appendix 2.5), and the PRC2: Read & Recommend sheet (Appendix 2.6), as well as their vocabulary notebook and pencil or pen.

## Using the PRC2 Questions Sheet

The PRC2 Questions sheet was developed to help scaffold discussion between the partners. It is important to note that, although the questions are general enough to be relevant to a wide variety of themes and texts, the "why" and "how" aspects of the questions should be fully explored. That is when deeper thinking around the text will happen. It is not enough to ask, "What was most interesting?" One partner should ask the other partner to think about *why* it was most interesting.

When working through the questions, the Project ALL team discussed the lack of knowledge of some of their students around the language of discussion. Some ELs didn't have enough understanding of the syntax of the English language to be able to extend discourse. We found it necessary to supply prompts for students to use to receive what the partner says, elaborate and extend an idea, clarify a statement, make connections, and add a different perspective. Students whose first language is English also benefited from explicitly learning the way to use language to extend thinking. In today's society, where sitting down for a family dinner and engaging in family discussions are becoming less common, all students need to review the language of discourse.

In the PRC2 process, we developed the PRC2 Questions sheet to get to the core of comprehension and discussion for ELs and struggling readers who had a hard time with other established questioning techniques. However, PRC2 is a broad enough process that allows modification of questions used. If you have established a questioning routine in your classroom or if your school uses a specific questioning style—for example, some of our schools used Question–Answer Relationship (QAR) (Raphael, 1986), while others referred to questions as "thick and thin" (Lewin, 1998)—continue using what works for your students.

## Using the WOW! Look at All I've Read! Sheet

The WOW! Look at All I've Read! sheet is used as a reading log (Appendix 2.5). Students write the dates and number of pages read, the title of the nonfiction book, the author, partners who read together (the students should change partners depending on the growth of reading), and whether they would recommend the book to others in the class. Although many teachers use a reading log as a formative assessment tool to know how many books students read and how long it takes them to read a certain number of pages, most reading logs include only fiction. Informational (nonfiction) books are rarely included in those logs. Most classroom libraries have extensive genre collections, the bulk of which are fiction. However, the 2009 NAEP framework uses 50 percent literary passages and 50 percent informational passages in fourth grade, 45 percent literary passages and 55 percent informational passages in eighth grade, and 30 percent literary passages and 70 percent informational passages in twelfth grade in its reading assessments. Students must learn to read informational genre for future success in school, on standardized tests, and later in life. Reading more nonfiction can lead to higher reading achievement (Kletzien & Dreher, 2004; Routman, 2003). By contrast, students with little experience reading nonfiction have difficulty comprehending informational texts and fail to determine the important information within (Stoodt-Hill & Amspaugh-Corson, 2005). Scholastic recommends that 40–60 percent of books in classroom libraries be nonfiction (the higher the grade, the higher the percentage of nonfiction texts). Does your classroom library reflect these percentages?

## Using the PRC2: Read & Recommend Sheet

The PRC2: Read & Recommend sheet serves as a self-reflection on the book (Appendix 2.6). With partners, students answer the questions, thinking about whether they would recommend the book. Questions prompt students to think about what they liked best, what they learned, and what they would have done to make the book better.

# Beginning PRC2

Now students are ready to read together. On the first day, partners preview the cover of the book and the table of contents together. After you have modeled and reviewed how to preview informational books, have students do an infor-mational book talk. With partners, have students talk about the theme of the book. What is the title of the book? What does the cover illustration say about the book? Ask students to discuss the following list and prepare answers.

I. Preview the cover of the book and the table of contents with a partner.

    A. What is the book about?

    B. How is it organized?

    C. Look through the book (a chapter-by-chapter walk-through) and notice:

        1. Organization: chapters and content

        2. Headings and subheadings

        3. Pictures and captions

        4. Illustrations

        5. Diagrams

        6. Boxed information

7. Highlighted vocabulary:

   a. **Boldface**

   b. *Italics*

   c. Boxed definitions

8. Resources in the book: glossary, index, suggested websites, and other books

9. Author's information and book-cover information

D. Make a list of highlighted words on a separate sheet of paper and have your vocabulary notebook ready so that you can write down important words.

---

Many of our students are ELs and struggling readers who need extensive practice and instruction with vocabulary. All students have notebooks that they use to explore words. (See Chapters 11 and 12 for more on vocabulary.)

Day 1 is over . . . and now the fun begins. Students begin reading the book as partners. As previously stated, teacher modeling of this part of the process should have been done extensively before students do it themselves. The core of PRC2 is students reading with leveled texts and discussing their comprehension with a partner for at least twenty minutes of uninterrupted time.

It is now time for students to begin reading. Below is the reading process of PRC2 that students should follow.

## II. Read the book with a partner (sharing one book).

A. Look at the first two pages of text; partners decide who will read page 1 and who will read page 2.

B. Read both pages silently, thinking about meaning.

C. Reread only the page that you will read aloud with the intention of reading aloud with good expression and pace.

D. Choose one of the four questions on the PRC2 Questions sheet (Appendix 2.2) that you want your partner to answer. (Or use other questioning.)

E. Read: Partner 1 reads the first page while Partner 2 listens and is ready to answer a question.

F. Ask a question: Partner 1 asks one question and Partner 2 answers. *If Partner 2 does not recall, he or she is given the book and finds information to answer the question.* The objective is to discuss what was read.

G. Switch: Partner 2 reads the page while Partner 1 listens. Partner 2 asks one question and Partner 1 answers. *If Partner 1 does not recall, he or she looks in the book and finds information to answer the question.*

H. Write down content words that are important to "go deeper." Transfer these words to your vocabulary notebook to learn the words during word study.

I. After twenty minutes of reading, bring the class back together and have students discuss one thing about what they read.

J. Repeat the cycle until the book is finished.

K. Partners fill out the WOW! Look at All I've Read! sheet together.

L. Students pick another book for the theme and continue the process.

Adaptations have been made for earlier readers. Frank DeJohns, a third-grade teacher at Murphy Elementary School in Chicago, has modified our PRC2 Questions sheet to accommodate his third graders (Appendix 2.4). Debbie Sheriff, the Lead Literacy Leader from Jenner School, developed a student poster for support as the primary students went through the process (Figure 2.1). For further information on using PRC2 in a second-grade class, see Chapter 5.

Because partners are reading at their instructional or independent level, the text is accessible to them. The first time the partners both read the two pages is to understand what the author wants them to learn about. In informational text, if the student only reads the second page, he or she will miss things on the previous page that might explain concepts or ideas that are needed to make meaning of the second page. So reading both pages is extremely important. The first reread serves two purposes: one is to prepare to make a performance read; the other is to think of a question that is applicable to the text. The second rereading of only the page originally read provides an opportunity for the reader to read aloud and the partner to practice listening skills. Many students have commented about how much they like reading only to their partner because it is less scary than reading aloud to the class. The National Reading Panel (2000) concluded that reading fluency is an important component of the reading process. Researchers (Dowhower, 1987; Rashotte & Torgesen, 1985; Rasinski, 1990) have shown that repeated readings help with students' fluency. By giving students books appropriate for their independent reading level and allowing for rereading, teachers enable students to become fluent readers who are able to comprehend better what they read.

## Steps for PRC2

1. Sit shoulder to shoulder.

2. Pick 2 pages to read.

3. Read both pages silently.

4. Read your page silently and write a question to ask your partner.

5. Left side read aloud and ask your question.

6. Right side read aloud and ask your question.

7. Complete your sheet.

(Deborah Sheriff, 2007)

After reading each book, students are encouraged to do the following:

III. Reflect on the book.

A. Partners share what they liked and learned from the text.

B. Partners fill out the PRC2: Read & Recommend sheet.

C. Partners check the words and enter the new terms they choose as important in their vocabulary notebook, using the book for definitions, pictures, examples, and other information. (This is a nice shared activity, with both partners contributing to the other's entries.) Partners ask each other: "Do we have more questions?" "Do we want to read another book on the same topic?" and "Do we want to share interesting information?"

Keep in mind that in a classroom of thirty-two students, you can have anywhere from four to fifteen different books, encompassing varying levels of reading ability. Because all the texts are around one theme, content is being learned using the language of appropriate levels. If, for example, you are teaching Ancient Egypt in sixth grade, most books, independent of what reading level they are, will target certain content words (or their derivations): mummies, mummification, mummify, Egypt, archaeologist, hieroglyphics,

Student using his PRC2 notebooks.

and so on. The word *hieroglyphics* appears in the text and glossary of *The Ancient Egyptians* by Lila Perl that Scholastic levels as Lexile level 1320; it also appears in the text and glossary of *Egypt* by Kevin Supples that National Geographic levels as Lexile level 590. They share three more words in their small glossaries. Having students share their texts accomplishes a few things: Students see connections between books; all students share a common vocabulary that they can bring to their textbook; and all students have some information to share, which provides motivation and voice to all readers.

In the beginning, the PRC2 process is complex. However, students catch on quickly because PRC2 provides a structure that helps them gain confidence in their use of informational books, helps them use content vocabulary in real-world situations through discussions, allows them time for interacting with text that is in their zone of proximal development, and provides a safe situation where everyone has a voice.

# References

Allington, R. (2006). Critical factors in designing an effective reading intervention for struggling readers. In C. Cummins (Ed.), *Understanding and implementing reading first initiatives: The changing role of administrators.* Newark, DE: International Reading Association.

Dowhower, S. L. (1987). Effects of repeated reading on second-grade transitional readers' fluency and comprehension. *Reading Research Quarterly, 22,* 389–406.

Kletzien, S. B., & Dreher, M. J. (2004). *Informational text in K–3 classrooms: Helping children read and write.* Newark, DE: International Reading Association.

Lewin, L. (1998). *Great performances: Creating classroom-based assessment tasks.* Alexandria, VA: Association for Supervision and Curriculum Development.

National Reading Panel. (2000). *Report of the National Reading Panel: Teaching children to read. Report of the subgroups* (NIH Publication No. 00-4769). Washington, DC: U.S. Department of Health and Human Services.

Pearson, P. D., & Gallagher, M. (1983). The instruction of reading comprehension. *Contemporary Educational Psychology, 8,* 317–344.

Raphael, T. E. (1986). Teaching question-answer relationships. *Reading Teacher, 39,* 516–520.

Rashotte, C. A., & Torgesen, J. K. (1985). Repeated reading and reading fluency in learning disabled children. *Reading Research Quarterly, 20,* 180–188.

Rasinski, T. V. (1990). Effects of repeated reading and listening-while-reading on reading fluency. *Journal of Educational Research, 83,* 147–150.

Routman, R. (2003). *Reading essentials: The specifics you need to teach reading well.* Portsmouth, NH: Heinemann.

Stoodt-Hill, B., & Amspaugh-Corson, L. (2005). *Children's literature: Discovery of a lifetime* (3rd ed.). Upper Saddle River, NJ: Pearson Merrill Prentice Hall.

## Student References

Perl, L. (2005). *The ancient Egyptians.* New York: Scholastic.

Supples, K. (2005). *Egypt (Civilizations past to present).* Washington, DC: National Geographic.

**Appendix 2.1** Partner Reading and Content, Too (PRC2) Student Guide

## PRC2 Student Guide

### Getting Ready to Read Together

- Choose a book together.
- Find a place where you can sit next to each other.
- Come prepared with your PRC2 folder with PRC2 Questions sheets, WOW! sheet, Read & Recommend sheet, as well as your vocabulary notebook, and pencil or pen.

### Previewing

- Look at the cover and title, and ask each other, "What do we think this book is about?"
- Look for a table of contents, and ask, "How is this book organized?"
- Look through the book together and ask, "Does the book have . . .?"
  - Chapters
  - Headings
  - Pictures and captions
  - Special marked vocabulary
  - Diagrams
  - Maps
  - Charts
  - Index and glossary
  - Author information
  - Book jacket
- Talk about these features.

### Reading the Text Together

- Take turns reading the pages of this book by first deciding who will read page 1, and who will read page 2 aloud.
- Both read the first two pages silently, thinking about what they mean. If there are some words you don't know how to say, ask your partner. If your partner doesn't know, raise your hand and ask the teacher or use the glossary.
- Silently reread the page that you will read aloud, thinking of good expression and pace.
- Choose one of the four questions on the PRC2 Questions sheet (Appendix 2.2) you want to ask your partner.
- The first person reads his or her page aloud, while the other partner listens and thinks about the ideas.
- The reader asks the listener the question he or she chose for that page. The listener explains what he or she thinks. The partners talk about ideas and any questions they have.
- Then the other partner takes a turn and reads page 2 aloud to the partner. The listener thinks about the ideas.
- The reader asks the listener the question he or she chose for that page. The listener explains what he or she thinks. The partners talk about ideas and any questions they have.
- Continue taking turns until you are finished.
- Fill out the WOW! sheet.
- Be ready to share one thing about your reading together with the class.

### Thinking and Talking about the Text

- After reading the pages, share what you liked and learned about the text.
- Attend to the vocabulary you wrote down on the PRC2 Questions sheet.
- Together fill out the PRC2: Read & Recommend sheet

Ask yourselves the following questions:

- Are there words we want to remember? (If so, write them in your vocabulary notebook.)
- Do we have more questions?
- Do we want to read another book on the same topic?
- Do we want to share any interesting information or thoughts with the class?

(Ogle & Correa, 2006)

Appendix **2.2** PRC2 Questions Sheet

| PRC2 Questions Sheet | |
|---|---|
| Name: _____ Partner: _____ | |
| Title: _____ Date: _____ Page ____ to Page ____ | |
| **What was most important? Why? (Explain)** | **What was most interesting? Why? (Explain)** |
| | |
| **What connections can you make? How? (Explain)** | **What could the author make clearer? How? (Explain)** |
| | |
| **Vocabulary: What are important words to remember?** | |
| | |

(Ogle & Correa, 2006)

## Bookmark

Receiving what the partner says
- Thank you.
- Those are good ideas.
- That was interesting.
- You helped me understand this in a new way.

Asking for more elaboration and extension of the idea
- Can you tell me more?
- What does that mean?
- Can you think of another example?
- What you said reminds me of . . .

Asking for clarification
- Can you explain that a little more?
- I'm not sure what you mean; can you say it in a different way?
- Where in the text did you find that idea?
- Can you tell me why you think that?

Making connections
- That's an interesting connection; I was thinking of something else.
- I make that connection with . . .
- I think this is like . . .
- I remember when . . .
- I remember reading about . . .
- It reminds me of . . .

Add a different perspective
- That's interesting.
- I hadn't thought of it in that way. I was thinking something different.

(Ogle & Correa, 2006)

**Appendix 2.4** Questions Sheet for the Primary Classroom

---

### PRC2 Questions Sheet: Adapted for Third Grade

Name: _____ Partner: _____

| What was the most *important* thing you learned from this text? Why is this important? | What was the most *interesting* thing you learned from this text? Why did you find it interesting? |
| --- | --- |
| _____ | _____ |
| _____ | _____ |
| _____ | _____ |
| _____ | _____ |
| _____ | _____ |
| _____ | _____ |
| _____ | _____ |

Partner
Reading
and
Content,
TOO!

| List some vocabulary words you think the author wants you to remember. | Draw a picture of something that interested you from your reading. |
| --- | --- |
| _____  _____ | |
| _____  _____ | |
| _____  _____ | |
| _____  _____ | |
| _____  _____ | |
| _____  _____ | |

(Frank DeJohns, 2007)

| WOW! Look at All I've Read! | | | | |
|---|---|---|---|---|
| **Name:** _____ | | | | |
| Date(s) and Pages Read | Title | Author(s) | Partner(s) I Read With | Recommend? YES/NO |
| | | | | |
| | | | | |
| | | | | |
| | | | | |
| | | | | |
| | | | | |
| | | | | |
| | | | | |
| | | | | |
| | | | | |

(Ogle & Correa, 2006)

**Appendix 2.6** PRC2: Read & Recommend

## PRC2: Read & Recommend

Partner: _____

Partner: _____

Title: _____ Author: _____

1. Would you recommend this book?

     _____ Highly Recommended ☺

     _____ Good and Interesting ☺

     _____ Not Recommended ☹

2. What did you like best about this book? _____

   _____

   _____

   _____

   _____

3. What did you learn? _____

   _____

   _____

   _____

   _____

   _____

4. How would you make the book better? _____

   _____

   _____

   _____

   _____

(Ogle & Correa, 2006)

# Developing Academic Talk

## Providing Guidance and Structure

**?** How can I improve the quality and quantity of student talk in PRC2?

In this chapter, **Amy Correa**, Co-Director of Project ALL, addresses the challenge of improving student talk in content area reading.

Amy is Co-Director of Project ALL and is one of the directors of the Literacy Partners, a collaboration among National-Louis University, the Chicago Public Schools, and the Chicago Community Trust. Amy began her career as a dual-language teacher in Chicago and then served as an area reading coach and as a Coordinator for the Office of Literacy of the Chicago Public Schools.

38

Chapter
Three
Developing
Academic Talk:
Providing
Guidance and
Structure

In the first year of PRC2 implementation, we quickly noticed that student conversations weren't what we had anticipated. In fact, there was little student talk going on at all. We observed an interaction that modeled what students have experienced in schools for far too long: One student would ask a question, already knowing the "right" answer, and the other student would answer it. The student who asked the question would either confirm that the other student's answer was right or wrong and then follow with another question or just stop "discussing" and move on, and the partner would begin reading the next page. The students were displaying a discussion, or talk, pattern that reflected what they had seen modeled by their teachers.

Teachers (myself included) have modeled this discussion pattern because it was part of our own school experience. As teachers, we know what the right answer is. It is our job to "teach" students. We *initiate* the discussion by asking a question of what has been read. We look for a student to *respond*. We *evaluate* the student's response and the moment. If the answer is correct, we initiate another question for another student to answer to be able to evaluate that student's answer. If the response is incorrect, we continue to look for the "right" answer; responding kindly, perhaps, "Nice try, Michael, but, Suzy, could you help Michael?" This type of so-called discussion is what Cazden (1986) has referred to as I-R-E (Initiation-Response-Evaluation). In research conducted by Almasi (1995), 85 percent of teacher-led discussions fit this I-R-E–type discourse. Our students were using the only model they knew. Sadder yet, Almasi found that discussions were dominated by the teacher, who was responsible for asking 93 percent of the questions and for talking 62 percent of the time.

Not only are students unaccustomed to engaging in true discussions at school, but also, in today's society, they have less time to practice the art of discourse at home. Thirty years ago, having dinner as a family and talking about the events of the day were a daily occurrence. Today, with mom picking up Joey from school to drive him to soccer practice and then to karate lessons while dad picks up Steven from the after-school program and grabs some fast food that they eat in the car before Steven's piano lesson, there is less opportunity for discourse. Or Mary may come home to an empty house, heat up the supper her mom left for her, and do her homework until her mom comes home from work. With schedules like these, families have to plan for a dinner together, perhaps once or twice a week. Time for extended talk is precious!

# How Did We Get Students to Talk?

Teachers working on Project ALL were challenged to develop a classroom culture in which student talk was a focus. This wasn't easy. Some of our teachers were similar to Almasi's teachers, who were asking almost all of the questions and talking most of the time. Others were just the opposite, letting the students talk about anything—but not necessarily academic subjects. We asked teachers to try various activities throughout the day and subjects that promote student talk. Those activities included Turn and Talk, T-P-S, T-P-S Square, and, of course, PRC2. Slowly, a classroom culture that encouraged and respected the importance of student talk began to develop.

Although having a climate in which student talk is encouraged was important, we found that students needed scaffolding to learn the basics of polite discussion. Some students did not have the cultural understanding of American classroom discourse; other students were not always tactful about how to disagree with another viewpoint. The Project ALL team created a guide for discussion stems that some teachers made into bookmarks on how to encourage academic talk with a partner or in a group. We discussed what we thought were important moves (how to receive what a partner says and then how to ask for appropriate elaboration) in shared discussion. We listened to students while they were engaged in PRC2 and made notes of how they expressed ideas. From our brainstorming and refinement, we developed some general exchanges that needed to occur regularly for rich discussion to develop. We gave these to students so they could expand their own speaking. They are on the question guide (Appendix 2.2) and in a bookmark format.

In working with students and modeling these responses, we decided that students should see some basic discussion stems for themselves, not just listen to and copy our oral modeling. We found that by including the prompts in a bookmark (see Appendix 2.3), the list was less cumbersome for students to use. The prompts fall under five general categories: receiving what the partner says, asking for more elaboration and extension of an idea, asking for clarification, making connections, and adding a different perspective.

*Receiving what the partner says*

- Thank you.
- Those are good ideas.
- That was interesting.
- You helped me understand this in a new way.

40

Chapter
Three
Developing
Academic Talk:
Providing
Guidance and
Structure

*Asking for elaboration and extension of the idea*

- Can you tell me more?
- What does that mean?
- Can you think of another example?
- What you said reminds me of . . .

*Asking for clarification*

- Can you explain that a little more?
- I'm not sure what you mean; can you say it in a different way?
- Where in the text did you find that idea?
- Can you tell me why you think that?

*Making connections*

- That's an interesting connection; I was thinking of something else.
- I made that connection with . . .
- I think this is like . . .
- I remember when . . .
- I remember reading about . . .
- It reminds me of . . .

*Add a different perspective*

- That's interesting.
- I hadn't thought of it in that way. I was thinking something different.

# Now That They're Talking . . . How Do I Know That It Is Academic Talk?

For content area teachers who see their students for only forty-five minutes a day, many do not have an opportunity to really get to know what their students know if it isn't in a test. We have learned that when teachers develop a PRC2 segment of their class period, they can create a space to listen to their students. We experimented with ways to take notes on these conversations and finally developed a form for this purpose. See an example of this form, Observation Notes for PRC2, in Appendix 3.1 at the end of this chapter. Teachers can use this when they want to assess how well students are engaging in PRC2. The teacher needs to sit close enough behind the two students to be able to hear their exchanges. The top section of the Observation Notes form allows teachers to record how fluently students read orally to each other. The next section is for notes of their discussion as students talk about the text: are the exchanges focused, do the students elaborate on ideas, are key points identified, and do the students use the academic vocabulary? The bottom section is for teachers' reflections on what they have observed and for ways they plan to follow up to help students in their reading, in use of academic discussion, and in understanding of the content. As students are engaged in PRC2, teachers have found they can observe two to three student pairs each day. If PRC2 is done daily, by the end of a week teachers will have observation notes on the entire class. For content area teachers, this information is invaluable. Teachers can verify not only whether the talk is academic but also, more importantly, what content information students are comprehending.

Let's look at a real-life example. Alma and Maria are fifth-grade students who are learning about Native Americans. Alma and Maria are reading National Geographic's *The Iroquois: People of the Northeast* by Rudy Maile. Alma has just finished reading her page out loud. This is what she read:

> The Iroquois are a group of Native American nations. The Iroquois lived south and east of Lake Ontario. This area is now upstate New York. French settlers named these people the Iroquois, but they prefer the name Haudenosaunee. The word means "people of the longhouse." The name comes from the houses the people lived in.

Partners enjoy sharing the book content.

41

Now That They're Talking . . . How Do I Know That It Is Academic Talk?

42

Chapter
Three
Developing
Academic Talk:
Providing
Guidance and
Structure

The Iroquois are a group of five nations, the Mohawk, Cayuga, Onondaga, Oneida, and Seneca. Once, these people were at war with each other. But they made peace and came together to form the Iroquois Confederacy, also called the League of Five Nations. The League was formed around 1570.

Although each nation had its own beliefs, all followed the laws of the League. The most important was the Great Law of Peace. It said that the Iroquois should not kill each other. In 1722, another nation called the Tuscarora joined the Iroquois Confederacy, making it the League of Six Nations. (p. 6)

The following is a transcription of Alma and Maria's discussion:

*Alma:* Now, my question is what was most interesting about the south and east of Lake Ontario?

*Maria:* That, that, that this was, now is New York City and a lot of people live there. Also, upstate New York, and that the Iroquois lived there and they had many peoples. The French settlers named these people the Iroquois, but they were called the Handensee (pronunciation) so that's sad. What about you . . . what do you think?

*Alma:* I think that, yea, I agree with you, it is important . . . interesting it is now upstate New York and it is cool if you ever go to the north of New York, you go upstate you think . . . like wow, like all the Indians and group of people they were here, they were actually here. Could you tell me more about the Iroquois?

*Maria:* The Iroquois are a group of five nations and those five nations they were all fighting, but they came together and had peace. They have . . . the great law of peace and everyone followed that. And basically said not to kill each other.

*Alma:* So, but what exactly does the Great Law of Peace mean?

*Maria:* It means that the Iroquois Nations cannot kill each other.

*Alma:* That's interesting. More people should follow that law.

As I jotted down notes on the Observation Notes for PRC2 form, I noticed that Alma (as well as many other students) had trouble with the pronunciation of the various nations. I need to use this information to guide my instruction. I need to review the pronunciation of the nations, perhaps allowing students to chorus read them with me until their pronunciations are accurate. As I jot down notes on the Talking About the Text section, I find that Alma and Maria are focused on their discussion about the text. They were talking politely and were able to extend the discussion and elaborate on ideas. They used several of the academic vocabulary words in their discussion, including terms such as *Lake Ontario*, *upstate New York*, *Iroquois*, *Haudenosaunee* (although mispronounced), *five nations*, and *Iroquois Nations*. They were able to discuss such concepts as the Iroquois lived in present-day upstate New York; French settlers named the Haudenosaunee tribe "Iroquois"; the Iroquois was one of five Indian nations that were at one time at war but joined forces in peace; and the Great Law of Peace, which the Iroquois nation has to follow, is not to kill each other.

Using the Observation Notes for PRC2 form, I create anecdotal records of student learning, giving me tangible evidence that student talk helps students with comprehension. Alma, who is a second-language learner, is benefiting from PRC2. This approach to learning encourages students to use their English even though it is imperfect. Vygotsky (1978) has pointed out the importance of social interaction for academic success. Alma has what Vygotsky calls the "knowledgeable other"—in this case, Maria, who helps Alma in her comprehension of the text. You may notice that Alma's response, which is general, uses her questions to Maria to help clarify meaning.

## How Do You Move Student Dialogues Forward?

Explicit instruction on what constitutes good dialogue is necessary for students before they can be expected to engage successfully in academic discourse. Although using the prompts and showing students when to use which stems may seem awkward at first, teachers are able to model good dialogue. We have found that with practice student discussions become second nature. Teaching that good questions are often a precursor to good discussion helps students learn to engage in good dialogue.

Students engaged in academic discussion in a comfortable corner of their classroom.

44

Chapter
Three
Developing
Academic Talk:
Providing
Guidance and
Structure

Modeling how to ask good questions as well as modeling good discussions is important. You may have to model how to engage in academic discourse several times. Some teachers model with another teacher as a partner and have students write down what they notice about their discussion and then share with the whole group what they noticed and why they think it was important to the discussion. Other teachers model with a student as a partner and have the other students critique the dialogue. Still other teachers invite former students to come back and model good discussion. The more opportunities students have to see what the expectation is, the more likely those students will be successful.

Some teachers use the fishbowl technique to spotlight good partner dialogue. The students sit in a circle and two partners sit in the middle. The partners begin a dialogue and the other students take notes on what they observe. This technique serves two purposes: First, the spotlighted partners receive positive reinforcement, and, second, the students who are observing realize that if classmates are able to do it, they are too. Note that it is not just the "good" readers who can or should be spotlighted. Because the materials the students are reading from are at their independent or instructional level, the discussion is the focus. Every student could have a rich discussion if he or she is able to understand the text.

Another way to have students explore and analyze what makes academic discussions rich is to have them listen to audiotapes of other students. Project ALL has several audiotapes of students at various grade levels discussing text. Teachers are able to use audiotapes of students from different schools for their students to critique without worrying about any social repercussion. Anonymity has a way of making the students be free to evaluate without feeling that someone's feelings could be hurt.

Finally, teachers have encouraged student talk to move forward through the use of self-evaluation or partner evaluation. Students can check off rubrics on their perception of how well they did using academic discourse after each PRC2 session. Alternatively, students can fill out exit slips explaining what part of their discussion from that day they want to share and including concrete examples that made their discussion a good one.

Oral language skill is one of the aspects of PRC2 that promotes academic discussion between partners. Gambrell (1996) explains, "Discussion brings together listening, speaking, and thinking skills as participants engage in exchanging ideas, responding, and reacting to texts as well as to the ideas of others" (p. 26).

# References

Almasi, J. F. (1995). The nature of fourth graders' sociocognitive conflicts in peer-led and teacher-led discussions of literature. *Reading Research Quarterly, 30*(3), 314–351.

Cazden, C. B. (1986). Classroom discourse. In M. C. Wittrock (Ed.), *Handbook of research on teaching* (3rd ed., pp. 432–463). New York: Macmillan.

Gambrell, L. B. (1996). What research reveals about discussion. In L. B. Gambrell & J. F. Almasi (Eds.), *Lively discussions! Fostering engaged reading.* Newark, DE: International Reading Association.

Maile, R. (2007). *The Iroquois: People of the Northeast.* Washington, DC: National Geographic.

Vygotsky, L. (1978). *Mind in society.* Cambridge, MA: Harvard University Press.

## Observation Notes for PRC2

Partner 1: _____ Title of book: _____

Partner 2: _____ Date: _____ # of sessions with book: _____

| Partner 1 | Partner 2 |
|---|---|
| **Oral Reading Notes** | **Oral Reading Notes** |
| Attends to punctuation, pronunciation, phrasing; attends to new or unfamiliar terms; uses fix-up strategies. | Attends to punctuation, pronunciation, phrasing; attends to new or unfamiliar terms; uses fix-up strategies. |
| **Talking about the Text** | **Talking about the Text** |
| On topic; key points identified; focused dialogue; good listening; use of key academic terms. | On topic; key points identified; focused dialogue; good listening; use of key academic terms. |

**Teacher Reflections**

Partners' social behaviors, communication, pacing, motivation, level, lack of understanding of content (comprehension), instructional needs, follow-up plans, etc.

(Ogle & Correa, 2008)

# Change Across Time

## A Look at One Sixth-Grade Classroom

**?** How can I differentiate content area instruction for the range of my students' reading abilities?

In this chapter, **Adam Geisler**, a classroom teacher, addresses the challenge of differentiation in content area reading.

Adam is a sixth-grade social studies and language arts teacher at Bateman Elementary School in Chicago, Illinois. He has also taught in Atlanta, Georgia, and Beijing, China. When not teaching about ancient history, he coaches the school's chess club. He enjoys the diversity of his students, whose families come from throughout the world, from Mexico to the Philippines.

48

Chapter
Four
Change Across
Time: A Look at
One Sixth-Grade
Classroom

Teaching social studies and science from textbooks presents a challenge in a classroom with readers of many levels. The vocabulary alone is often at a level that proves difficult for on-grade-level readers. Factoring in more complex sentence structures in the text and the limited background knowledge of many students shows that content area instruction can be daunting.

Enter PRC2. When my school's Lead Literacy Teacher offered me the opportunity to access leveled books on Ancient Egypt, I accepted immediately. My sixth-grade class had an upcoming unit on the topic. I soon discovered that the project that I was joining included an innovative method to incorporate the supplemental texts.

Over the next two years, I experimented with different applications of PRC2. This chapter focuses primarily on my initial attempts to use PRC2 and the adjustments I made. Although it also includes some of the changes I made during the second year, my first encounters with the project will more likely give prospective or current teachers a more realistic idea of PRC2's immediate value. The purpose of this chapter is to show how the various strategies and components of the project can be feasibly worked into a classroom routine. In addition, I hope to convince teachers that PRC2 can become an important asset to a rich literacy-based classroom.

# Background on My Classroom

Our school is on the north side of Chicago in a diverse neighborhood. Several countries are represented by the children within each classroom. In my two years as a sixth-grade teacher, our room welcomed children from Colombia, Dominican Republic, Ecuador, Guatemala, Mexico, Algeria, Liberia, Bosnia, Philippines, Thailand, and Vietnam. Bilingual education is offered through fifth grade. From sixth through eighth grades, the students receive EL instruction from a resource teacher. Over 90 percent of the students within the school receive free or reduced-cost lunch. The building functions as a neighborhood school with an enrollment, as of 2008, of 840 students in grades PreK through 8. In the 2006–2007 school year, the sixth grade was divided among four teachers, one of whom taught a group selected for the school's gifted program. My class had an average of twenty-five students, with transfers in and out occurring throughout the year.

# Beginning the PRC2 Journey

Once I found out that the PRC2 project would be ongoing, I felt that I should inform the students that they would get to be a part of it. With enthusiasm, I held up one of the Egypt books with a colorful cover, declaring, "We're going to take a trip outside the textbook to start our Ancient Egypt unit!" I told the students that we would officially begin in about two weeks, but that I would share the books in the classroom library to give them a chance to see the books ahead of time.

## Preparing the Classroom and the Schedule

After learning the PRC2 procedure in a series of seminars, I had to determine the best way to include it in my daily classroom schedule. Social studies had already been spread over four days during the week, with forty minutes for each lesson. I decided to place the partner-reading element every other day. The forty minutes would be split into three components: introduction/mini-lesson (five minutes), reading (thirty minutes), closing/sharing (five minutes). The components are explained in more detail later in this chapter.

In preparing the classroom environment, I had to visualize what I wanted the classroom to look like while partner reading would be taking place. Spatial-arrangement considerations included proximity of each pair of readers, access and storage of materials, and ease of teacher monitoring. To avoid the potential cacophony of twenty or more students reading aloud simultaneously, I discussed the following key points with the students to keep in mind during partner reading:

- Use "six-inch voices" when reading and discussing (that is, speak loud enough for your partner to hear you but not so loud that the nearest group is disrupted).

- Face a different direction than the two nearest groups.

- If a nearby group is too loud or disruptive, politely ask them to quiet down (for example, "I can't hear my partner, can you please talk quieter?").

- If a group does not comply, approach the teacher to follow through with the request.

Initially, the leveled books were the only item used during partner reading. After the first few practice reading sessions, I introduced composition

50

Chapter
Four
Change Across
Time: A Look at
One Sixth-Grade
Classroom

notebooks. (Later in this chapter, I discuss how I used other materials to create a more organized and efficient system.) Finally, to ensure that I could roam the room with relative ease, I sketched a diagram of desk, table, and open-space arrangements.

## Administering Pre-Assessments

Before I could begin using PRC2 in the classroom, I had to administer a Classroom Fluency Snapshot to ascertain the current reading levels of each student. The results of the snapshot, a sixty-second reading assessment, would be used to place the readers in pairs. It is essential to have the reading partners on similar levels in order to match proper texts to the partners. I chose to do these snapshots during the independent reading block of my daily schedule. This allowed me to complete the snapshots for the entire class within two days. I compiled the results from all twenty-four students and paired them from lowest to highest, beginning with the two lowest-level readers. There was, as expected, a relative bell curve. This actually allowed me some flexibility in grouping, to match compatible personalities.

Next, to get a base of the students' prior knowledge of ancient Egypt, the four pre-tests (Visual Interest, Idea Web, Table of Contents, and Morphology) were administered. (See Chapter 6 for more explanation.) It was important to introduce each handout separately so that the students knew what was expected. The two pre-tests that needed the most explanation were the Visual Interest Inventory and the Morphology Assessment. I found it necessary to emphasize that only one book could be selected from each row on the Visual Interest Inventory. Meanwhile, for the Morphology Assessment, the students benefited from a read-aloud of the directions, as well as an explanation of the difference between a syllable and a morpheme. Of course, as a pre-assessment, I wanted to determine what the students knew, so I avoided using any of the items on the page (other than the provided example) to explain morphology.

## Introducing PRC2 to the Students

The next step in preparing the students to begin using PRC2 was to establish a reliable procedure. Any classroom routine lives or dies by its modeling. The first session would need to be a basic introduction of the PRC2 method, followed by questions that the students might have. To effectively model the method, I asked Juan to serve as my partner. At the front of the room, using the book *Egypt: Past and Present* (Brega, 2006), we went step-by-step through the following partner-reading techniques, recording each on chart paper.

1. **Preview the book.** We demonstrated a conversation about the features of an informational book that typically stand out: table of contents, pictures and captions, headings, highlighted vocabulary words, and other eye-catching elements. We asked each other questions like, "What is this book about?" "How is it organized?" and "What looks interesting to you?" It naturally turned into a conversation about our expectations of the book's contents.

2. **Decide which side of the book each partner will take.** This is an important detail to model. I emphasized that this allows each reader to concentrate on his or her side of the book's main points and anticipate what the partner's side would reveal.

3. **Silently read your page and write a comprehension question.** While Juan read silently, I informed the students that the first reading is an opportunity to become familiar with the words and ideas of your assigned page. I then asked them to describe a good comprehension question. I recorded their ideas on the chart paper. One student, Gloria, said that they should not be *yes/no* questions; they should be able to be answered from the page that was read (not from previous knowledge); and they should be "not too easy and not too hard." I asked for clarification on that last suggestion. David compared it to the research questions we had recently discussed for independent research projects the students were working on. We had decided that *what, how,* and *why* questions were the best way to get deeper ideas.

4. **Read your page aloud to your partner.** Before reading, I reminded the students of the importance of the six-inch voice, although our demonstration was loud enough for the entire room to hear.

5. **Ask your partner your comprehension question.** Juan was able to answer the question. However, I asked the students to consider what should be done if the partner is unable to answer. They first suggested that the reader should think of a different question. I responded that although that may be possible, might the student find another way to answer the initial question? They surmised that the partner could be allowed to review the text that was read.

6. **Repeat the procedure for the next page.** I emphasized that both partners are equally involved. While Partner A reads, Partner B listens intently, and vice versa.

52

Chapter
Four
Change Across
Time: A Look at
One Sixth-Grade
Classroom

Reviewing the steps in PRC2 to check student understanding.

Rather than transitioning immediately to the vocabulary component of the unit, I wanted to allow the students some time to acquaint themselves with the PRC2 procedure. After the introduction, I asked the students to review the step-by-step method, as I recorded it on chart paper, with the title Partner Reading and Content, Too (PRC2).

Following the review, I fielded questions that the students had: "What do we do if we don't know a word?" "What do we do when we finish the book?" "Are we always going to have the same partner?" "How long do we have?" "Do we pick the book?"

I complimented them on their strong questions, happy to see them so curious and eager. We discussed each important question with the following suggestions:

*". . . don't know a word?"*

- You can ask your partner for help.
- You can refer to the Vocabulary Strategies poster (which we already had on the wall).
- You can write the word down to investigate later.

*". . . when we finish?"*

- You can talk about the book.

- You can review the book.
- You can check the words you didn't know.

I also took this opportunity to tell them about the PRC2: Read & Recommend form (see Appendix 2.6) that they would be using.

*". . . have the same partner?"*

- You will have the same partner for at least the whole book.
- If your partner is absent, you will either be matched with someone else without a partner or join a pair of readers.

I explained the purpose of the Classroom Fluency Snapshot and how the leveled books are matched to each student's instructional reading level. I let them know that there will be multiple snapshots throughout the year and that the partners may change as a result.

*"How long . . . ?"*

- You will usually have about thirty minutes to read.
- There will often be an introduction or a focus before beginning to read.
- There will be about five minutes at the end of every session for sharing interesting facts or cool ideas.
- Some days the reading time will be shorter so that you can complete an activity related to the book.

*". . . pick the book?"*

- Most of the books will be assigned, but there will be times when you finish a book and can choose another.
- You will likely read at least three books during the unit, which lasts four weeks.
- All the books will be available for browsing during independent-reading time.

That introduction took forty minutes, so I felt confident that we had a good launching point. I was anxious to get the books into the students' hands. With fifteen books and twenty-four students, I had enough for all partners to begin with a text. The reading levels didn't match each student exactly, but they fell into an instructional range that I felt was adequate for the purpose of partner reading.

54

Chapter
Four
Change Across
Time: A Look at
One Sixth-Grade
Classroom

# Practicing Partner Reading

Two days later, to pique the students' interest for the second session, I announced the title of each book, followed by the partners who were going to read it. I informed the students that this first session would be a chance to practice the PRC2 method of partner reading that we would be using. We reviewed the procedure that was recorded on chart paper two days before. On an overhead transparency, I had drawn a bird's-eye-view diagram of the room's arrangement. Each area of this room was assigned a number and, as I handed a book to every pair of students, they sat at the appropriate location. I wrote in the initials of each student on the diagram, so it would expedite the process of finding their spot next time. Figure 4.1 shows this form with student initials indicating where they would be sitting.

As soon as all students had found their spots, I got their attention one more time before they began to read. I asked the students to recall the expectations for respecting the other groups while reading, referring to the chart paper that had been posted. Finally, I told the students that I'd be floating around the room, offering assistance, answering questions, and listening in.

That first full reading session went fairly smoothly. Of course, there were a few groups who needed some redirection. I reminded them that while today they are just reading and asking questions to practice the PRC2 method, in future sessions, they will be expected to respond more in writing. One issue that arose was the uneven distribution of text from page to page. For instance, in one book, the left-hand pages contained the majority of the content, while the right-hand pages were more illustration-based. I asked the two students how that problem could be overcome. They suggested switching sides. I had them determine first, whether that pattern persists through the whole book (which it did). Next, they took the total number of pages in the book and cut it in half to find the place where they would switch sides. (Sneaking a little math in never hurts.) This did not solve the problem, however, of what to do about the reader who has the illustration side while the other student silently read the text on the content side. Jennifer offered the idea of using that time to write down questions about the illustrations. I also added that there would be opportunities to work on vocabulary during that time.

With ten minutes remaining, I asked the students to finish the page they were on and to talk about the content of their books. As they wrapped up, I asked the students to return to their seats so that we could discuss how our first attempt at partner reading went. On chart paper, I drew a T-chart with titles: "What went well/What didn't." The students responded:

Figure 4.1 Bird's-Eye View of Classroom

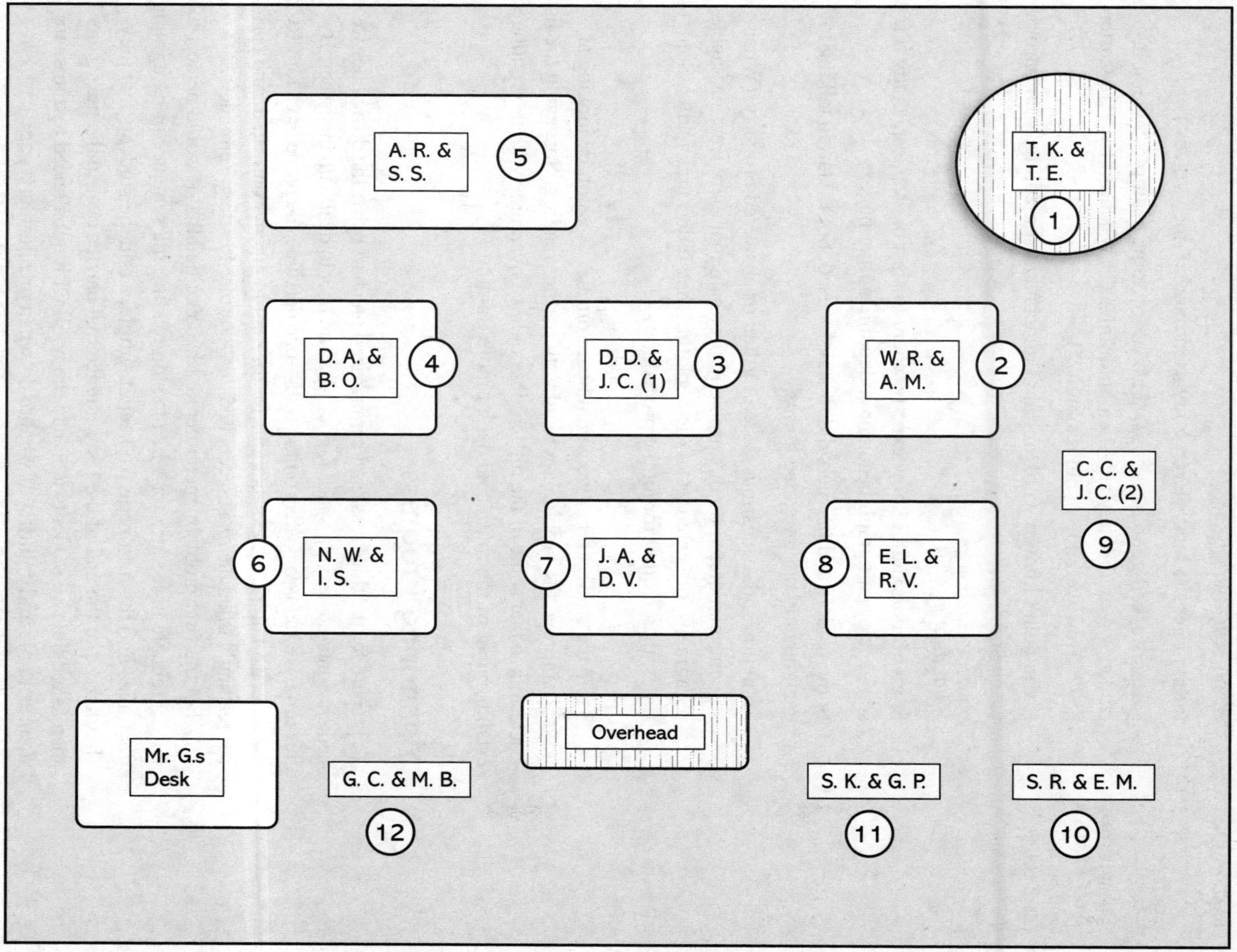

55

56

Chapter
Four
Change Across
Time: A Look at
One Sixth-Grade
Classroom

*What went well*

- It didn't get too loud. (Everybody used their six-inch voices.)

- Partners asked good questions. (I asked for some examples, which included: "Why did they call them mummies?" "What did Howard Carter do?" "How were the pyramids built?")

- If you didn't know a word, or didn't understand something, your partner was helpful.

*What didn't*

- Some readers didn't know exactly where to start or stop, especially if a sentence or paragraph began or ended on another page.

- Some readers and listeners didn't stay focused. Some started talking to each other about unrelated topics.

- Sometimes, the questions weren't asked or answered properly. (When students elaborated on this problem, they said that there were passages, paragraphs, or sentences in the book that they didn't understand. Sometimes, they simply forgot the procedure.)

I told the students that we would begin our next session by looking at ways to improve the problems we had with partner reading. Surveying the list, I determined that some of the difficulties could be overcome with the continued establishment of the routine, and a bit more training.

## Monitoring Progress

To prepare for the third session, I summarized on chart paper the difficulties we had encountered, leaving space for our ideas on how to deal with the issues. By this time, we had two posters on the wall—one detailing the procedures for PRC2, the other explaining the expectations for the classroom environment during partner reading. I titled the most recent addition "Partner Reading Reminders."

For the first problem encountered, I had decided that it would be best to have a reliable procedure for when to stop reading if a sentence or paragraph continues into the next page. To keep it simple, I told the students that they should read to the end of the last sentence that carries over to the next page. I then asked the two students who had the book with unbalanced text to share their example and solution of what to do when one partner's page has few words. I recorded: "If the pages on the left and right don't have equal text, you and your partner may decide to switch sides halfway through the book. (Check to make sure that the pattern is the same for the whole book before you decide. There may be just a few pages with this issue.)" I informed the students that as we continued with partner reading, we would find more activities that can be done while waiting for a partner to finish the silent reading. One student reminded us that the partner who doesn't have any text on his or her page could write questions about the pictures. This was an excellent suggestion!

Next we took a couple minutes to reinforce the expectations of what to talk about during partner reading. To condense it to a ready reminder, I wrote: "After you and your partner have read two pages together, you can talk about the main idea(s) of the passage, what was interesting, what was confusing, and what connections you could make." I added that the usual classroom rules applied. In this case, if a student disrupts an activity, he or she would receive a verbal warning. If the student does not heed the warning, he or she would have a five-minute time-out. Regarding the activity at hand, the partners would need to separate for that time, reconsider their choice to be off-task, and then return to the activity. Finally, we discussed the matter of asking and answering questions, and I recorded the following: "If you have trouble under-standing what you're reading, first talk with your partner to see if she or he can help make it clear. If that doesn't work, you may raise your hand to ask the teacher for assistance."

Ready to begin, I flipped the switch on the overhead projector to show the students the seating chart from the last session. As I called off the names of the partners, I handed them their books and off they went. This time, I was prepared to take observational notes using the prepared form. (See Appendix 3.1.) I estimated that I could visit three to four groups in the thirty-minute session. As the students began reading, I sat down between two groups. With partners occasionally reading silently, I figured that while one group was quiet, I could observe a nearby group. This would serve as a tool to drive my instruction and help determine follow-up plans.

The focus of this first round of observations was to informally assess the oral reading fluency of the students. I was specifically listening for pronuncia-tion, phrasing, pacing, and expressive interpretation. With four readers in my vicinity, I made sure to listen to each student read at least one full page. In ad-dition, I made sure to catch two conversations per group. The notes were sim-ple and direct so that they could be interpreted easily when I returned to them.

We ended the third session by coming back together and sharing cool facts, interesting connections, impressions of the book designs and layouts, and ex-pectations of what the students anticipate learning during the next session. I informed the students that the next session would have a new component: idea and vocabulary notebooks. Upon reflection, I noticed a general enjoyment of the experience among the students.

58

Chapter
Four
Change Across
Time: A Look at
One Sixth-Grade
Classroom

## Introducing Writing Responses

Now that the students had been exposed to the reading method, the next step would be to incorporate the use of a notebook. Its purpose would be for the recording of questions, key ideas, and vocabulary. I handed out to each student a 200-page composition book. To demonstrate how it would be used, I performed a read-aloud/think-aloud/write-aloud using an overhead transparency and a copy of one of the Egypt-theme books. This time, I let the whole class be my collective partner to keep the students engaged.

At the top of the transparency, I wrote the date and the title of the book. I skimmed through and stated a few of the ideas that came to mind while highlighting the graphic features (headings, images, captions, bold words, tables, and maps). I recorded three words that I pretended to not recognize and explained that I would look for context clues when my partner or I got to those words. Next, I returned to the first page and began reading. I stopped after the first paragraph and summarized aloud an idea that interested me, jotting it down on the transparency as well. In the second paragraph, I picked a word to struggle with. Immediately, hands popped up and I accepted the help of an eager student. I referred the students to the poster that recommended what to do if you don't know a word. The word was added to the transparency. As I ended the last sentence on the page, I wrote down the page number and the question to ask my partner. I also wrote down two more words that I thought were important.

We were ready to practice using the PRC2 notebooks. I asked the students what they thought a good goal would be for the amount to write in the notebooks for their first practice. We came up with a list: at least three questions, three important ideas, and five vocabulary words. The students had about twenty-five minutes remaining for reading time. Off they went with fresh notebooks in hand.

With ten minutes remaining, I suggested the students take a quick look at how many items they'd written. I asked the students to trade notebooks with their partners to check each other's progress. At the conclusion of the reading time, we came back together to share questions, ideas, and words. Some of the highlights included questions like Derese's "What did you think about when they were talking about finding the tomb?" I also noticed vocabulary words that were found on the pre-tests (like *archaeologist* and *hieroglyph*). As I reflected on that session later, I noted that some of the less proficient readers had struggled with completing the tasks in the notebook. During the next session, I made sure to meet with those partners early in the activity to help them properly use their notebooks.

Whole-class sharing at conclusion of PRC2 session.

## Building Connections Across the Unit

With the students fully engaged in PRC2, I wanted to see how the information the students were gathering was being applied to their overall understanding of the ancient Egypt civilization. I decided to devote the next lesson to a return to the textbook, encouraging the students to make valid connections to the knowledge they had acquired from the leveled readers.

We began the session with an open sharing of interesting facts and ideas obtained from the PRC2 books. Juan remarked that he was "shocked that King Tut was so young when he got killed." The first section in the textbook about ancient Egypt concerned the geography and early settlement of the region along the Nile River. I asked if any students had read about the Nile. Hands shot up! Naturally, I followed with requests for specific information. Dominique declared, "People used the water from the Nile for lots of stuff." Like? "Washing clothes, drinking, and boats." As we continued our preview of the section, students continued to offer connections between some of the key ideas in the textbook and what they had read about in their leveled books.

This engagement validated PRC2 as a substantial motivator. Many students were clearly interested in sharing their acquired knowledge about ancient Egypt. With PRC2, vocabulary that may have been out of reach through use of the textbook alone seemed far more accessible for struggling readers.

60

Chapter
Four
Change Across
Time: A Look at
One Sixth-Grade
Classroom

Mark, for instance, accurately, if uniquely, described a sarcophagus as a "mummy's shell."

For the remaining three weeks of the unit, we maintained the balance of the leveled readers and textbook lessons. By the second week, some partners finished their first book. I decided to find a couple of texts near the readers' instructional level from which they could choose. Before beginning the new book, however, I asked them to complete a PRC2: Read & Recommend form. (See Appendix 2.6.) Eventually, these were shared with the rest of the class and posted on the wall above the shelf where the books about Egypt were kept. Of the thirteen books, only two received a "not recommended" rating. Fortunately, when students were given a choice for their second texts, they actually recommended those books. Alyssa even wrote, "I liked this book better because it was more interesting and the pictures were nicer."

## Wrapping Up the Unit

As the unit drew to a close, the final activity for the students was to retake the four tests offered at the beginning. While they worked on the assessments, I conducted follow-up Classroom Fluency Snapshots. The results of the post-assessments are addressed in Chapter 6. I was pleased to see that the class average increased in each of the categories. Equally significant was the overall climb in fluency rates among the readers in the room. One of the more notable achievements was the acquisition of more academic language for Tokawon, a recent immigrant from Liberia. For the first reading, he only recognized eight words. His fluency rate improved 800 percent in just four and a half weeks!

However, some students did not show appropriate gains in either their fluency rate or the vocabulary concepts. I interpreted this to mean that I needed to spend more time on explicit vocabulary activities, while also incorporating more fluency strategies within the context of partner reading. Also, the fluctuation of students' reading rates indicated that certain partners would need to be reassigned for the next session of PRC2.

## PRC2 in Transition

As I continued to attend seminars related to the PRC2 project, several weeks passed before the next official PRC2 unit was introduced. However, in the interim, several students did apply the partner reading techniques to *Weekly Reader*

Students expand use of PRC2 in a variety of texts.

magazines to which our class had subscribed. At one point, I noticed Gabriel and Ismael sharing a magazine and having a detailed discussion of one of the articles. At the conclusion of the *Weekly Reader* time, I asked them to share their experience, emphasizing the inclusion of the reading and conversational strategies.

The next unit was about the solar system. This presented a slightly different challenge, as we did not have a corresponding textbook in our room. Astronomy is covered in fourth grade, according to our curriculum, but the seventh-grade state assessment includes astronomy questions. Therefore, a refresher course would be beneficial for the students.

To prepare for this unit, I decided to create a more efficient system for the use of the materials. Because the students were familiar with the notebook component, I chose to have the students store their notebooks with a folder that would also house their selected text. In turn, the folders would be kept in an accessible crate. By this time, the project leaders had developed a reference sheet for student questions and conversation tips. (See Appendix 2.2.) This form was also added to the folder so that students could have the questions available. In the end, each partner shared one folder that contained two composition notebooks, one leveled reader, and the question reference sheet.

The first session for the Solar System unit began with an unveiling of the new books. Sixth graders aren't too old to still be fascinated by space, so the

62

Chapter
Four
Change Across
Time: A Look at
One Sixth-Grade
Classroom

anticipation was evident. After reviewing the key PRC2 components, I introduced the question reference sheet and modeled how it could be used to enhance the conversations about the books. The students completed the corresponding pre-assessments and were ready to go again.

Their familiarity with the PRC2 method allowed for a more immediate connection with the content. During the sessions, I took observational notes, first concentrating on those students who had not made gains during the previous PRC2 unit. When students struggled with fluency, I analyzed their approach to the text. A wider variety of reading levels were represented in the span of books about the solar system than were available for the unit on ancient Egypt. In a couple instances, I asked the partners if they would like to try a different book, and they responded favorably. I also intervened when necessary to help clarify passages or concepts. For those students who had had previous difficulties with carrying on conversations, the reference sheet did help. Sheila, an EL, initially went straight down the list, filling in phrases. However, after a couple sessions, she appeared to have internalized many of the statement starters. At one point, I overheard her saying, "What you said reminds me of the Egypt book I read."

We had only three weeks to devote to this unit, but it did culminate in a field trip to the Adler Planetarium in Chicago. The prospect of the trip served as a strong motivation for students to acquire knowledge of the solar system. At the planetarium, students confidently talked about aspects of the solar system. I observed Juan and Pablo standing by a large model of the Milky Way comparing the inner and outer planets.

*Juan:* I know Earth is an inner planet.

*Pablo:* Aren't the outer planets gas?

*Juan:* Yep. It says right here [pointing to an exhibit caption]. Plus I remember that page in the book we read that had the inner planets on one side and the outer planets on the other side.

Music to a teacher's ears.

## Second-Year Adjustments and Additions

At the end of the first year of using PRC2, I reflected on its efficacy in my classroom. My overall impression was that the students enjoyed the process. In an end-of-the-year activity, I have students share memories of their time in sixth grade. David remarked that he was happy to "go outside the text-book" to learn about ancient Egypt, a topic he took a great liking to. Many students described the field trip to the planetarium, with Sheila suggesting that it was a better trip because she "got to read about stars and planets before going."

In preparing for the next school year, I definitely wanted to maintain the PRC2 units on ancient Egypt and the solar system. I also had a set of books about ancient Rome. With an even deeper understanding of the strategies and techniques, I began the second year with enthusiasm.

Despite having slightly less time in the schedule available for social studies, we actually expanded the Ancient Egypt unit because of our access to Field Museum materials that were used in a culminating activity. (The Field Museum of National History loans museum artifacts, specimens, audiovisual materials, and activity kits to area schools.) I also added a few books to the text set to allow for more choice within the reading-level range. For the selection of partners, I decided to go a bit beyond a simple Classroom Fluency Snapshot by adding a set of three comprehension questions to the test passage. I took this step because I noticed in the year before that a few students had fluency rates that were higher than their comprehension level, causing a mismatch in partners. Use of the comprehension questions proved to be a better measure for more effectively pairing readers.

Both the Ancient Egypt and the Solar System units were successful in the second year. Unfortunately, we did not take another field trip to the planetarium. We did, however, design a bulletin board that the students took pride in that displayed facts, figures, and terms on a canvas of stars. For Ancient Egypt, I set up learning centers that involved the materials on loan from the Field Museum. Students got the opportunity to use hieroglyph stamps, play an ancient Egyptian board game, and build a model of a tomb. These enhancement activities enriched the experience of the students. Yet they would have had less lasting meaning if the students had not acquired the background knowledge through PRC2.

With the addition of the ancient Rome text set, I had an opportunity to start a new unit afresh. The sixth-grade team decided to include a research project as part of the unit. We began with a general introduction to ancient Rome (having just completed a separate unit on ancient Greece). I paired the students up for a three-week PRC2 exploration. During the first week, students selected a topic for research. I found that this prompted the students to share a considerable amount of information between each other. Naturally, that meant more conversations and applications of new vocabulary.

64

Chapter
Four
Change Across
Time: A Look at
One Sixth-Grade
Classroom

## Conclusion

After two years of using PRC2, I can say with confidence that my classroom is a richer learning environment because of it. Most students not only improved their reading levels but also increased their familiarity with informational texts. This is an often overlooked skill in elementary and middle schools. By differentiating the materials available and "going outside the textbook," the students were able to read and understand content that was relevant to the curriculum.

There were, as mentioned, a few snags in the fabric. The most notable issues were the unequal distribution of text and graphics within books and partner conflicts or absences. Students were generally able to work out the reading assignments, but I was occasionally called in to assist with finding a solution. It almost always amounted to a matter of dividing the text equally. As for the partner concerns, when a student's partner was absent, I gave the student the option of joining another set of readers to follow, or reading the text independently and checking in with me to expound on what he or she had read.

The overall effectiveness of using PRC2 can perhaps best be illustrated by the fact that students used the skills and techniques in settings other than those designated by me. *Weekly Reader* has become a regular partner reading opportunity. When students were working on their research projects, they would often sit together to share pertinent information. These are just a few examples of the intrinsic value students found in PRC2. Andrea, one of the second-year students, shared an appropriate closing thought in a reflective piece of writing, "We've learned [about] Egypt in other grades but not as much as we have learned [from] PRC2 and social studies."

## Student Reference

Brega, I. (2006). *Egypt: Past and present*. Washington, DC: National Geographic.

# Developing PRC2 in a Primary Classroom

# 5

**?** How can I motivate my primary students using informational text?

In this chapter, **Avni Patel**, a primary classroom teacher in a multiage classroom at Louis J. Agassiz Elementary School in Chicago, explains how she addressed the challenges of teaching strategies to help young students comprehend informational texts. She includes several examples from her classroom showing how she guided her six- to eight-year-olds in reading, discussing, and thinking about content.

Avni is now working as an early childhood education facilitator with Erikson Institute's New Schools Project. She consults with and coaches teachers at another Chicago public school, helping them provide their students and families with instruction and developmentally appropriate practices for their early childhood students.

*The classroom's bright, fluorescent lights flicker as a hot, sticky breeze swoops through the room, reminding my children that today promises to be another sweltering, almost unbearable day in our un-air-conditioned school. Jermaine wipes the sweat off his brow as he and Agrim flip through a nonfiction text about anacondas, finally stopping at a chapter titled "Predators." "Ooh! Here it is! Page 23!" Agrim exclaims. In another corner of the room, two girls fan themselves as they whisper-read a book together. Several children are working together at our round table, hovering over an oversized copy of* The Great Kapok Tree *and writing observations on index card after index card. "Read the picture! Look! What does it tell you?" Kiara says, mimicking my words as she helps her partner. "Our research project fair is in five days! Come on!" whispers Mimi, waving feverishly to Elina as she walks toward their half-completed diagram, balancing plates of paint, paper towels, and paintbrushes in their hands.*

*A colleague pops her head into our classroom and whispers, "Omigosh! How did you get them to work like that? My class won't do anything in this heat!" Smiling, I listen as the continuous buzzing of my students' voices fill my ears. The bustling of little bodies moving busily within our classroom, engaged in whispered conversations, reading together while sprawled across the library rug, and excitedly jotting down notes for their research projects calls. It's time for me to get in on this action!*

If my colleague had walked into my classroom during my first year as a primary classroom teacher, the sight would have been completely different. Amid a buzz of chattering voices deeply engaged in conversation, she would have seen students working in small groups at brightly labeled literacy centers. If she had stepped closer, though, she may have heard Hannah talking to Kiara about the birthday party she had attended the night before, or Mimi whispering to Elina that Rebecca's hair looked cute. If she had stayed a little longer, she may have also seen me leaving my guided reading group for the third time to attend to a brewing conflict between Sam and Elijah over the best headset in the listening center. She would have noticed the detour I took on my route back to my guided reading group to redirect Mimi and Hannah to their respective center activities. Upon my return to the guided reading group, she would have heard me sigh as I attempted to regain the attention of my youngest students, who were playing freeze tag on the rug while I was away.

How did I advance from those first experiences as a teacher to a point in my professional practice in which my class was interdependently engaged in high levels of thinking on one of the hottest days of the school year? I think back to our earliest months together. Although the years of experience since my first year had provided lessons in strengthening classroom management, my literacy block had evolved rather unevenly. A missing link quickly emerged. My students were proving to be great readers with soaring reading levels and rising comprehension scores with fiction, but their lackluster growth interacting with nonfiction left me puzzled and desperately searching for a better strategy. I tried several strategies before I finally took a course so that I could achieve my reading endorsement. This is when I was introduced to the process that changed my nonfiction reading instruction forever. Enter Partner Reading and Content, Too (PRC2)!

I was introduced to PRC2 as a strategy for teaching nonfiction reading skills during a graduate-level course in reading comprehension. Immediately intrigued by the PRC2 process, I began a year-long trial to adapt the intermediate and upper elementary strategy to my first- and second-grade primary students' developing literacy needs. In this chapter, I recount, step by step, my class's journey as we adapted PRC2 for the early childhood primary student.

# Modeling and Introducing PRC2 to My Students

I began this process by enthusiastically introducing PRC2 to my students during our large-group time on the rug. Our literacy coach had been working with a group of struggling fifth graders on the strategy and volunteered two of her students to model the procedure for my students. Before their visit, I modeled the procedures of listening attentively and asking relevant questions to prepare them for their PRC2 exhibition. I created a poster-sized chart listing the standard procedure for PRC2 and I discussed each step with my students. In doing so, I hoped to create reference points for them to make connections when observing the two fifth graders model the procedure. I also created two enlarged copies of the PRC2 question sheet for each fifth grader to record his or her discussions according to the process so that my children were able to see clearly how the fifth graders used the forms.

After introducing themselves, Deanna and Mariah, the fifth-grade models, discussed how they learned the PRC2 process and shared their opinions about using this reading tool: "I like PRC2 because we get to talk to each other when we are working, and we get to learn more because we're talking about what we're reading," Mariah said. My students exchanged smiles and excited glances, later explaining that the thought of having conversations like older children does made them feel grown up and eager to try the process themselves.

My colleague had also introduced the concept of the personal social goal. She explained that much of the PRC2 process involves working cooperatively with a partner and respecting the developing reading abilities and opinions of the partner. The goal of each partner was to support the other in his or her reading and thinking. Each model then explained her personal social goal to work on during the session and identified specific behaviors that indicated her practice of this goal. For example, Deanna stated that her social goal would be to "listen actively without interrupting." She explained that when she was taking notes on her scratch sheet of paper, she was writing her thoughts quickly instead of interrupting her partner to voice them. Deanna also told my students that she would try to look her partner "in the eyes" while she was speaking, to demonstrate that she was actively listening. Mariah discussed her social goal, explaining that she would try to "speak clearly and concisely." She explained to my students that when she paused before it was her turn to speak, she was stating her thoughts "in [her] mind" first, before verbalizing for her partner.

After the modeling session, we held a question-and-answer session in which my students asked the models questions about the PRC2 process. The questions included the following:

- Is it fun to listen to your friend read?
- Is it hard to listen to your friend read to you?
- Do you have a hard time doing PRC2?
- What do you like about PRC2?
- What do you think is hard about PRC2?
- Is it hard to remember your social goal when you are talking to your friend?
- Do you think it's hard to look into your partner's eyes when you're talking?
- Do you really say everything in your head before you say it out loud? Do you say it better when you do that?
- Do you ever get to talk about anything else?

Providing an opportunity for my students to observe PRC2 in action served a number of purposes. Most important, my students were able to see firsthand the full PRC2 experience. This opportunity created a universal schematic reference for each child in my classroom to access when participating in the introductory lessons I taught. In addition, my students were given a model to follow when participating in the PRC2 process themselves. If they had not seen the two fifth-grade girls, sitting side-by-side, maintaining eye contact, and speaking clearly as they conducted their discussion, my students' initial attempts at PRC2 might have been widely diverse and based solely on individual visualizations of past discussions.

After the fifth graders left our room, my students also became interested in the social goals that each girl identified and worked toward. An engaging discussion ensued about how the fifth graders came up with their goals, what a good social goal would look like, and how my students would know if a goal was a social goal or a reading goal. I explained that a *social goal*, as my colleague had referred to it, was one that focused on how "you can work well together so that both of you feel important, confident about your thinking, and accepted by your partner." Together we made a chart listing all the skills that they would need to be able to have successful conversations about their readings. The following is a list of social, speaking, and listening skills that the students would need:

- Listen actively to your partner's thinking.
- Respond relevantly to your partner's thinking.
- Maintain eye contact when listening to your partner.
- Maintain eye contact when speaking to your partner.
- Speak in a clear, loud voice when talking to your partner.
- Speak with an idea in mind.
- Speak concisely to help your partner stay attentive.
- Think before speaking or responding to your partner.
- Disagree respectfully with your partner.
- Agree with your partner.
- Agree and add on to your partner's thoughts.
- Ask your partner (clarifying) questions for more information.
- Ask your partner for time to think.
- Ask your partner to restate the question.
- Ask your partner to restate his or her response.

Finally, from their observations of Deanna and Mariah and through their interactions in the question-and-answer session, my students were able to make connections with the models—an experience that allowed them to see themselves in the models. "They seemed a little nervous to talk to each other like that," noticed Mimi. "I think that they were trying to talk about things that can be hard to talk about because you have to use your head to think—and sometimes I get confused, too, so I have to say my thoughts in my head before I say them out loud, too," explained Agrim. "I liked that they tried really hard to talk to each other and looked into each other's eyes," said Hannah. Once my students were able to associate with Deanna and Mariah on this level, the PRC2 process became less foreign and more achievable in their eyes.

## Creating the Learning Environment

After analyzing the PRC2 process, I spent a considerable amount of time experimenting with how best to implement the process within the time constraints of my literacy block.

Originally, to attend to my diverse, multiage group, my language arts program consisted of a combination of reader's workshop, writer's workshop, self-made literacy centers, and the daily five. I extended my school's mandated language arts instructional time from sixty minutes to 125 minutes. Within the first forty-five minutes, I gave a seven- to ten-minute mini-lesson on a reading or writing strategy and allowed the remainder of the time for independent student reading or writing. During this time, I conferenced with my students, individually or in small-group guided settings, modifying my instruction based on the students' developmental needs. In the following sixty minutes, my students moved through daily five centers or language arts learning centers I created to allow for review and practice of previously taught skills. While students were working interdependently in small groups, I was able to circulate through the room, attending to specific children who needed extra support. In the final fifteen to twenty minutes, the students shared their work through author's chair, share clubs, or centers stars, practices that promoted a level of accountability throughout our language arts instruction and encouraged students to celebrate their developing strengths.

I analyzed my literacy schedule to locate the most effective time slot to teach this process. I decided I would embed PRC2 into my reader's workshop time, using the gradual release of responsibility model (see Chapter 2). During this time, I would model a focus skill or component of PRC2 for five to seven minutes, thinking aloud to allow my students to witness the metacognitive awareness I had during the process. Then I would allow students to practice working cooperatively with PRC2 for approximately thirty minutes, while I planned to work in guided settings with flexible groups or pairs of children on individualized and group learning goals. Finally, we would end the session by sharing student successes and observing positive behaviors from that day's lesson—essentially I was mimicking my reader's workshop schedule with an added PRC2 twist. Because I intended to teach PRC2 each day, I also substituted other literacy centers (for example, ABC center, phonics center, and research center) with independent reading and writing centers to supplement my students' loss of self-selected reading and independent writing time. I also created other pockets in the daily schedule for self-selected reading, buddy reading, free writing, and publishing opportunities.

In creating a learning environment suitable for using PRC2, I recognized a need to provide more nonfiction books at my students' wide range of reading levels. Because my students' interests varied considerably, I organized the nonfiction books in my classroom library by genre and subject. I created an inventory of the nonfiction books in my classroom as well. In our project-based Science and Social Studies units, students were then learning about various natural disasters and weather formations. However, other students in my room were still deeply engaged in readings from our previous unit on occupations and communities. Still other students in my room were constantly asking for more books about animals. After assessing the classroom inventory with my students' interests in mind, I checked out or purchased seventy or eighty books, at Fountas and Pinnell reading levels reflected in our classroom and in a number of subject areas. By creating a library of nonfiction texts well-suited for the reading levels of my students, I was able to ensure that there would be a surplus of literature to choose from.

The original PRC2 model suggested that students be intentionally placed in pairs by the teacher based on a reading inventory designed to create optimal fits for student performance in PRC2. I began by assessing my students' individual reading fluency, including percentage accuracy and reading rate. I also used Fountas and Pinnell's Benchmark Assessments to determine my students' reading-comprehension capacity and reading level—an assessment tool I regularly relied on for valid, reliable student data. After I had assessed each of my students, I organized my data by locating each child on a vertical continuum based on their scores. In doing so, I was able to systematically group students according to their current reading ability.

## Building a Foundation for Practicing PRC2

With the physical environment and organizational structures in place, I decided to create specific learning goals for my students in order to lay a solid foundation for navigating and fluently interacting with informational texts. I would teach mini-lessons on the external features of nonfiction text and create opportunities for students to practice applying their new knowledge in daily literacy centers. To further support student understanding of these features, with each mini-lesson I added to an anchor chart with descriptions and pictures of the current focus. Students used the anchor chart as a reference when identifying new features or practicing their new learning in literacy centers.

We began by reviewing the basic differences between fiction and nonfiction informational texts. In a shared writing activity, we created a simple T-chart to list the distinguishing characteristics of each type of text. During library center, students would sort a set of books that I had purposefully selected during preparation into fiction and nonfiction piles, engaging in discussions to determine where each book should be placed. Students used the Fiction vs. Non-Fiction T-Chart as a reference for their discussions and decision making. Each small group elected a "Writer" who recorded the differences between texts on a simple data table that highlighted the characteristics outlined in the chart. Furthermore, to explain their reasoning and document their thinking, I asked my students to also record the "clues" that influenced their decisions during the sorting activity.

Once a solid understanding of these distinctions was demonstrated, my students began surveying the features on the covers of our texts: the title, author, and visual representation (illustrations, photographs, and so on). I emphasized the importance of "reading" all the features of the cover before opening the book for "right there" information—information that is explicitly identifiable on the page—as well as thinking based on their schema. For example, in a book titled *Volcanoes*, a student may deduce that the text would be about volcanoes. However, the collage of pictures on the cover may show a number of different volcanic eruptions, allowing the student to predict that the book will discuss various types of volcanoes and eruptions. My students and I spent a number of lessons, through the gradual release of responsibility framework, examining covers to make predictions about the facts inside the book, eliciting questions based on our observations, and discussing how our thinking led us to such conclusions. In learning centers, students examined nonfiction book covers, collaboratively made predictions about the possible content, and independently created sample pages for the book—including illustrations and the corresponding text to represent their thinking.

As my students became more comfortable with previewing the cover, we started to study the table of contents and index in various texts. I conducted think-alouds to demonstrate how a reader might use the table of contents or index to search for information or to gain a better understanding of what the book will be about. We discussed the purpose of page numbers and practiced using the pagination in the table of contents and index to locate information. During literacy center time, students analyzed different table of contents and index pages to extract information, made predictions about the text, and searched for answers to simple questions. Our study of the table of contents and index led my students to discover chapters, headings, and subheadings. They realized that the chapter titles and headings in the text matched the chapter titles and headings in the table of contents. They also recognized that many of the words or terms found in the index were bolded in the text. Naturally, we began an exploration of words printed in bold type and eventually found ourselves in the glossary, making connections between the bold words found in the text and their identical twins at the back of the book.

In response to my students' discoveries, I created a Vocabulary Exploration page to give my students the opportunity to delve deeper into understanding the new words they were learning. My students began exploring content vocabulary through this graphic organizer on a regular basis and soon became accustomed to scanning a text for words they did not recognize. They found these words in captions, diagrams, and within the text. This form is shown in Figure 5.1.

As in many primary early childhood classrooms, my students' unexpected discoveries and their authentic inquiries paved our path, guiding me in planning subsequent mini-lessons through the remaining external features of nonfiction text. With each focus lesson, my students became more and more familiar with navigating through nonfiction text. The following are the mini-lessons my class and I focused on, in sequential order:

- Nonfiction versus fiction
- External features of nonfiction text
- Title
- Author
- Table of contents
- Index
- Chapters
- Headings
- Page numbers
- Bold words
- Glossary
- Content vocabulary: Vocabulary Exploration
- Maps
- Diagrams
- Pictures/photographs
- Illustrations
- Captions
- Facts-to-know page

**Figure 5.1** Vocabulary Exploration

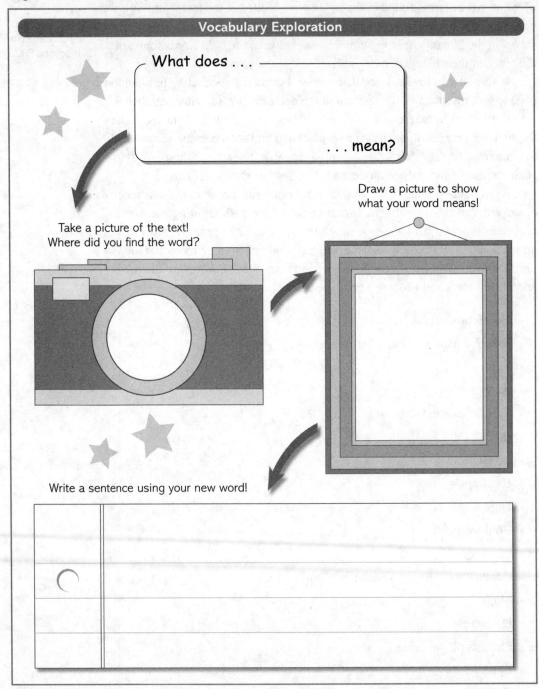

74

# Adapting PRC2 to the Early Childhood Learner

Now that my students had built a strong foundation to approach nonfiction texts with experience and prior knowledge, it was time to redefine the step-by-step procedure for the PRC2 method. Because I knew my students' collaborative work skills were still developing, I broke down the steps of the PRC2 process to create a more primary-friendly method. I also renamed PRC2; I called it Reading and Thinking with My Buddy to explicitly label, in student-friendly language, the purpose of the process my students would be carrying out. In doing so, I hoped to keep this as a consistent reminder that as successful readers, my students were to maintain a metacognitive awareness while reading or listening to their partner. I selected a fluent reader from my class to model the procedure with me. Together we moved step-by-step through the motions of Reading and Thinking with My Buddy. Originally the process was similar in procedure to the PRC2 model meant for intermediate and upper-grade elementary school students (see Chapter 2). After initial experiences with this model, however, I inserted two new steps to accommodate my primary students' developing needs and the texts they read (see Figure 5.2). I also supplemented our daily practice of Reading and Thinking with My Buddy with a number of mini-lessons to address conflicts that arose, challenges that emerged, and successes that my students achieved. Following is the Reading and Thinking with My Buddy procedure, along with related mini-lessons, after its evolution:

1. **Preview the text! Talk time!** When previewing the text, my students used a separate anchor chart to help them through the steps. We discussed how to (1) look at the cover; (2) read through the table of contents; and (3) look through the book, paying special attention to photographs, illustrations, diagrams, tables, maps, and so on. We also talked about various discussion prompts that students could use when previewing the text. When examining the cover, students could say, "What do you think this book will be about?" or "This picture on the cover makes me think _____." While reading through the table of contents, students were prompted to ask questions like, "Do you want to read the first chapter title?" and "Which chapter title seems interesting to you?" They also were encouraged to take turns reading the chapter titles—a strategy that ensured active participation and involvement from both partners. Finally, as students began scanning the text, I encouraged them to "read" the pictures.

Figure **5.2** Anchor Chart

# Reading & Thinking with My Buddy!
## A Primary Adaptation of PRC2

1. Preview the text!  Talk Time!

2. Choose which chapter you will read.

3. Divide your text!

4. Read the <u>whole</u> text independently.

5. Read the <u>whole</u> text together aloud!

6. Read your part to your buddy!

7. Ask questions! Discuss your thinking!

8. Switch roles and do it again!

*Mini-Lessons to Address Step 1*

- How to preview a book cover
- How to talk to your partner about a book cover
- How to do a self-guided picture walk
- How to talk to your partner during a picture walk
- How to preview a book
- How to talk to your partner during a book preview
- How to preview the table of contents
- How to talk to your partner about the table of contents

2.  **Choose which chapter you will read. Talk time!** Because the nonfiction books my students were reading were aligned to their reading levels, the text was simple and short. Each chapter was anywhere from one page to four pages long, with a limited number of lines on each page. To accommodate this difference, I asked most of my students to choose one to two pages to read within the chapter. Those students who were reading at more advanced levels selected entire chapters that they would be responsible for reading.

*Mini-Lessons to Address Step 2*

- How to decide what to read
- What to do when you disagree about what to read

Students engaged in previewing a book together.

3. **Divide your text! Time to count!** I added this step later, after students began exhibiting a need for consistent conflict-resolution support following Step 2. The original procedure assumes that the selected chapter will have enough text for students to equally divide and share responsibility for reading. However, as I mentioned earlier, in the primary nonfiction books my students used, chapters were often a single page with a single passage. Because my students did not know how to divide the passage equally, conflicts began to erupt. To prevent this from happening, I designed a process to help my students divide the number of lines on a page so that both partners would read an equal number of lines.

a. Students would count the number of *lines* in the selected passage (for example, sixteen lines in a passage).

b. Students would begin counting lines from one through sixteen aloud.

c. With each line counted, each partner would take turns holding up a finger. (Student A: 1, 3, 5, 7, 9 . . . 15. Student B: 2, 4, 6, 8, 10 . . . 16.)

d. By the end of the count, each student would have an equal (or approximately equal) number of fingers raised. This is the number of lines they would read.

e. If both partners could decide on who would read the first and second sections independently, they were free to do so. However, if they were not able to reach an agreement, the student who counted first would read second.

In learning this counting procedure, my students could independently divide their text and continue moving through the process of Reading and Thinking with My Buddy.

*Mini-Lessons to Address Step 3*

- How can we divide our reading?
- How do we count the lines?
- How do we use finger counting to divide the text?
- I have three pages, she has two! No fair!
- How can we decide who reads first?

4. **Read the *whole* text independently. Shhh!** I modified this step to create a pattern of repeated reading to support my students' developing comprehension skills. Because early childhood readers gain a deeper level of understanding with each repeated experience with a text, I asked that both students read the chapter silently, or in a whisper voice (whichever was developmentally appropriate, or "just right," for them). When they were done reading they could

let their buddy know by looking up from the text. Once both partners looked up, they knew they could move to the next step.

*Mini-Lessons to Address Step 4*

- How can I whisper-read so that it doesn't bother my buddy?
- What can I do when I'm done reading?
- My buddy is taking too long! What can I do?
- How can both buddies use pointers to read?
- My buddy wants to hold the book. I can't read that way. What can I do?

5. **Read the *whole* text together aloud!** I added this step after I found that students were still having difficulties reading the text fluently. Although the text was aligned with their reading levels, the content vocabulary was proving to affect their fluency and, in turn, their partner's ability to actively listen while they read. In reading the text aloud together, each student was able to help his or her partner decode difficult words.

*Mini-Lessons to Address Step 5*

- How do I give my buddy reading space when we read together?
- I need help reading a word. What can I say?
- My buddy won't use a pointer. I want to use one. What can I do?
- My buddy doesn't pay attention when we read. What can I do?
- My buddy reads too slow. What can I say?
- My buddy reads too fast. How can I make him or her slow down?

6. **Read your part to your buddy!** In modeling this step, I focused primarily on my students' developing listening and speaking skills. We discussed the importance of speaking clearly, using a pointer to help track the words and lines in the text, and using a loud voice that their buddy could understand. Although I did not use the term *six-inch voice*, my students and I discussed the difference between speaking loudly and clearly versus screaming and disrupting their neighbors. After a few humorous dramatizations, they seemed to get the hang of it! We also discussed "what good listeners look like." The children made a list to qualify an active listener's behavior:

*Active Listeners . . .*

- Look at the speaker while he or she is talking or follow the pointer while he or she is reading.

- Think about what the speaker is saying while they listen.
- Try to "push away" other noises and voices that they hear in the room.
- Ask the speaker or reader to repeat the words if they need a second chance.

After my students reviewed the behaviors of active listeners and clear speakers or readers, they were able to practice applying these skills during this step. I also developed a guide for the students to use when listening to their partner on which they learned to make notes. See Figure 5.3 for an example of this form.

### Mini-Lessons to Address Step 6

- How do I give my partner reading space when he or she reads?
- Why do I give my partner reading space?
- How do I ask my partner for reading space?
- How do I follow along as my partner reads?
- I need help reading a word. What can I say?
- My partner keeps trying to help me, but I don't want help. What can I say?
- My partner won't use a pointer. What can I do?
- My partner doesn't pay attention when I read. What can I do?
- My partner reads too slow. What can I say?
- My partner reads too fast. How can I make him or her slow down?

7. **Ask questions! Discuss your thinking! Talk time.** To facilitate a lively discussion between the partners, my students and I spent a considerable amount of time on various aspects of a Reading and Thinking with My Buddy conversation. We reviewed the listening and speaking behaviors we had previously outlined and we discussed the variations in behavior while in conversation versus during buddy reading. For example, when actively listening to a reader, a student can follow his or her partner's pointer or look directly at the reader. When actively listening to a partner in conversation, however, it is important to maintain eye contact with that person. I also reviewed the list of social skills and created a series of mini-lessons and dramatization opportunities based on each one. As my students' skills with practicing Reading and Thinking with My Buddy began to develop, I allowed them to guide my planning again. Whenever they demonstrated a successful self-made modification to a skill or displayed difficulties during conversations, I created a mini-lesson to address it. In responding to their developing needs as we all experimented with this process, I was able to facilitate their growth as informed conversationalists.

Figure 5.3 Active Listening Notes

## Active Listening Notes

Name: _____

Date: _____

Listen to your partner read. Write the active listening note in the small box. Then write your idea in the big box.

* I think something is important.
? I have a question.
+ I already know this.
! Wow! I think this is interesting.

*Mini-Lessons to Address Step 7*

- I don't understand the question. What can I say?

- I don't know what to say! I need more time.

- I need help thinking about how to respond.

- How do I ask my buddy to read it again?

- What do I do if I am confused?

- What do I do if I have too many thoughts?

- My buddy keeps interrupting me. What can I say?

- My buddy doesn't listen when I read. What can I do?

- I have trouble remembering my thinking. What can I do?

- I am having trouble asking questions. What do I say?

- If my buddy answers, "I don't know," I can say . . .

- If my buddy gives me a short answer, I can say . . .

- My buddy's answer is too long! I can't pay attention. What can I do?

- If I want to agree with my buddy's thinking, I can say . . .

- How do I disagree respectfully with my buddy's thinking?

- How do I ask my buddy for help recording our answers?

I developed other guides for students to use during their discussions (see Figures 5.4 and 5.5).

   8. **Switch roles and do it again!** These steps now complete the adapted PRC2 model for my primary students. See Figure 5.2 for the anchor chart I developed to help them use the complete process.

# Using Reading and Thinking with My Buddy in Integrated Units

As my students became practiced in using Reading and Thinking with My Buddy to make better sense of informational texts, an interesting phenomenon began to emerge in my classroom. Prior to introducing Reading and Thinking with My Buddy, my students had grown accustomed to the sharing session we had at the end of reader's workshop. Originally, during this time, my students would share new strategies they had used to try to decode a hard-to-read word or they would explain how they had found a "just right" book or how they had accomplished the focus goal of a past mini-lesson. Once we began Reading and Thinking with

**Figure 5.4** Reading and Writing with My Buddy: Asking
and Answering Questions

**Reading and Writing with My Buddy**

My name: _____ My buddy: _____

Text/book: _____

I asked my buddy:

❑ Did you think something was interesting?

❑ Did you wonder about anything?

My buddy said: (Draw and Write)

—— I agreed with my buddy! ☺

—— I did not agree with my buddy ☹, but I respect my buddy's thinking!

**Figure 5.5** Reading and Thinking with My Buddy: Asking and Answering Questions

| Reading and Thinking with My Buddy |
| --- |

Name: _____ Buddy: _____

Our book title: _____

| What was the most <u>important</u> part? Why do you think so? | What was the most <u>interesting</u> part for you? Why do you think so? |
| --- | --- |
| | |

Words we had trouble figuring out _____

_____

Question we had _____

_____

_____

### Things to say:

**If my buddy says "*I don't know*," I can say:**
- Try to think about it.
- Do you want me to read it again?

**If my buddy gives me a *short answer*, I can say:**
- Tell me more.
- Why do you think so?

- I didn't get that. Can you say that in a different way?

**If my buddy is *done*, I can say:**
- That was smart thinking!
- You really listened to me read!
- Good job! Are you ready to read yours?

My Buddy, my students and I continued with this practice. Either I would ask a student to share a successful strategy from our mini-lesson or students would ask permission to share their own strategies for reading and thinking in the process. Soon after we delved deeper into practicing Reading and Thinking with My Buddy, my students began excitedly asking permission to share new learning they had acquired from their reading. Our sharing time became filled with readers, one after another, explaining their newly acquired knowledge of a veterinarian's work or a community fire department's work schedule. Little did I know that soon our sharer's circle would become the setting in which my students would decide our next integrated unit. This day's sharer's circle began like any other. As students were cleaning up from a session of Reading and Thinking with My Buddy, several students approached me with requests to share their new knowledge. Sam, a second grader, wanted to share what he had learned in the *Magic Tree House* informational book he was reading. When it was his turn to read, he exclaimed, "Michael and I learned that volcanoes form almost the same way mountains do, but they don't just have a hole at the top! The hole is a huge crack that goes all the way down into the ground! And that's where the lava comes from!" Tyrell blurted out, "What's a volcano?" The room erupted with conversation as the students turned to Tyrell to explain their understanding of a volcano. Amid the buzz of conversation, Mimi approached, with wide eyes and an eager smile, with a question. "Mrs. Patel? Can we do this for our next unit?" It was in this moment, with my students engaged in content-specific conversation, that I decided this time our interdisciplinary unit would be different. I would capitalize on my students' developing abilities to practice Reading and Thinking with My Buddy and create a research-based unit that would demonstrate the deeper levels of inquiry and understanding that we were acquiring.

As with most of my thematic, interdisciplinary units, I began documenting the children's discussion. They mentioned facts and some misconceptions about volcanoes and also began discussing their knowledge and misconceptions of tornadoes, hurricanes, and geysers. I decided that I would propose that we begin a research study of various natural disasters.

# Creating the Family Research Project

Once my students agreed to my proposal to conduct a research study on natural disasters, I spent the next few days filling our classroom library with developmentally appropriate informational texts about natural disasters. My hope was that if my students' level of interest and engagement remained high, we could use Reading and Thinking with My Buddy as a vehicle for feeding their thirst for knowledge about the topic. With greater understanding of the informational texts, I hoped that my students would begin to further develop their reading and research skills. This hope was realized soon after I introduced my students to the new additions to the classroom library. Some parents approached me with supportive comments regarding their student's reading ability. Others questioned how their child could read informational text with such rich content when their reading skills were not fully developed. Several more parents told story after story about their child's insistence on visiting the library and bookstores to get more information on natural disasters. Because of the immense parent inquiry and family involvement I was receiving, I decided to create and plan a research project that families could work on with their child. My objective was to create an opportunity for my students' parents to participate in their child's learning and developing abilities as a reader of informational texts.

While I planned the details and prepared the materials for the family research project, I continued to create opportunities for my students to acquire and demonstrate their knowledge of natural disasters. We continued practicing Reading and Thinking with My Buddy in a formal workshop setting during our literacy period. We also devoted a section of our literacy block to developing our skills in asking questions and researching answers. We created large-group inquiry charts to document our findings. I created graphic organizers to support my students' inquiries and introduced many of the organizers during our small-group learning sessions. My students began learning how to take active listening notes while their buddy read or spoke. (See Figure 5.3.) I created lessons to teach highlighting important information and other active reading strategies. In building my students' research skills, their interactions with one another during Reading and Thinking with My Buddy evolved further as well. To help them focus their reading during their research process, I developed the asking-questions guide shown in Figure 5.6.

In the afternoons, a time I generally reserved for multiple intelligence–based learning, I planned for self-selected centers-based activities that students could participate in. While some students spent afternoons creating clay sculptures and information cards of natural disasters, others wrote and revised new reports that they would later deliver as Channel 205 news anchors in our dramatic play area. I created a music studio center where students could choose to use their knowledge to write and perform a song about a natural disaster. In the art center, students created picture stories on large sheets of chart paper that we later glued together to make a story mural. The students in the writing center also used large chart paper to write collaboratively a realistic fiction story about a family experiencing a natural disaster. In the creation station, students worked with various materials to make diagrams of volcanoes they

| Research Notes | | |
| --- | --- | --- |

Name: _____ Date: _____

Title of the story: _____

| I have a question! | Proof from the text | Answer |
| --- | --- | --- |
| | | |
| | | |
| | | |
| | | |
| | | |

had learned about. They later labeled each part of the volcano and displayed their work outside our classroom.

Because my students became more and more interested in learning about natural disasters and our winter vacation was fast approaching, I decided to move forward with the family research project. First, my class and I brainstormed a list of questions that we still had about natural disasters. From this list, we created an inquiry question that tied all of our "small questions" together. To notify the parents about the project, I created a general information packet to outline the purpose of the project, highlight the important dates, and offer support for materials acquisition and technological needs. In the project, I asked that students choose a natural disaster to research with their family during winter break and explained that our class would be presenting their findings during a presentation fair after we returned to school. Students and families were responsible for creating a presentation board to document their findings. They would also have to select three activities from a tic-tac-toe grid of multiple intelligence–based activities that I had developed. I filled the grid with activities that we had already done in class so that each student had prior experience with the tasks. I also included a parent grade report and student grade report for my families to have ownership of the overall evaluation of the research project. In these reports, students were assessed on their research and content, high-quality work, and presentation and speaking skills. Finally, I organized information and question-and-answer sessions in which parents could come to our classroom before or after school to ask questions, gain clarity, and address their concerns about the project. This proved to be valuable for some parents who needed more clarification regarding the expectations of the project and their children's work.

When my students returned from their winter vacation, we held our research project fair. I invited our students' families, the school administration, faculty, and other primary classrooms to visit the fair, ask my students questions about their projects, and support their efforts. I was truly amazed on this day! My students were confident in their knowledge and could explain their research with little or no support. They beamed with pride at their creations and showed off their work to each visitor that passed by.

## Using PRC2 in the Primary Classroom

Using PRC2 in the primary classroom proved to be a highly beneficial experience. The greatest impact from implementing the primary-classroom adaptation of PRC2 was clearly evident in the level and rate of student growth as well

Children studying a research project display board that
includes a report by a parent on his experience in an
earthquake.

as in the opportunities for enhanced learning. My students' ability to navigate
informational texts was hugely affected by the implementation of this process.
They became well versed in identifying external features of nonfiction text and
could apply their knowledge in varied situations. My students learned a great
deal about how to use informational texts as resources for finding answers to
their questions. Their comprehension skills while reading nonfiction text began
to climb significantly higher in a short amount of time, increasing to levels
comparable to their fictional text comprehension.

In adapting the PRC2 process for the early childhood learner, I practiced
varying levels of differentiated instruction to meet the needs of all my students. I
used my collection of informational texts as a differentiation tool to meet the
varied needs of my developing readers, while planning and implementing

mini-lessons to address large-group trends and classwide areas for growth. Implementing the PRC2 adaptation in the format of a reader's workshop schedule also allowed me to circulate the room while partners worked together to read and think. In doing so, I was able to provide individualized support for specific students while the remainder of the class worked interdependently to facilitate their own learning. Because of my freedom to move systematically from student pair to student pair, I was able to gain an objective understanding of the developmental needs for supplementation that my students were exhibiting. Documenting my observations allowed me to purposefully modify and accommodate the PRC2 process for the early childhood learner.

Although implementing the PRC2 adaptation Reading and Thinking with My Buddy was largely successful, I did find some areas to reflect on further. For example, I noticed that flexibly grouping students into partners for Reading and Thinking with My Buddy was a valuable procedure. However, because my students were acquiring more advanced reading skills at varying rates, the student pairs I assigned were constantly becoming imbalanced. Continually assessing student growth with formal evaluations (such as a reading inventory or the Fountas and Pinnell Assessment) in such frequency is something I felt conflicted about. As an early childhood educator, I am always informally evaluating my students' progress through anecdotal records, checklists, and so on. These low-anxiety assessments allow me to collect valuable information regarding my students' development while avoiding the pressures and stress that more formal assessments bring. As a result, I found myself torn between a decision to formally assess my students more frequently and a decision to use less informative anecdotal notes to essentially make an educated guess when reorganizing their partnerships.

In the end, creating a primary adaptation for PRC2 offered my students the missing link in literacy instruction that I was yearning to provide for them. Reading fictional texts for pleasure requires a completely different set of skills than does reading nonfiction texts for information. It is our responsibility as educators to prepare our students for a life of autonomous thinking, competence in a competitive environment, and a sense of belonging in their community. One's ability to navigate through and interact with informational texts plays a large part in achieving these three goals. From one educator to another, my advice is to take the plunge. Use Reading and Thinking with My Buddy or create your own adaptation of PRC2 for your early childhood readers. Not only will you be able to show them how much fun reading for information can be, but you'll arm them with an arsenal of skills that will carry them through the rest of their lives.

# Assessing Students' Interests, Knowledge, and Concepts

**6**

? How do I assess what students know and the progress they are making in learning?

In this chapter, **Christine Kamp Seidman**, a literacy facilitator, addresses the challenge of using assessment information to help teachers and students see what they know and need to learn and to inform teaching as well as to monitor progress.

Christine's work focuses on the ongoing assessments in PRC2, including the rationale for assessing knowledge, the construction of assessment tests, and directions for administering the tests. She is part of National-Louis University's Chicago Literacy Instruction Partnership (CLIP) project team and is a facilitator for Project ALL.

92

Chapter
Six
Assessing
Students'
Interests,
Knowledge,
and Concepts

In PRC2, informal assessments are used throughout a unit of study to pair students and to inform teachers about their background, their conceptual and vocabulary knowledge, and their organizational knowledge of the topic. For relevant learning to occur, teachers need to be aware of their students' prior knowledge, reading level, and progress. Then they are better able to individualize instruction to meet the learning needs of their students (Ogle, 2008). In PRC2, students should be reading at their independent reading level and should be paired with a partner at a comparable reading level (Allington, 2006). As explained in Chapter 7, a one-minute Classroom Fluency Snapshot is given individually to students to help the teacher match students with partners of similar reading development. Classroom Fluency Snapshots are given three times during the school year for progress monitoring. In addition, several short content assessments are given at the beginning and completion of each unit to ascertain students' background knowledge and understanding of central concepts and academic vocabulary essential for the unit. Ongoing observational assessments take place throughout the unit of study to inform teachers and students on a daily basis about how the students are progressing on the topic and how well they are mastering the partner reading protocol (see Chapter 3). Teacher Assessment is at the core of the PRC2 program.

# Implementation of Pre- and Post-Assessments

The learning of the content in social studies and science is the goal of these PRC2 units. Therefore, at the beginning of each of the units we have developed a series of short, instructional assessments that help both teachers and students assess their entry knowledge and familiarity with the structures and concepts foundational to the topic of study. We wanted assessments that were interesting, that were fun for students to complete, and that would quickly provide feedback. By using these assessments, teachers have been able to adjust their instructional focus and tailor their activities to students' level of knowledge. For example, the unit on the solar system turns out to be one for which the students in our schools already possess a great deal of knowledge. Some teachers shortened this unit; others added more sophisticated activities and projects for individual and group work. Academic vocabulary was more challenging across the units. The most difficult assessment we developed turned out to be the morphology test, one that asks students to break academic terms into their underlying morphemic structure, using knowledge of affixes, roots, and base words. In some schools, teachers have decided to extend their teaching of morphology both in language arts and in the content areas. This chapter explains each of these assessments and how they are being used within the units.

## Pre-Tests

Pre-tests inform teachers of the students' prior knowledge of the topic and their preparation for reading. Knowing what students know and what they need to know is critical information for informed instruction and learning. Teachers often activate students' interests and help them call up their knowledge that is pertinent to the topic by engaging the whole class in a K-W-L (Ogle, 2008). However, teachers also need to know what each student brings to the learning, and some individual assessments are very useful. In our work to provide strong personalized instruction to all students, we developed a set of short, engaging assessments. We devised pre-tests for a Visual Interest Inventory, as well as Table of Contents, Idea Web, and Morphological assessments of the vocabulary. Having an understanding of the students' familiarity with and knowledge of a topic helps the teacher plan for instruction. The pretests, presented as an introduction to the vocabulary, activate the students' prior knowledge of the topic. This knowledge serves as a metacognitive base that helps both teacher and students plan for and assess their learning.

The students' background knowledge of the topic that they are about to study provides students with an opportunity to reflect on their knowledge of the subject and their readiness for learning. Students become aware of the topic's vocabulary and concepts and quickly realize what they know and do not know. They can also think about the major categories that define the area they will study (through the Table of Contents Assessment) and use these as anchors for what they learn. Students become more responsible for their learning as they form questions about what they do not know and seek answers to those questions, which serve as their purpose for reading. This best-practice principle of asking questions leads teachers to front-load or activate the students' thinking about the topic (Daniels & Bizar, 2004; Ogle, 2008).

## Setting the Stage for Vocabulary Development

The pre-tests are also used for introducing the unit academic vocabulary to the students. The vocabulary words may be known, familiar, or unfamiliar to the students. Concept words are often unfamiliar to students if they are part of a

94

Chapter
Six
Assessing
Students'
Interests,
Knowledge,
and Concepts

topic students know little about. As mentioned earlier, knowledge and rein-forcement of academic language is critical for learning in the content areas (Bear, Invernizzi, Templeton, & Johnston, 2006; Marzano, 2004). Academic language is very difficult for some English speakers as well as for bilingual speakers. If the topic is familiar, students may know most of the words; if not, confronting the new vocabulary activates students' thinking for future encoun-ters with the words, even if they do not know the word or meaning, and it alerts them to note these words when they occur in oral and written texts. If students are familiar with the concepts, the words will activate their prior knowledge. Meeting the vocabulary in the pre-tests sets the stage for student learning.

Students become more responsible for their learning when they are aware of what they don't know. Pre-tests were developed to encourage student self-assessment as well as to monitor student learning. The ultimate goal is to encourage students to become independent learners. The pre-tests were given to the students prior to introducing partner reading for the new topic. We found that having students grade their own pre-tests was beneficial. Having students go through the process of grading their own work makes them more aware of what they know and what they need to know and, ultimately, more responsible for their learning. Involving students in discussion focused on the grading of the pre-test becomes a primary learning experience for the stu-dents. They immediately realize what they don't know, and this builds capac-ity for future learning.

As we developed the units of study, we also sought input from the stu-dents in participating classrooms. In questionnaires given to students after they had completed the unit of study, many students regularly responded that learning vocabulary helped them to be better readers, to read fluently, and to perform better on tests. When asked, "Did PRC2 help your reading?" one fourth-grade student replied, "I got to learn more and I can read better." Another wrote, "It helped me read more carefully in my other reading that I do." Many said that it taught them to reread when they don't understand the material they were reading.

## Post-Tests

Because nonfiction reading in the content areas is the major focus of PRC2, we felt compelled to be able to ascertain the growth students achieved in learning the content. The same pre-tests are used as post-tests to monitor and measure student growth. The tests are given at the conclusion of each PRC2 unit of study.

Most classrooms worked on a PRC2 unit for three to four weeks, either before the prescribed curriculum unit of study or in conjunction with the prescribed curriculum. In a sampling of seventy-five sixth-grade students in three classrooms, there was notable growth (30–40 percent) between the pre- and post-test Table of Contents and Idea Web assessments. The improvements on the Morphology Assessment was 16–49 percent.

# Visual Interest Inventory

Students tend to choose and read those books that are familiar to them. Nonfiction text is usually not selected by students unless they have a special interest in or knowledge of a particular topic, especially in classrooms where fiction dominates. The Visual Interest Inventory was designed to encourage students to think critically about choosing a book they would want to read. This initial activity gives the students a sampling of what to expect. It alerts the students to the topic, concepts, and vocabulary. It also can help teachers match students and books; for example, one student wrote, "I like mysteries." This gave the teacher a clear indication of which of the content books to suggest to this reader. The teacher had two books that seemed appropriate during the unit on ancient Egypt: one focused on a lost pyramid and one on the question of the boy king. They were full of information and intriguing to the student.

An important component of the PRC2 program is reading visual material—that is, maps, graphs, photographs, drawings, captions, and so on—which is explained in Chapter 10. Helping students to get information from a book cover is also an important reading skill that encourages activating prior knowledge and prediction. Many students have never been encouraged by their teachers to use this kind of visual information in their preparation for reading. This activity helps model a skill common to expert readers.

## Construction of the Visual Interest Inventory

The Visual Interest Inventory pre-test includes a total of nine book covers:

- three nonfiction books from the text set
- three fiction texts related to the topic
- three fiction texts unrelated to the topic

96

Chapter
Six
Assessing
Students'
Interests,
Knowledge,
and Concepts

The book covers are scanned onto a worksheet with one book from each category in each row, making three rows. Students are asked to choose one book from each row. Lines are provided under each row asking students to explain their choice. A color transparency of the page could be put on an overhead projector. Showing the students the actual book covers would be optimal to avoid poor reproduction quality. Students should be able to read the titles, subtitle, and any other information on the cover. A black-and-white reprint is often not of adequate print quality. We found that print clarity was critical for students to be able to make an informed choice.

## Scoring Student Inventories

In the fourth-grade unit on Native Americans, student responses ranged from "It looks interesting" and "I like stories about horses" to "I like to learn about Native Americans" (Figure 6.1). An in-depth evaluation of students' comments demonstrated that their choices often depended on how carefully they viewed and read the cover, whether they carefully read the title and subtitle, their knowledge of English, and what initially sparked their interest. Students' genre preferences also were clear. For example, "I like mysteries," "I want to read about history," and "I want action" are explanations that help teachers find books for particular students. In scoring responses, one point is given for each nonfiction title selected in each row, for a total of three points. As we reviewed student responses to these choices, we chunked their responses and found several types of answers, including the following:

- Intrigue of the cover
- Familiarity with the topic
- Interest in the genre (that is, "I like mysteries")
- Interest in the topic
- Wanting to learn more about the topic
- Recommended by someone
- Prediction

# Table of Contents Assessment

Gaining information about a book from its table of contents is one of the first strategies a good reader uses before reading a nonfiction text. The table of contents gives the student an overview of the book, allowing the student to gain information about the text to facilitate predictions of what's to come, a critical

Figure 6.1 Visual Interest Inventory: Pre-Test and Post-Test 97

## Visual Interest Inventory

Name: _____ Date: _____

Which one of these books would you most want to read and why? Place a
check (✓) next to the cover picture/letter and explain in the lines beneath why
you would want to read that book.

____ A        ____ B        ____ C

Why? _____
_____
_____

____ A        ____ B        ____ C

Why? _____
_____
_____

____ A        ____ B        ____ C

Why? _____
_____
_____

98

Chapter
Six
Assessing
Students'
Interests,
Knowledge,
and Concepts

strategy in reading nonfiction (see Chapter 10). The organization of the book as outlined in the table of contents helps students categorize learning and locate specific information they need. This activity demonstrates the importance of giving students the opportunity to reflect on the information they know about the topic and to predict what might be encountered during their reading. Activating thinking through prediction is another best-practice strategy that is equally important when reading content text as it is when reading fiction. Students need to have some understanding of the topic in order to successfully complete the pre-test, as well as an understanding of the information they gain from a table of contents. This assessment demonstrates the students' knowledge of the topic and subsets of the topic, as well as their knowledge of chapter organization.

## Students' Responses

In Figure 6.2, we can see that this fourth-grade student knows something about simple machines. He knows that they do work, and he mentioned three simple machines. Does he know the other three? He also knows something

**Figure 6.2** Table of Contents Pre-Test, Example of Student Work

Name: _Derek_ _____  Date: _____

We are beginning a unit on simple machines. On the two tables of contents below, fill out what types of chapters you might read about. Using what you know about machines and skateboards, what are important topics that should be included as possible chapter titles?

| Simple Machines | Skateboards |
|---|---|
| Chapter 1 _How they work_ | Chapter 1 _What they do_ |
| Chapter 2 _How they help_ | Chapter 2 _Different kinds of skateboards_ |
| Chapter 3 _Wheels and axles_ | Chapter 3 _How are they made?_ |
| Chapter 4 _Inclined planes_ | Chapter 4 _Who made them?_ |
| Chapter 5 _Screws_ | Chapter 5 _Why are they fun?_ |
| Concept: Machines Do Work | Concept: An In-Depth Look at One Machine |

about skateboards and chapter organization. Knowing how to organize and connect ideas is a key to learning new content; as students begin a new unit, they need to think of the ways experts organize information. The table of contents activity is a simple way to help students begin to adopt the expert organizing framework and to think of key categories that define topics they study. Teachers who use this activity regularly can also direct students to think about the internal structure of ideas suggested by the table of contents. For example, a book about Egypt that has a table of contents with chapters titled First Pharaohs, The Golden Age, Later Rulers, and Cleopatra and Roman Rulers clearly indicates a chronological frame. Another text, with chapters titled Culture, Religion, Class System, and Education, indicates an organization by topics, or main ideas. In science, the organization of the table of contents will depend on the topic; some tables of contents are clearly classification and description, others problem-solution and compare-contrast. Students can learn to use the table of contents as a way to think about the organization of key ideas by experts. They can then be better prepared to make choices in their own writing so that they select the organizing frame that works best for them.

## Construction of the Table of Contents Assessment

The Table of Contents Assessment presents students with a broad topic from the unit of study (for example, the solar system) and a biographical or specific reference (for example, Mars), depending on the topic. Both the more general and the specific tables of contents are connected to what students will be learning. The Table of Contents Assessment for the Native American unit includes *Native Americans* and *Pocahontas*. Students need to think about the organizational structure of each topic and list the chapters they might find in each book. Each heading has five chapters. *Native American* could include topics focused on the homes, rituals, food, locations, and various nations. *Pocahontas* would include chapters devoted to her life story (that is, early life, family, conflicts, and accomplishments).

## Scoring the Table of Contents Assessment

The Table of Contents Assessment is scored by counting the number of correct answers (ten). As we piloted this assessment, we used it for two units in the same classes. Most students improved on this assessment between the pre- and post-tests. The mean total scores for four sixth-grade classes on the Ancient Egypt unit showed an increase of 35–43 percent on this assessment

100

Chapter
Six
Assessing
Students'
Interests,
Knowledge,
and Concepts

Figure 6.3 Mean Total Scores Based on Number Correct

| Grade 6—<br>Ancient Egypt | Table of<br>Contents<br>Pre- (10) | Table of<br>Contents<br>Post- (10) | Change |
|---|---|---|---|
| Class 1 | 5.67 | 9.913 | 4.333 |
| Class 2 | 4.714 | 8.143 | 4.368 |
| Class 3 | 5.652 | 9.235 | 3.529 |
| Class 4 | 4 | 8.091 | 3.778 |

(Figure 6.3). When these same students did a subsequent PRC2 unit, the mean total score on the post-test ranged from 7.5 to 9.8 out of ten (75–98 percent). This reflected the students' understanding of the organizational format as well as the topic. On the Student Questionnaire, several students commented that reading the table of contents was something they learned to do in PRC2. Students became more cognizant of the table of contents in the books they read and were able to use the information the table of contents provided to predict what they would learn from the text. At the beginning, many students were not familiar with the information they could gain from a table of contents. Once they learned this reading strategy, both their pre- and post-test scores improved. Familiarity with the organizational format helps students develop a strategy for future reading.

## Idea Web Assessment

The Idea Web Assessment asks students to look at academic vocabulary and categorizes words associated with the topic. Academic vocabulary is a stumbling block for those students who are unfamiliar with the concepts. Helping students gain the vocabulary they need for a given unit of study allows them to become successful readers (Blachowicz & Fisher, 2002; Marzano, 2004). In the pre-test, students are given a list of words that will be important in the unit of study and are asked to chunk these terms on a graphic organizer with major headings identified. Many students are confronted with vocabulary that they may not know. Based on what they do know, they can use prediction strategies to try to unlock the meaning of the words. The categories in social studies units are general words or concepts that students are familiar with, such as religion, economics, people. The categories in science are specific to the topic.

## Construction of the Idea Web Assessment

In this graphic word sort, students are given two to five categories on a spider map and a list of corresponding words taken from the vocabulary of the text sets (Figure 6.4). The words chosen should be those that are most frequently used and important for understanding the topic. Each word is used once. Teachers are careful to include some words that all students know at least at some basic level. We don't want this initial encounter with the concepts and vocabulary to be defeating; a mix of unfamiliar, challenging terms with some more well-known terms is more inviting for students. The number of words included on the list will vary, depending on the topic and the number of content-specific vocabulary words.

### Scoring the Webs

As students create their own webs, they quickly realize the advantage of crossing off words as they use them. The Idea Web Assessment is another visual indicator of what the students know and what they need to learn. One point is given for each correct answer. Having students grade their own pre-test helps them to see their errors, and the assessment instrument becomes a learning tool. In a sixth-grade class of striving readers (the majority reading below grade level), students showed a 30 percent increase in growth between the pre- and post-tests. In a sixth-grade gifted class, students showed an increase of 71 percent between the pre- and post-tests. This reflects the advantages that attention to concepts throughout a unit and engaging students with reading in the PRC2 format offer all students regardless of their ability level. The students see their own growth.

# Morphology Assessment

The Morphology Assessment asks students to break words into parts: prefix, root or base word, and suffixes. The ability to recognize word parts, prefixes, and suffixes determines students' reading ability (Bear et al., 2006). English learners are often not aware that many of the words they meet are cognates of

102

Chapter
Six
Assessing
Students'
Interests,
Knowledge,
and Concepts

**Figure 6.4** Idea Web Assessment: Pre-Test on Prior Knowledge;
Post-Test on Knowledge Learned

## Idea Web Assessment

Name: _____ Date: _____

**Directions:** Choose words from the lists below and put them under the appropriate category or concept. Use as many of the words as you know and only use the word once. Some categories may have blank spaces even though you used all the words.

| | | | |
|---|---|---|---|
| asteroids | astronaut(s) | astronomer | booster rocket |
| comets | crew | Earth | Galileo |
| Jupiter | launch pad | Mars | Mercury |
| meteor | mission specialist | moon | Neptune |
| planets | remote manipulator system | robot arm | Neptune |
| planets | remote manipulator system | robot arm | satellites |
| Saturn | shuttle | space station | Uranus |
| Venus | Yuri Gagarin | cargo bay | |

**Orbiting Objects**

_____
_____
_____
_____

**People**

_____
_____
_____
_____

**Solar System**

**Planets**

_____
_____
_____
_____

**Spacecrafts**

_____
_____
_____
_____

words that they know (August & Shanahan, 2006). The English words may not look familiar to ELs. And, without looking closely, many of those students give up. The base or root of the word frequently comes from Latin or Greek and is the same or similar in English and Spanish, for example. It is often the case that words that are common in Spanish are more esoteric in English; this can give Spanish speakers a real boost in confidence if they take advantage of this strength. Beginning at fourth grade, all students should build their understanding of the common base and root words, prefixes, and suffixes in order to increase their vocabulary knowledge. Students may find these kinds of activities confusing if they are unfamiliar with looking for and identifying meanings contained in word parts. They need to learn to ask, "What clues can we get from the parts of a word to help us with its meaning?"

## Construction of the Morphology Assessment

Ten words are selected from the vocabulary lists or glossaries of the text sets. They should be words that are critical to the unit of study. The correct number of boxes is given for the word parts. Students are asked to divide the words into their meaning units and then also define the words on the line beneath each word (Figure 6.5). Students receive a point for each correct word part and meaning. Depending on the words, the number of word parts will vary. There are ten definitions.

## Knowledge Rating Chart

In some units, only a few words can be defined through the use of word parts. For example, the Simple Machines unit had very few words that were appropriate for the Morphology Assessment. Instead, we developed a knowledge rating chart for sixteen vocabulary words. Students rated the word by checking the appropriate category: Don't Know It, Seen or Heard It, Know It Well. Then they were asked to use the word in a sentence and draw a picture of it (Figure 6.6). The student in Figure 6.6 demonstrates that she knows most of the vocabulary. She is clear about what she doesn't know, and the way she used the word *slope* in the sentence shows that she has some understanding, but she indicates some uncertainty. Her ability to illustrate her knowledge, as well as to use the vocabulary in sentences, informs us that she has a strong understanding of the vocabulary. We know exactly that she needs to learn about friction, and we need to reinforce the meaning of *slope*.

Both of these assessments give the teacher a very clear picture of the students' understanding of the vocabulary and their knowledge of the concepts.

104

Chapter
Six

Assessing
Students'
Interests,
Knowledge,
and Concepts

**Figure 6.5** Morphology Assessment

## Morphology Assessment

Name: _____ Date: _____

As we learn new vocabulary, it is often helpful to keep breaking words into parts—some of which can help us figure out what the word means. For example, what does it mean if you buy something that is imported? If you break this word into its word parts, you can get more meaning.

*im* = into
*port* = to carry
*ed* = happened in the past

| im | port | ed |

So the word *imported* probably means that it was carried into someplace (from somewhere else).

**Directions:** Use the boxes to divide these words into their parts. Write what you think the words can mean.

1. dehydrate
Probably means _____

2. decomposing
Probably means _____

3. mummify
Probably means _____

4. embalmer
Probably means _____

5. pictogram
Probably means _____

6. hieroglyphs
Probably means _____

7. surveyor
Probably means _____

8. Egyptologist
Probably means _____

9. archaeologist
Probably means _____

10. claustrophobic
Probably means _____

## Figure 6.6 Pre- and Post-Assessments (Vocabulary)

**Knowledge Rating Chart**

Name: _Berta_ _____ Date: _____

Read the words and check the ones you know well. Write a sentence or draw a picture of each of them. For words that you are uncertain of or don't know, check the appropriate box.

| Word | Don't Know It | Seen or Heard It | Know It Well | Use it in a sentence. | Draw a picture of it. |
|---|---|---|---|---|---|
| forces | | | X | We have the force to move the feather. |  |
| pulley | | | X | A pulley can pull things up. |  |
| lever | | | X | We push levers to make things move. |  |
| mechanical | | | X | Some people use mechanical pencils. |  |
| friction | X | | | | |
| catapult | | | X | They used to launch catapults. |  |
| slope | | X | | There is a big slope of sidewalk the streets. | 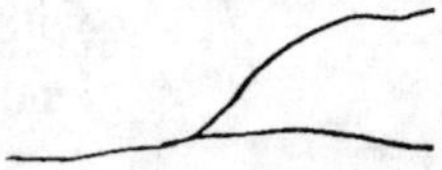 |
| load | | | X | The load is part of a seesaw. |  |

106

Chapter
Six
Assessing
Students'
Interests,
Knowledge,
and Concepts

The students, too, can use these pre-tests to help them set their own learning goals and monitor their practice of the terms. Morphology is one area in which the students showed the least growth between the pre- and post-tests. One teacher reported after having done the unit and looking at the Morphology Assessment results that she should have spent more time on the vocabulary and especially the root or base words. In the future, she would incorporate more of the vocabulary activities into her teaching. She thought that the time spent on the prefixes and suffixes had helped her students in the statewide exams.

## Assessment Protocol

An assessment protocol for creating your own unit of study to correspond to a curriculum unit is provided in Figure 6.7. First you want to create a text set that includes the reading ranges of the students in your class. The vocabulary words are taken from these books. Creating the assessments is relatively easy using our suggested formats. The key is helping your students gain success in academic language even though they do not have the language skills or the background knowledge. The partner reading and discussion in these units give them the confidence and knowledge they need to understand the grade-level texts. Take some time to peruse the Native American Content Unit Guide on the DVD that accompanies this book. It gives you a model to follow.

## Final Reflections

Not all leveled trade books will cover all of the information for every unit of study that you want the students to learn. Students will probably only complete one or two books during PRC2 for a unit. Once students are familiar with the process and their reading improves, the number of books read may increase. Because this is a supplement to your curriculum, you should not be concerned that every student is gaining all of the information required. Rather, PRC2 is a process that will comfortably expand the students' present knowledge level and will prepare students for the learning that will occur during the actual unit of study. It provides for and enhances the students' background knowledge.

### Discussion, the Knowledge Builder

As previously mentioned, discussion is a critical component of PRC2. Students discuss their reading during partner reading, discuss their responses to

| Getting Started |
| --- |

1. Select subject appropriate **leveled texts for each unit set** that represent the instructional reading levels of your students. Number the book sets. (All books of a set should have the same number so they can be easily sorted and filed.)

2. List the titles, authors, and reading level of each book. Reading levels, if not listed on the back of the book, can be found in the publisher's catalogue or on its website. Also check www.lexile.com, www.scholastic.com, or www .fountasandpinnellleveledbooks.com/.

3. Create a Word document table or Excel spreadsheet and record all highlighted or targeted vocabulary words in each text. Words that are common to most texts and that represent key content terms will become the featured academic vocabulary for the topic.

4. Fill in the **Theme at a Glance** page including the book's number (#1 above), title, and reading level (#2 above). List the theme vocabulary taken from the text sets (#3 above). (Not all texts will have identical vocabulary.) Select the appropriate state standards.

5. Fill out the **Text Set Specifics** page including the title, author, publisher, ISBN, reading levels; book parts and features (not all books are written in the same format); vocabulary; and content (a brief synopsis).

6. List the **Cognates** that are specific to the theme.

| Assessment Tools |
| --- |

Not all assessments are applicable for all themes. Choose at least four that will give you the information you need about your students' background knowledge for the theme.

1. Choose nine book covers for the **Visual Interest Inventory** (three books from the text sets, three fiction texts related to the topic, and three fiction texts unrelated to the topic). The book covers are scanned onto a worksheet with one book from each category in each row, making three rows. Lines are drawn under the rows asking students why they made that choice. A color transparency of the page could be put on an overhead projector. Showing the students the actual book covers would be optimal to avoid poor reproduction quality. Students should be able to read the titles and subtitles and gather any available information from the covers. A black-and-white reprint is often not adequate print quality. We found that print clarity was critical for students to make an informed choice.

2. Choose ten vocabulary words from the texts that you want your students to learn based on grade-level standards. Word choice should include affixes, roots, base words, and cognates that are grade level appropriate. Enter them on the **Rate Your Knowledge** template.

3. Select fifteen to twenty-one vocabulary words for the **Idea Web Assessment**. Select three or four categories that represent the key concepts. Enter them on the Idea Web template.

4. Select two concepts, one broad and one narrow, within the theme for the **Table of Contents Assessment**. These will depend on the theme. Examples are Simple Machines—Simple Machines and Skateboards; Solar System—Planets and Earth; Ancient Egypt—Ancient Egyptians (People/Cultures) and Cleopatra (Biography).

5. Select ten vocabulary words for the **Morphology Assessment** template. Create the teacher's key as you look up the words to verify their meaningful parts.

108

Chapter
Six
Assessing
Students'
Interests,
Knowledge,
and Concepts

the texts, and share information at the end of each session. "What did you learn or discover today?" is an easy way to include all students in the discussion even though they read different books.

Sharing of interesting facts and new discoveries builds the collective knowledge of the class. Sharing and discussion also gives the opportunity to use the new academic vocabulary words beneficial to mastery.

## Students Become More Responsible for Their Learning

It is important for students to know the purpose of PRC2. How well they understand its purpose is reflected in their post-test scores. In our initial class work, those who were diligent and responsible showed gains between their pre- and post-tests. In three classes of twenty-five students each, the mean gain was fifteen to twenty-three points on their fluency scores, and at least 30 percent on the Idea Web, Table of Contents, and Morphology post-tests. Figure 6.8 shows how one teacher kept track of changes and tallied the scores of her sixth-grade class of striving readers on the Solar System unit. In this class, most students substantially increased their fluency scores during the year, the Idea Web scores increased by almost 30 percent, the Table of Contents scores increased by 37 percent, and the Morphology scores increased by 15 percent. The spreadsheet gives a clear picture of individual student needs and accomplishments. The teacher noticed the need to focus on vocabulary and word parts. In the next unit, she incorporated more vocabulary activities and spent more time talking about words and their derivations.

Students who are familiar with the protocol and test formats show higher achievement than other students. One teacher reported, "The assessments work best in two regards. First, they are a good measure of background knowledge. Second, comparing the pre- and post-test documents allowed for a concrete example of progress. The students responded favorably to the activities, often sharing facts and ideas well after a lesson."

## Evaluation Surveys

Teacher and student surveys were created as part of our strategy to assess the effectiveness of PRC2. We wanted to know how often they did PRC2 during the week and how many units they had done during the year. When asked "To what degree do you feel that your students benefited from using PRC2?" one teacher replied, "It was extremely beneficial. The students became critical

Figure **6.8** Classroom Data over Time, Solar System Unit

| Grade 6— Solar System | Fluency Snapshot Fall | Fluency Snapshot Spring | Change | Idea Web Pre- (27) | Idea Web Post- (27) | Change | Table of Contents Pre- (10) | Table of Contents Post- (10) | Change | Morphology Pre- (27) | Morphology Post- (27) | Change |
|---|---|---|---|---|---|---|---|---|---|---|---|---|
| Dominique | 154 | 161 | 7 | 26 | 19 | -7 | 1 | 9 | 8 | 1 | | |
| Jennifer | 139 | 181 | 42 | 25 | 27 | 2 | 7 | 8 | 1 | 5 | 5 | 0 |
| Mark | 89 | 137 | 48 | 20 | 24 | 4 | 3 | 7 | 4 | 5 | 8 | 3 |
| Gabriel | 107 | 122 | 15 | 25 | 25 | 0 | 10 | 9 | -1 | 6 | 8 | 2 |
| Joshua | | 92 | | 22 | 26 | 4 | | 9 | | 4 | 6 | 2 |
| Cheyenne | 64 | 87 | 23 | 22 | 23 | 1 | | 8 | | 2 | 4 | 2 |
| Juan | 82 | 87 | 5 | 24 | 27 | 3 | 10 | 10 | 0 | 5 | 6 | 1 |
| Derese | 70 | 79 | 9 | 26 | 26 | 0 | 3 | 9 | 6 | 5 | 10 | 5 |
| Talmas | 95 | 73 | -22 | 24 | 25 | 1 | 2 | 10 | 8 | 4 | | |
| Sarah | 122 | 113 | -9 | 21 | 26 | 5 | 4 | 8 | 4 | 3 | 5 | 2 |
| Beatris | | 169 | | 13 | 24 | 11 | | 10 | | 5 | 3 | -2 |
| Gloria | 116 | 113 | -3 | 19 | 27 | 8 | 4 | 7 | 3 | 4 | | |
| Sheila | 71 | 88 | 17 | 16 | 25 | 9 | 1 | 4 | 3 | 4 | 8 | 4 |
| Alyssa | 40 | 87 | 47 | 14 | 27 | 13 | 1 | 7 | 6 | 7 | 6 | -1 |
| Willie | | 28 | | 13 | | | | 4 | | 6 | | |
| Ismael | 116 | 146 | 30 | 26 | 24 | -2 | 2 | | | 8 | 7 | -1 |
| Sergio | 50 | 75 | 25 | 21 | 26 | 5 | | 8 | | 7 | 7 | 0 |
| Richard | 91 | 139 | 48 | 22 | 16 | -6 | 10 | 10 | 0 | 9 | | |
| David | 122 | 149 | 27 | 26 | 27 | 1 | | 10 | | 5 | 8 | 3 |
| Nathaniel | 102 | 159 | 57 | 22 | 26 | 4 | 4 | 10 | 6 | 6 | 10 | 4 |
| | | | | | | | | | | | | |
| TOTAL | 1630 | 2285 | 366 | 427 | 470 | 56 | 62 | 157 | 48 | 101 | 101 | 24 |
| | | | | | | | | | | | | |
| MEAN | 95.9 | 114 | 22 | 21.4 | 24.7 | 2.9 | 4.429 | 8.263 | 3.7 | 5.05 | 6.73 | 1.6 |

110

Chapter
Six
Assessing
Students'
Interests,
Knowledge,
and Concepts

thinkers and enjoyed discussing books. It integrated social studies and science content that was meaningful and taught the students to learn while reading." His response was similar to many who responded; their reflections were positive and indicated ways they were adapting the process to their own settings.

We knew the growth that students were making on the assessments and through our observations, but we also wanted to know how PRC2 had affected their learning. Most important, we wanted to give students the opportunity to reflect on their learning during PRC2. Many students responded on the Student PRC2 Questionnaire (Figure 6.9) that their reading improved, they

**Figure 6.9** Student PRC2 Questionnaire

## PRC2 Questionnaire

Name: _____ Grade: _____

1. What aspect of PRC2 was most helpful to you? _____
   _____
   _____

2. What aspect of PRC2 was least helpful to you? _____
   _____
   _____

3. Did PRC2 help your reading? (Circle one.)    Yes       No
   If you responded yes, explain **how** it helped your reading. _____
   _____
   _____

   If you responded no, explain. _____
   _____
   _____

4. Did your vocabulary knowledge improve with PRC2? (Circle one.)    Yes       No

5. What strategies did you learn from PRC2 that you can use in your reading throughout the day? _____
   _____
   _____

6. Do you use PRC2 strategies in your reading in other subjects?
   (Circle one.)    Yes       No

Thank you for your thoughtfulness in filling out this questionnaire.

became more fluent, they were better at vocabulary, and they were better readers in all content areas. One student replied, "PRC2 helped me know that there are tons of strategies." Jocelyne said, "It helped my reading by helping me understand more." Most students said that they like partner reading because their partner can help them with words they don't know or understand. Others said that they learned to use sticky notes, that they learned to ask themselves questions while they read, and they learned to reread when they do not understand what they are reading. We encourage students to use the strategies they have learned in PRC2 in their reading throughout the day. Reading strategies are being reinforced throughout the PRC2 program. When students understand and incorporate these strategies in their reading, they become independent readers and learners.

In closing, the true value in these assessment tools is in looking at the results. Yes, there is value for the students in helping them see what they need to know and how they are progressing as they strive to become independent learners. And there is value for the teacher, who needs to be aware of where the students are in their knowledge of the topic, in their vocabulary knowledge, and in their ability to follow the PRC2 protocol. This gives the teacher insight into developing meaningful instruction (Popham, 2008). Assessment is at the core of using PRC2 in the content units.

# References

Allington, R. L. (2006). *What really matters for struggling readers: Designing research-based programs* (2nd ed.). Boston: Allyn & Bacon.

August, D., & Shanahan, T. (Eds.). (2006). *Developing literacy in second-language learners: Report of the National Literacy Panel on Language-Minority Children and Youth.* Mahwah, NJ: Lawrence Erlbaum.

Bear, D. R., Invernizzi, M., Templeton, S., & Johnston, F. (2006). *Words their way: Word study for phonics, vocabulary, and spelling instruction.* Upper Saddle River, NJ: Pearson Prentice Hall.

Blachowicz, C., & Fisher, P. J. (2002). *Teaching vocabulary in all classrooms.* Upper Saddle River, NJ: Merrill Prentice Hall.

Blachowicz, C. & Ogle, D. (2008). *Reading comprehension: Strategies for independent learners* (2nd ed.). New York: Guilford.

Daniels, H., & Bizar, M. (2004). *Teaching the best practice way: Methods that matter, K–12.* Portland, ME: Stenhouse.

112

Chapter
Six
Assessing
Students'
Interests,
Knowledge,
and Concepts

Marzano, R. J. (2004). *Building background knowledge for academic achievement*. Alexandria, VA: Association for Supervision and Curriculum Development.

Ogle, D. (2008). *Coming together as readers* (2nd ed.). Thousand Oaks, CA:
Corwin.

Popham, W. J. (2008). *Transformative assessment*. Alexandria, VA: Association for Supervision and Curriculum Development.

# Teacher Ongoing Assessment

## 7

**?** How can I monitor students' progress and document their learning?

In this chapter, **Debbie Gurvitz** addresses the challenge of monitoring student progress in both reading and concept development.

Debbie is Assistant Professor of reading and language at National-Louis University, National College of Education, Chicago, Illinois, where she directs the Reading Specialist Program and Summer Reading Clinic on the Chicago campus. Prior to joining National-Louis University, Debbie was a school district Reading Specialist, building Reading Specialist and Literacy Coach, and classroom teacher. As a member of the Project ALL team, Debbie's role as a university facilitator focused on data collection, observation of PRC2 in a variety of settings, and development and use of formative and performance assessments to inform PRC2 instructional practice and student learning.

Ongoing performance assessment is embedded within the PRC2 model of instruction. Data from the ongoing assessments assist teachers in determining students' prior knowledge about the readings or subject, what they understand from the materials read, and how they apply their knowledge to the readings. Teachers use the data from the ongoing assessments to differentiate instruction, monitor progress, group students, and inform present instructional practices. The ongoing assessments administered within the PRC2 model were carefully chosen to align with the Illinois State Board of Education (ISBE) language arts, science, and social studies learning standards, performance descriptors, and classroom assessments (ISBE, 2000–2002).

The importance of including ongoing assessments and observations rather than traditional assessments was based on current research in assessment (Afflerbach, 2007). The RAND Reading Study Group (2002) and Afflerbach concur with the importance of ongoing performance assessment as a means to discover how students read, think, and learn. Although traditional or standardized reading tests often provide summative data, they do not provide a full account of how well students read and apply what they understand from the readings (Wiggins, 1998).

Four ongoing performance assessments were carefully chosen to help teachers. These include fluency snapshots, observation notes, audiotapes, and vocabulary monitoring. Each informed the teacher about the instructional needs of the students, the effectiveness of the instruction, and how well students read unfamiliar content material, and provided pre- and post-assessment data. The assessments also provided a plethora of information to support instructional practice based on the students' background knowledge of the content before, during, and after the reading; an application of the text to the content; and an interpretation and clarification of the reading through conversation and understanding of word use within the content and during the reading.

## Classroom Fluency Snapshot

A concern for classroom and content area teachers is how to determine where the students are in relationship to the classroom materials that they currently use in content reading. A one-minute Classroom Fluency Snapshot is a quick initial screening that informs oral reading fluency and can readily be used for instructional decision-making. Administering a Classroom Fluency Snapshot at the beginning of the unit helps teachers choose appropriate materials at the students' high instructional (95–97 percent accuracy) or independent level (98–100 percent accuracy) and determine partnerships based on how students read the materials. Current research supports this choice and concurs with the notion that the ability to read fluently (rate, accuracy, and porosity) highly correlates with reading competence (Fuchs, Fuchs, Hosp, & Jenkins, 2001).

## Administering the Test

Administering a one-minute Classroom Fluency Snapshot is quick and efficient. Students read grade-level passages that may be chosen from grade-level texts, published materials, or reading inventories. Because the focus of PRC2 is content reading, we chose grade-level, long expository passages from the *Basic Reading Inventory* (Johns, 2005) for the one-minute Classroom Fluency Snapshot.

To administer and score the one-minute fluency snapshot, follow this procedure:

1. Choose a content grade-level passage of approximately 200 words.

2. Make two copies of the passage so that you have one to mark and the student has one to read.

3. Have the student read the text for one minute.

   a. Time the student using a stopwatch or timer.

   b. Mark errors (/), insertions (^), omissions (O), supplied by teacher (T).

      i. You may tell the student the word if he or she is not able to read it within two seconds.

      ii. If time permits, write the errors above the word that was read incorrectly.

   c. Self-corrections and repetitions are not counted as errors.

   d. Use a double slash (//) to mark the last word that the student read.

4. Count how many words the student read in one minute. Subtract any errors that were made (insertions, substitutions, omissions, told).

**Figure 7.1** Classroom Profile of Fall Fluency Scores Using Sixth-Grade National Norms

| Students | Fall National Norms |
|---|---|
|  | 170 |
|  | 160 |
| Beatrice 152 Dominique 154 | 150 |
|  | 140 |
| Jennifer 139 | 130 |
| David 122 Sarah 122 | 120 |
| Ismael 116 Gloria 116 | 110 |
| Gabrielle 107 Nathan 102 | 100 |
| Richard 91 Eli 95 | 90 |
| Juan C 82 Edison 82 Mark 89 | 80 |
| Sheila 71 Dernite 71 | 70 |
| Cheyanne 64 | 60 |
| Erik 59 | 50 |
| Ilysa 40 Joshua 45 Talmas 46 | 40 |
| Willie 38 | 30 |
|  | 20 |
| Takawah 8 | 10 |

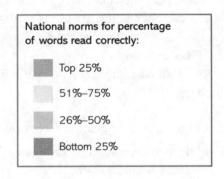

National norms for percentage of words read correctly:

Top 25%

51%–75%

26%–50%

Bottom 25%

5. The result is the student's fluency rate in words correct per minute (WCPM).

6. Chart the results on the fluency Snapshot Scoring Chart (Figure 7.1), ranking the students by WCPM.

In Figure 7.1, notice how easy it is for the teacher to determine partners based on the students' WCPM. It is also important to consider students' disposition toward reading, background knowledge, and home language when pairing students and selecting the text.

Administering one-minute Classroom Fluency Snapshots as an ongoing assessment is a quick way to determine if students are making adequate progress, determine changes in PRC2 partnership and instructional materials, and, again, determine if grade-level materials are within the majority of the students' instructional reading levels. Teachers often administer Classroom Fluency Snapshots fall, winter, and spring, or when beginning a new content unit of study.

Figure 7.2 charts fall and winter one-minute Classroom Fluency Snapshots of Mr. A's sixth-grade class. Each student's fall and winter WCPM is charted in comparison to the sixth-grade national oral fluency norms (Hasbrouck & Tindal, 2006). When examining the chart, the teacher can determine if the students have made adequate progress. Although Cheyanne made significant progress, from 64 WCPM (fall) to 97 WCPM (winter), her fluency rate remains in the bottom 25 percent of the country. Mr. A pointed out that Gloria might have been overlooked if he had not reviewed Figure 7.2. Gloria scored 116 WCPM in the fall, but her score dropped to 92 WCPM in the winter, which now placed her in the bottom 25 percent.

It is important to note fluency growth rates; however, of equal importance is ensuring that during PRC2 students are well matched with their partners and their materials. The use of the Classroom Fluency Snapshots provides an ongoing assessment tool that will help teachers determine instructional level materials and partners for success in PRC2.

# Observational Notes for PRC2

Systematic teacher observation of students is an important ongoing assessment tool that is embedded within the PRC2 instructional model. A question often asked by classroom and content area teachers is how to determine if students are actively engaged in learning when participating in PRC2. Observational notes provide teachers with a systematic approach in the collection of anecdotal notes on students' literacy development when reading content materials. This requires structured time that provides an opportunity for teachers to observe students' oral reading skills, discussion of materials read, knowledge and use of vocabulary, social behavior, communication, pacing, motivation, and comprehension, and then to plan follow-up instruction based on needs determined by the observational anecdotal notes. Current research supports the importance of systematic teacher observation to ensure proper placement in instructional grouping and materials with an end result of successful academic growth (Ediger, 2007).

**Figure 7.2** Comparison of Fall and Winter One-Minute WCPM: Using Sixth-Grade National Norms

| Students | Fall National Norms | Winter National Norms | Students |
|---|---|---|---|
|  | 170 | 170 |  |
|  | 160 | 160 | Dominique 167 |
| Beatrice 152 Dominique 154 | 150 | 150 | Jennifer 156 Beatrice 156 |
|  | 140 | 140 |  |
| Jennifer 139 | 130 | 130 | David 135 |
| David 122 Sarah 122 | 120 | 120 | Ismael 124 Nathan 125 |
| Ismael 116 Gloria 116 | 110 | 110 | Richard 118 Gabrielle 116 |
| Gabrielle 107 Nathan 102 | 100 | 100 | Sarah 104 Eli 108 Mark 109 |
| Richard 91 Eli 95 | 90 | 90 | Pablo 91 Gloria 92 Cheyanne 97 |
| Juan C 82 Edison 82 Mark 89 | 80 | 80 | Joshua 80 Deresa 87 Juan 87 |
| Sheila 71 Dernite 71 | 70 | 70 | Serio 72 Ilysa 74 Shelia 69 |
| Cheyanne 64 | 60 | 60 | Talmas 68 Erik 65 Takawah 64 Alexis 62 |
| Erik 59 | 50 | 50 | Sergio 50 |
| Ilysa 40 Joshua 45 Talmas 46 | 40 | 40 |  |
| Willie 38 | 30 | 30 | Willie 36 |
|  | 20 | 20 |  |
| Takawah 8 | 10 | 10 |  |

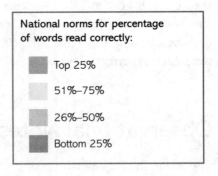

National norms for percentage of words read correctly:

Top 25%

51%–75%

26%–50%

Bottom 25%

# Conducting the Observation

Appendix 3.1 was developed to provide teachers with a framework for observing students during PRC2. To conduct the observation, use the following procedure:

1. Try to be unobtrusive as you focus your observation on students' oral reading and discussion about the text. Sit behind the partners. Listen but don't interfere with their work.
2. Write the observation notes on the PRC2 recording sheet.
3. Note the participation of each student.
4. Upon completion of or during the observation, teacher notes and reflections of student behaviors inform instructional needs of the students and follow-up plans.

## Ongoing Assessment

Completing and recording observation notes for PRC2 provides teachers with ongoing authentic, informative assessment data of students' oral reading and discussion when reading content materials. It is another way to determine if students are actively engaged as readers, if changes in the PRC2 partnership are warranted, and if the instructional reading materials are at the appropriate level for student understanding of the content presented.

Figures 7.3 and 7.4 are observation notes for PRC2 made during a fifth-grade social studies class in an urban school. Both Dulce and Sophie's first language is Spanish, and their current instructional reading level is at fourth grade. The readability of the materials chosen was within each student's high instructional level; however, Ms. T had some concern in pairing the students because neither girl participated in class discussions and both appeared to have little background knowledge in this subject.

Ms. T conducted Dulce and Sophie's first PRC2 observation on November 5 (Figure 7.3) and noted that both students' oral reading was fluent; Dulce clearly articulated her words, and Sophie used an index card to help her keep her place so that she could maintain fluency. Ms. T. also noted that both students provided simple answers to the questions, which did not necessarily elicit further discussion. As noted in the teacher reflection portion of the observation notes, both students needed additional instruction on how to facilitate discussion. Follow-up instruction presented and modeled ways to

**Figure 7.3** Teacher Observation Notes from November 5 Session with Two Fifth-Grade EL Students

| Observation Notes for PRC2 | |
|---|---|

Partner 1: _Dulce_    Title of book: _Columbus and the Americans_
Partner 2: _Sophie_    Date: _11-5_    # of sessions with book: _2_

| Partner 1 | Partner 2 |
|---|---|
| **Oral Reading Notes** | **Oral Reading Notes** |
| • Maintained a good pace, which allowed her to clearly articulate the words<br>• Paused and looked at illustration when she came to an unknown word | • Tracking with a piece of paper, which helped her keep her place<br>• Maintained fluency<br>• Followed punctuation<br>• Difficult to hear her—"face in the book" |
| Attends to punctuation, pronunciation, phrasing; attends to new or unfamiliar terms; uses fix-up strategies. | Attends to punctuation, pronunciation, phrasing; attends to new or unfamiliar terms; uses fix-up strategies. |
| **Talking about the Text** | **Talking about the Text** |
| • Answered yes/no questions matter of fact and then went on to ask a question not comment on question or elicit further discussion.<br>• Answered yes/no question<br>• **Although they were polite to each other, neither student elicited further discussion. | • Provided simple answers to the questions<br>• Had difficulty coming up with questions and when she did only yes/no answer<br>• Talked quietly—difficult to hear her—similar to oral reading<br>• **Although they were polite to each other, neither student elicited further discussion. |
| On topic; key points identified; focused dialogue; good listening; use of key academic terms. | On topic; key points identified; focused dialogue; good listening; use of key academic terms. |

| **Teacher Reflections** |
|---|
| • Students followed the steps of PRC2—used PRC2 bookmark<br>• Students need further instruction on how to facilitate discussion<br>• Have students develop bookmark to prompt discussion—similar to PRC2 bookmark because it helped with the process of PRC2<br>• Work with Sophie on speaking louder and book away from her face |
| Partners' social behaviors, communication, pacing, motivation, level, lack of understanding of content (comprehension), instructional needs, follow-up plans, etc. |

**Figure 7.4** Teacher Observation Notes from November 18 Session after Implementing Support for Partner Discussion

| Observation Notes for PRC2 | |
|---|---|

Partner 1: _Dulce_    Title of book: _Columbus and the Americans_
Partner 2: _Sophie_    Date: _11-18_    # of sessions with book: _Final Session_

| Partner 1 | Partner 2 |
|---|---|
| **Oral Reading Notes** | **Oral Reading Notes** |
| • Read confidently<br>• Used a paper to track print (which is what Sophie did on first observation)<br>• Interesting—she added her opinion in the middle of reading the page and didn't wait for a response just kept on reading after her side comment.<br>"Look at this—I think Columbus looks different than he did at the beginning—it looks like they are getting along—what do you think?" | • No longer using paper to track print but was able to follow the print easily—fluent—good attention to punctuation<br>• Clear loud voice (YEAH!) |
| Attends to punctuation, pronunciation, phrasing; attends to new or unfamiliar terms; uses fix-up strategies. | Attends to punctuation, pronunciation, phrasing; attends to new or unfamiliar terms; uses fix-up strategies. |
| **Talking about the Text** | **Talking about the Text** |
| • Asked good questions—variety of QAR<br>• Answered with "I think" when she had an opinion<br>• Pointed out to her partner something on the page to begin the conversation (nice strategy that she put into place)<br>• Used bookmark to assist in asking questions and making comments | • Initial questions that she asked during discussion were yes/no, but after Dulce answered with 2 or 3 words she referred to the bookmark and said "Why do you think that?" Made Dulce provide additional information<br>• Used the PRC2 steps to facilitate the conversation |
| On topic; key points identified; focused dialogue; good listening; use of key academic terms. | On topic; key points identified; focused dialogue; good listening; use of key academic terms. |

**Teacher Reflections**

Both students applied strategies that were modeled during class discussions and read-alouds and from guided instruction. Bookmark and visuals continue to be a great help. For next PRC2, will meet with Dulce and Sophie to continue instruction on further development of questioning and conversation.

Partners' social behaviors, communication, pacing, motivation, level, lack of understanding of content (comprehension), instructional needs, follow-up plans, etc.

ask questions and create conversations. For additional support during PRC2, Dulce and Sophie created a conversation and questioning bookmark.

On November 18, Ms. T conducted a follow-up PRC2 observation (see Figure 7.4). As noted, both students read with confidence, but this time Dulce also used an index card when reading the text. In addition, Ms. T noted the change in discussion, where it was more fluid with both students asking good questions and responding with clear, accurate comments. Although the girls had made progress, Ms. T noted that additional modeling of ways to locate information, ask meaningful questions, and create fluid conversations was still an area of need.

As a result of the observations, instruction was provided that helped the girls expand their talk about the text as well as set guidelines for higher-level thinking and questioning. The observation notes provide teachers with invaluable information on how students read, discuss, and interpret the text.

# Audiotapes of Student Conversation

Audiotapes of student conversations provide the teacher additional insight into students' oral reading skills and talk about the text. In addition, audiotapes allow students to hear themselves read and discuss the text, as well as provide an opportunity for student self-reflection.

## Taping the Conversation

Use the following procedure to tape the conversation:

1. Locate a tape recorder and microphone for the taping.
2. Try to place the tape recorder in an area that is unobtrusive yet close enough to be able to record the voices of the students.
3. Transcribe the audiotape and complete the observation notes form.
4. Identify student behaviors that will inform follow-up plans supported by the audiotape and observation form.

## Ongoing Assessment

As discussed previously, language is the heart of learning. The coupling of the audiotape and PRC2 observation form provides the teacher with in-depth information on student conversations; specifically, it shows how students use and process the academic language throughout the academic discourse. By audiotaping the PRC2 sessions, teachers have an opportunity to capture authentic conversations and critically evaluate students' academic and social discourse. Teachers use this information to plan instruction in language and to provide students with strategies to support practice with new terms and vocabulary. Teachers might also consider collecting samples from fall, winter, and spring PRC2 sessions and then comparing and contrasting each audiotape to establish students' growth in language and use of academic language.

Another valuable use of the audiotapes is to have the partners listen to the audiotape. Students often learn a lot through the metacognitive self-reflective process, as was the case for Ms. Jones and her fifth-grade students. Javier and Pedro, students in Ms. Jones's class, had one PRC2 session audiotaped. They listened to the audiotape and completed a self-reflection of their oral reading and their active role as participants and discussants during PRC2. Based on their self-reflection, the students set a goal for the next PRC2 session (Figure 7.5).

The use of audiotapes provides an ongoing assessment tool that assists teachers in pinpointing how students read and process content materials, and it provides students with an opportunity to observe themselves as readers and thinkers. Based on this information, teachers make informed instructional decisions and students take responsibility for their individual learning.

## Academic Vocabulary

As discussed in previous chapters, developing academic vocabulary is a key component for success in school. Chapters 11 and 12 present ways to enhance and support teacher-selected content vocabulary through playing games, working at stations, and using technology.

Another component to learning and using academic vocabulary is having students self-select additional words they need to learn. Research supports the effectiveness of student self-selecting vocabulary and making connections (self, text, and world) with words they are reading, using the selected words in conversation, and recording the self-selected words in vocabulary logs for future reference and use (Wagner & Quinn, 2007). Ruddell and Shearer (2002) found that the use of self-selection of vocabulary words enhanced students' motivation and achievement in learning new words. During PRC2,

Figure **7.5** Audiotape Partner Self-Reflection

| Audiotape Partner Self-Reflection | |
|---|---|
| Partner 1: _Javier_ | Partner 2: _Pedro_ |
| Title of book: _____ | Date: _____ |

| Partner 1 | Partner 2 |
|---|---|
| **Oral Reading** | **Oral Reading** |
| What I did well . . .<br>Read all the words right<br>Took my time<br><br>What I need to work on . . .<br>Stop at periods.<br>Don't make everything sound boring. | What I did well . . .<br>No mistakes<br>Read the hard words—one I didn't know<br><br>What I need to work on . . .<br>Talk louder—I couldn't hear myself read.<br>Why didn't you tell me that you couldn't hear me? |
| **Talking about the Text** | **Talking about the Text** |
| What I did well . . .<br>Made a connection and told my partner<br>Had a lot to say<br><br>What I need to work on . . .<br>Let my partner talk, too<br>Talked when my partner talked—not good, but I had a lot to say | What I did well . . .<br>Asked good questions about what the book said<br>Was nice to my partner<br><br>What I need to work on . . .<br>Talk, too, not just say yes or no or shake my head. |

How did we do as partners:
We were nice to each other. We listened and tried hard.

Next time we will . . .
Ask better questions.
Listen and talk—each take turns.

students self-select words of interest. Discourse and academic conversations develop as students discuss and clarify the meaning of the self-selected words. Furthermore, as students discuss their rationale for the selection of the words, it helps them clarify the meaning of the words and builds the students' vocabulary knowledge. Note in the following dialogue how the two girls discuss the words they will add to their vocabulary notebooks.

Student working with words in her vocabulary notebook.

*Emily:* I don't know which words to choose.

*Lily:* You should do this one. It was new.

*Emily:* What words are you going to do?

*Lily:* I'm going to do carbon dioxide, cardiac, and oxygen.

*Emily:* I'm going to use contract . . . Con . . . tract, contract. Then, I'm going to do blood vessel.

*Lily:* Let's write the pages down so we don't forget the page we're on. Yes, so I'm going to write pages eight and nine.

## Procedure: Student Self-Selection of Vocabulary

When selecting vocabulary words, students attend to vocabulary that they wonder about in their reading.

1. Choose words of interest from the assigned page(s).
2. Discuss the words with the partner.
3. Record the new word in the vocabulary notebook, responding to the following (Figure 7.6):
   a. Description of the word
   b. Representation of the word
   c. New insights

Figure **7.6** Vocabulary Notebook Recording Sheet

**Vocabulary Notebook Recording Sheet**

Student name: _____ Date: _____

Title of book: _____

**Term/Word**



**My Description** (Tell about the word.)



**My Representation** (Tell what you see.)



**Author's Insights** (How did the author use the word? You may copy from the book.)



**New Insights** (What did you learn? Find something you never knew.)

## Ongoing Assessment

The use of a vocabulary notebook provides teachers with ongoing assessment data that capture how students choose, understand, and use the words that they self-select. When teachers review the notebooks, they can determine if the words chosen support the development of academic vocabulary or enhance their students' understanding of the content. If students' word choice does not include essential words, the teacher and student would each select one vocabulary word. Teachers evaluate student vocabulary growth by comparing early and later notebook entries. This provides a way to monitor vocabulary development over time.

## Summary

The ongoing performance assessments that were chosen for PRC2 provide teachers and students with a clear understanding of how students read and interpret content materials. Both students and teachers take an active role in the ongoing assessment process. Students demonstrate their learning in authentic ways (through discussion, self-selected vocabulary, self-reflection), and teachers observe and make instructional decisions accordingly. The ongoing performance assessments are especially effective in describing what and how students read and interpret content materials. They also provide guidelines for discussion and ways for students to become independent, responsible, and productive learners.

## References

Afflerbach, P. (2007). *Understanding and using reading assessment K–12.* Newark, DE: International Reading Association.

Ediger, M. (2007, September). Teacher observation to assess student achievement. *Journal of Instructional Psychology, 34*(3), 137–139.

Fuchs, L., Fuchs, D., Hosp, M., & Jenkins, J. (2001). Reading competence: A theoretical empirical and historical analysis. *Scientific Studies of Reading, 5*(3), 239–256.

Hasbrouck, J., & Tindal, G. (2006, April). Oral reading fluency norms: A valuable assessment tool for reading. *The Reading Teacher,* 636–645.

ISBE. (2000–2002). *Illinois learning standards: Descriptors and classroom assessment.* Retrieved from http://www.isbe.state.il.us/ils/html/descriptors .htm

Johns, J. (2005). *Basic reading inventory* (9th ed.). Dubuque, IA: Kendall/Hunt.

RAND Reading Study Group. (2002). *Reading for understanding: Toward an R&D program in reading comprehension.* Santa Monica, CA: RAND.

Ruddell, M. R., & Shearer, B. A. (2002). "Extraordinary," "tremendous," "exhilarating," "magnificent": Middle school at-risk students become avid word learners with the vocabulary self-selection strategy (VSS). *Journal of Adolescent & Adult Literacy, 45*, 352–363.

Wagner, K., & Quinn, K. B. (2007). *Choosing, chatting, and collecting: Vocabulary self-collection strategy.* Newark, DE: International Reading Association. Available from http://www.readwritethink.org/lessons/lesson_view.asp?id=296

Wiggins, G. (1998). *Educative assessment.* San Francisco, CA: Jossey-Bass.

# Using Partner Reading in Guided Reading

**8**

**?** How do small groups work in large classes?

In this chapter, **Kristina Utley**, a former classroom teacher, addresses the challenge of working in a large classroom of more than thirty students.

Kristina worked as a sixth-grade classroom teacher in Chicago until 2008, when she became the school's Literacy Leader. Her chapter reflects what she learned in the classroom. Her classroom was made up of thirty-one students, of whom 95 percent are Latino and 5 percent African American. Her students represented a wide range of abilities; six of the students received special education services and three were supported as English learners. Several students exceeded achievement levels on the state assessment, and others fell into the warning area.

130

Chapter
Eight
Using Partner
Reading in
Guided Reading

With more than thirty students in the classroom, I found it difficult to facilitate PRC2 as a whole class. It was hard for me to listen to the students with everyone talking and reading at once. I realized that if it was hard for me to hear, it was probably just as difficult (if not more difficult) for the students who were not only listening to discussions but also trying to comprehend what they were reading at the same time. This is when I decided to try PRC2 in small groups while the rest of the class worked at literacy stations (see Chapter 9 on literacy workstations).

I found working with students during PRC2 in a small group was most effective for my class. It allowed me to actively listen to what students were discussing. When I began the process, I often had to ask students to elaborate on what they were saying. However, by midyear I was able to sit back and, at times, not say one word throughout the entire discussion. Toward the end of the PRC2 block, when the students had finished discussing with their partners, students came back as a group to talk about different questions and ideas that had come up with their partners.

Teacher Kristina Utley encourages deeper partner engagement as students preview a science text.

Although literacy workstations bring students together to work and those students create some noise, the room was less loud than when all of the students were participating in PRC2 at the same time. I was also able to help facilitate the discussion and monitor the students working on PRC2. In addition, I found that by listening carefully to what the students were discussing I could get an authentic assessment of where they were in their reading development and what individual needs I had to address for each student. Sometimes I wrote these anecdotal observations down as the students were discussing. This was difficult, though, because it is hard to listen and write at the same time. I realized that writing a few quick key points after talking with the students was more beneficial. Although the assessment was informal, it gave me the most insight as to where each student was in terms of his or her reading achievement and understanding of a given content area.

In this chapter, I highlight some of the conversations between the teacher and students that took place when working in small groups with PRC2. The teacher must not intervene too much because the students need to come to an understanding of the material on their own. Usually, as the facilitator of the discussion, I listen and only speak up to clarify or ask questions that will further the student's critical thinking.

# Differentiating Instruction for a Range of Abilities

My sixth-grade classroom is in a school located on Chicago's south side where the population is 92 percent Hispanic and 8 percent African American. At that school, 99 percent of the students qualify to receive free lunch. Most of my students are ELs, and reading levels range from students reading at levels as low as pre-primer to students reading at levels as high as ninth grade.

Partner Reading and Content, Too, lends itself well to differentiating instruction, as students are always working together reading books at their level. I find that students who are reading at fourth-grade levels and above are able to create their own questions. I allow students who test below this reading level to use the PRC2 sheet with the four discussion questions (see Appendix 2.2). But I always encourage them to come up with their own discussion questions as well. I have students who are reading at a second-grade level and below read the entire text and then draw a picture to illustrate what they read. Then they write whether they agree with their partner's response to the text.

132

Chapter
Eight
Using Partner
Reading in
Guided Reading

As the year progresses, I constantly assess and modify how the students are responding. By the end of the year, I hope to have all the students creating their own questions and using the PRC2: Read & Recommend form (see Appendix 2.6). With my more advanced students, sometimes I do not have to say anything as they follow the PRC2 process and discuss the text. I listen and assess their understanding. When I'm working with students who are not as advanced, I probe and clarify more often. PRC2 can be adapted in many ways to meet the needs of any student.

# Examining Students' Small-Group Dialogue

Prior to beginning the PRC2 process, the teacher must build some background knowledge on a given content area (see Chapter 1). For example, we study ancient civilizations as part of the social studies curriculum. Many of my students have never heard of Egypt or even traveled outside the Chicago area. This is why it was important for me to build their background knowledge before they began PRC2. Partner Reading and Content, Too, is used as a supplement to what is already being taught in the given content area. In this particular situation, we had watched a movie and learned some basic information about ancient Egypt before the students started reading their PRC2 books.

## Previewing the Book

When they finally began the process, my students previewed the book by taking a book walk and noticing certain text features. This pre-reading activity allowed students to get an idea of what they were about to read and activated even more background knowledge.

The following is a conversation between two students as they previewed the book:

*Ana:* What do you think it's going to be about?

*Vivian:* I think it's going to be about pyramids and Egypt because it shows pyramids on the background of the book. And there are some pictures of Egyptian people on the cover.

*Ana:* I think it is going to be about pyramids also, and they are also going to talk about kings and queens because they have like two sketches of two people and their dressing might be queens and kings. And they also talk about how they built pyramids and what they are used for.

*Vivian:* What do you think that pyramids are used for?

*Ana:* I think they might be used to bury people inside of them, when they die and they get mummified. They might be put inside. What do you think?

*Vivian:* I think that also, but in the room where they put the tomb, or dead body, they might write some hieroglyphics of their life.

*Ana:* They'd also tell about where you lived, where you started, and why maybe they were so respected.

*Vivian:* How do you think they built the pyramids?

*Ana:* I think they probably, the people, would use big rocks, that were like bigger than themselves. And they used, well they didn't use any tools to build them, so probably it took many, many years before you could get one pyramid finished. Now, if you were in Egypt could you help build a pyramid?

*Vivian:* Probably, but I don't think I could carry the rock since it's so big. Would you?

When the students are previewing the book I limit my comments and listen, allowing the students to ask me any questions they might have as they encounter pictures and new vocabulary. In the previous dialogue, the students were having a meaningful conversation, so I focused on using polite conversation skills, utilizing the prompts listed on the bookmark (see Appendix 2.3). I wait until the students are finished previewing the text to tell them this, as I do not want to interrupt their conversation flow. When they finished, I said, "You did a nice job of discussing what the book is going to be about; one thing you may want to try is using the polite conversation techniques listed on your bookmark. So, Ana, after Vivian answers a question, you could say, 'Oh I hadn't thought about it in that way,' or what's something else you could say?"

Using PRC2 not only teaches the students to comprehend and think critically, but it incorporates everyday communication skills. For students who have the process down and seem to be doing well with the discussion, I encourage them to practice these skills. I also pay attention to see if the student is showing his or her partner that he or she is an active listener by making eye contact and not interrupting.

## Using Polite Conversation Techniques

After I explained to Vivian and Ana that they should try using polite conversation, their next conversation went like this:

*Vivian:* Would you like to live with Queen Nefertiti? Why or why not?

*Ana:* I'm not sure, it depends on if she's nice or not and, if not, then you don't know what will happen. What about you?

134

Chapter
Eight
Using Partner
Reading in
Guided Reading

*Vivian:* I would like to live with her because she has a lot of luxuries. You could do a lot of things and maybe she would let you wear her jewelry.

*Ana:* Yeah, that's true. Good answer.

At this point, I complimented Ana on using polite conversation when she said "Good answer." I then asked Ana to elaborate on what she thinks would happen if she were to live with Queen Nefertiti because her answer was very brief and I wanted her to explain what she meant. Often students (particularly ELs) have trouble explaining what they are thinking. Through PRC2 they are able to practice elaborating on their ideas using the partner discourse.

## Asking Questions

In this next example, two students read a different book than the one Ana and Vivian had read about ancient Egypt. They asked each other questions they came up with based on what they read and then discussed those questions. In this particular book, the students read that the tombs of ancient Egypt were often named after rulers or gods. I instructed the students to have a conversation and reminded them that both partners should answer the question and that they should have a lengthy discussion. I made sure to emphasize the fact that it does not matter how fast the students get through the book; I wanted them to have meaningful discussions.

*Lucy:* If you were supposed to build a pyramid, what would you call it? How would it look?

*Georgia:* It depends on who I built it for.

*Lucy:* You would name it after someone?

*Georgia:* Yes, like if I built it for Victoria then I would name it "Victoria." I would have it look like King Tut's pyramid because he is one of the most famous pharaohs and the person I built it for would be excited to feel as important as King Tut.

*Lucy:* I think that's what I would do, too. I would name it after someone I knew and make it look like King Tut's.

*Lucy:* Why do you think it is called a step pyramid?

*Georgia:* Well it says right here it looks like a series of steps.

*Lucy:* Oh, okay.

This conversation took place at the beginning of the year. After listening to these students in a small group, I encouraged them to talk about the different types of pyramids and how their structures are different. As the facilitator, I was always trying to further their thinking. However, the questioning needs to be balanced; if I probed too much, it might make the process tedious. It is important to keep the students engaged, but I did not want to ask students to analyze the text to the point where the analysis interferes with the reading.

## Reflecting in a Small Group

When twenty minutes is up, I bring the group back together to talk about interesting questions or facts that they considered while they were reading. The following conversation occurred among André, Miguel, Lindsey, and Stephanie during our Ancient Egypt unit. Coming together as a group and reflecting on what they had read allowed the students to review what they learned, listen to other perspectives, and bring closure to the PRC2 session.

*Teacher:* So what interesting questions or ideas came up while you were reading?

*André:* We were talking about why it was that Ramses lived for ninety years while most people [in ancient Egypt] only lived until thirty.

*Miguel:* Maybe there was not a lot of food and shelter for people with not a lot of money. Ramses had a lot of wealth, so maybe he had lots of food and shelter.

*Lindsey:* Maybe people were stung by animals or insects since they worked in the desert. Or, maybe, like you said, they didn't have the same amount of food; maybe they became dehydrated because they did not have enough water.

Listening to their conversation, I was able to see that three of the four students understood what they had read. They were able to take what they read to the next level and think critically about ancient Egyptians' longevity. If you noticed, Stephanie did not talk, so I asked her what she thought. This happens often that one student will sit back while the rest of the group is discussing. It may just be that Stephanie is shy, or it may be that she believes she does not have anything to add. Nevertheless, I needed to probe her to see if she understood the text. If she did not, then I would need to switch Stephanie into a group that is reading a book that better correlates with her reading level.

136

Chapter
Eight
Using Partner
Reading in
Guided Reading

## Making Connections

This next conversation occurred while students previewed a book on ancient Kush in Africa. This was one of many moments in which learning was completely student directed and occurred while I was working with a small PRC2 group. The students in this group were able to make connections to a book they had just finished on ancient Egypt. When I noticed that the two pairs of students were having similar conversations, I brought them together to have a group discussion.

*Cristin:* That's a god and that's a pharaoh. I remember this picture from another book I read.

*Liz:* [Pointing to text that says "Nubia, which later became Kush"] What does this mean? Were they two different civilizations?

*Justine:* I think maybe they were different.

While José and Cristin were previewing the same book, they had this conversation:

*José:* Why do you think Nubia became Kush?

*Cristin:* Well, Kush was probably more powerful and overtook Nubia's land.

*Teacher:* Can you share that with Liz and Justine?

*Cristin:* [Pointing to the map] It shows that it used to be Nubia and then became Kush, so I think maybe Kush fought Nubia for their land and won.

*Liz:* Oh, okay.

*Justine:* [Nods her head in agreement]

After listening to this conversation, I was able to see that the students were tapping into prior knowledge and making connections based on books they had already read. Although it was tempting to intervene and just give the answer, it was much more powerful for Liz and Justine to learn from their peers about why Nubia became Kush. It also empowered Cristin; she was able to teach something new to her group.

## Teachable Moments

Using PRC2, students have the opportunity to come to an understanding of and learn new insights about a topic through their own discovery. This next conversation occurred while a group was reading about ancient Greece and was one of those rare teachable moments when everything seemed to come together.

*Lupe:* Ms. Utley, [pointing to Greece] it looks like part of Greece came apart or something and left back little pieces of land.

*George:* Wow, that's weird.

*Teacher:* Well, Lupe, that's very interesting that you noticed that on the map because long ago it was all connected. Let me tell you about Pangaea. . . .

Lupe was not only inferring from the text but also using the pictures. She was able to discover on her own that the land of Greece used to be connected to other land parts. Because she came to this conclusion on her own, she is more likely to retain this information than if I had just told her. The PRC2 process offers a lot of opportunities for these types of teachable moments to occur. Students will realize things that have never occurred to me. I do not know the answers to all the questions that come up, but we resolve those questions together. Research shows that when we keep new ideas contextual for our students, they are much more likely to retain the information (Beck, McKeown, Hamilton, & Kucan; 1997; Guthrie, 2003).

## Vocabulary

As students read, they often encounter new vocabulary. When the teacher has the opportunity to work with students in a small group, it allows him or her to clarify meaning of the vocabulary words and terms. It also keeps the vocabulary contextual because it is related to what the students are learning. The teacher can encourage the students to break the word apart or use the context clues to try to determine the meaning of the word.

The following is a conversation that took place between Raul and Juan based on a book that incorporated ancient Egypt and math:

*Raul:* Why do you think they wrote their numbers differently?

*Juan:* Like, maybe they can understand it easier. . . . They would write it like this [showing with drawing]. It would make it easier, like the numbers, and like they learned to count from left to right or from right to left, or from top to bottom.

138

Chapter
Eight
Using Partner
Reading in
Guided Reading

*Teacher focuses on the word* decipher. *Do you know what* decipher *means?*

**Raul:** To find out.

**Teacher:** That's good, yes; to decipher each of these figures, to find out what these numbers are.

The PRC2 process lends itself well to building vocabulary skills because students read across the content areas from books at their reading level. Having conversations about new vocabulary words is one of the most effective ways for students to internalize word meanings. Discussion encourages students to figure out what the word means on their own and helps them remember this new information. I could have told Raul what the word meant, but receiving the information this way would not have been as meaningful as discovering it on his own. Instead, he was able to figure out what the word meant independently. Next time Raul comes across this word, he will most likely remember what it means.

# Teacher's Reflections on Using PRC2 in Guided Reading

## Advantages

Using PRC2 in a small group has many advantages. One of the most beneficial aspects is the smaller teacher-to-student ratio, which allows the teacher to have more individual time with the students. Many times throughout the day, there is one teacher with thirty students. Working in groups of four to six students with one teacher helps to build teacher-to-student and student-to-student relationships.

It is easier for the teacher to assess the students when students are working in small groups, rather than when students are working as one large group. The teacher can observe each group and determine which group or individual he or she should focus on. It also allows time for the teacher to give students immediate feedback on their discussion and how they are reading.

A small group of four to six students is easier to manage than a large group of thirty. The teacher can easily make sure that all students are on task during PRC2 when he or she can focus on a few students at a time. Because all students are reading books at their independent level, a lot of different books are being read at the same time. When students are working in a large group, it can get confusing as to who is reading what book. When students are working in small groups, however, it is easier to keep track of which book each group is reading.

A key component to PRC2 is allowing the students to get together with a few other students to reflect on what they talked about with their partner. This small-group discussion offers a way for students to recap all that they learned and discussed with their partner. It also allows them to listen to what other people have learned from PRC2. Reflection in a small group creates a less intimidating setting for students to share their thoughts. It also ensures that all students can participate in the discussion, and the conversation is more engaging than in a large group.

## Some Potential Difficulties

Even though there are many advantages to using PRC2, not every day will run smoothly. Knowing about some situations that may arise will better prepare you before starting this process. One of the most common difficulties is when students are absent. Because they are working with a partner, both students need to be in class. I try one of two solutions when a student is absent. One solution is to have the partner group up with his or her other group members and divide the book into three parts (instead of two). The next day when the absent student comes back, his or her partner can fill him or her in as to what they read about the day before. Another solution is to have the single student work with you instead of a partner. It helps sometimes to act as a student's partner; you can find a lot of insight as to how students are reading, questioning, understanding, and discussing if you work one on one with a student.

A die-hard student may come to school with a sore throat. His or her voice may be completely gone (which can be nice to reduce the talking during certain parts of the day, let's be honest), which creates problems with trying to discuss the reading material. When this occurs, I have the student still read his or her parts silently and come up with a question, but I have the other partner read all of the text aloud. As for the conversation piece, I allow students to write out their responses and realize that their discussions may not be as lengthy that day.

Some books do not have text on both pages for students to be able to divide evenly. Sometimes the text is only on one side. This happens often with the introductions to trade books. When this occurs, students can divide the text in half and read aloud their portion. (See Chapter 2 on PRC2 frameworks.)

Sometimes personality differences create issues, especially as children enter the adolescent years. This is where it is important to keep grouping flexible. Certain students may work better with others. You want children to be able

140

Chapter
Eight
Using Partner
Reading in
Guided Reading

to get along with everyone, but that is not always realistic. The priority with PRC2 is to group students so that they feel comfortable to exchange discourse easily with their partner. I have had situations where girls only want to work with girls and boys with boys. I want children to get other perspectives than just those of their friends, so I will group students with people they do not necessarily always talk to. If I notice that this is an issue, then I will switch the students to a more comfortable situation.

Determining when to switch the students' groups can be difficult because students finish their books at various times. I try to keep all the students at the same pace. When one group finishes ahead of another group, I may have them read a short article using PRC2 while they wait for the other groups to finish. When all the students have finished their books, I switch up the groups based on the latest data I have collected from my observations, anecdotal records, their read-and-response answers, and the most recent Classroom Fluency Snapshot results.

Most issues that occur during PRC2 can be easily resolved with minor modifications. The key is to realize that you need to learn what works best for you and your students. It may take a while to figure it out; once you do, however, PRC2 will run smoothly and students will be engaged in meaningful discussions centered on content area reading.

## References

Beck, I. L., McKeown, M. G., Hamilton, R. L., & Kucan, L. (1997). *Questioning the author: An approach for enhancing student engagement with texts.* Newark, DE: International Reading Association.

Guthrie, J. (2003). Concept-oriented reading instruction: Practices of teaching for understanding. In A. P. Sweet & C. E. Snow (Eds.). *Rethinking reading comprehension* (pp. 115–139). New York: Guilford.

# Using Literacy Workstations to Provide Scaffolded Learning

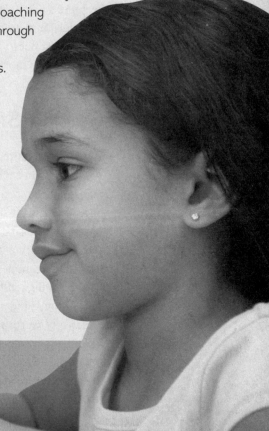

9

? How do I manage small groups in my classroom?

In this chapter, **Kristina Utley**, a former classroom teacher, addresses the challenge of organizing and managing small-group activities.

After working as a sixth-grade teacher, Kristina became the Literacy Coach of her school. She was responsible for training and coaching teachers as well as working with students in kindergarten through eighth grade. Kristina was able to help modify PRC2 and components of these literacy stations across all grade levels. She helped teachers create similar models in their classrooms. As a result, students across the school showed major gains and went up 12 percentile points on their statewide assessments.

142

Chapter
Nine
Using Literacy
Workstations
to Provide
Scaffolded
Learning

Prior to starting PRC2, I had been working with guided reading groups while the rest of my class participated in different literacy workstations. When I saw the PRC2 model, I thought it would be perfect for my guided reading groups. The students could work with partners but still receive guidance from the teacher. It also served as an authentic assessment when I was able to sit and listen to the discussions among the students. Literacy stations give students the opportunity to work independently, allowing me to meet with small groups for PRC2. When using literacy stations, students work in small groups of about four to six individuals for a full week on one project. Each day, twenty to forty minutes are allotted for literacy stations; during this time, the teacher pulls students to work in small PRC2 groups. At the end of the week, students are held accountable for their work at the literacy stations by either presenting their culminating piece to the entire class or turning in the work they have completed throughout the week. Each week the groups rotate to work at a new station. This rotation continues until all groups have completed each activity.

The classroom has many different stations, which I will explain. I usually change a few of the stations throughout the year to avoid monotony and to keep the students engaged. Throughout this chapter, I provide explanations, materials, directions, and rubrics for each station. These stations include current events, poetry, listening, readers' theater, homophones, jeopardy, computers, and word morphology (or reading rods).

## Getting Started with Literacy Stations

When I first started literacy stations, I had five different groups with five to six students in each group. Having fewer stations made it easier for me to manage the students. I also did not want to introduce too many stations at once, so I kept it simple.

After the first cycle of stations, I decided to try seven groups with four to five students in each group. I realized that when there were fewer students at each station, students were less likely to become off task. However, it would have been difficult to start with this many stations in the beginning.

I group students according to fluency level in order for PRC2 to work effectively. Surprisingly, students do not realize they are in leveled groups. I have them arranged in teams by numbers. Their number is random and does not correlate to the group's ability level. I keep the grouping flexible so that the students are able to work with different people and I am still able to rearrange groups after students have completed an entire cycle of stations.

## Model, Model, Model

A large concern about student-directed activities is classroom management. Often, while the teacher is working with other students, it is easy for the rest of the class to become off task. One way to alleviate this problem is by carefully modeling each station and explicitly clarifying expectations. For each station, I have created a rubric. The rubrics are very basic, but they let the students know what the requirements are. The rubrics are a work in progress. I find myself changing them for each new class or if I realize I missed something that I want the students to master. After the students have become used to the literacy stations, I have them help me create better rubrics for each one.

Literacy stations cannot start on the first day of school. Students must understand all procedures and routines in the classroom before the teacher begins to explain these stations. Depending on the class, it may take weeks or even a couple of months before literacy stations are implemented.

It is important to introduce each literacy station separately. It is also helpful to have students practice what they will be doing in each station before they begin. The week before work begins at the literacy stations, I have students practice one different station each day. There may not be time to complete the entire activity, but even a general idea can clarify misconceptions. It may take up to a week to model and explain each station. The more clearly the students understand what is expected of them, the smoother the literacy stations will run.

## Classroom Setup

Classrooms are often crowded and have minimal space for movement. If possible, move the desks into collaborative groups of four to six desks per grouping. Also, label bins for each workstation. The bins can be stored on a shelf and are mobile. These bins are usually inexpensive and sold at many department stores for close to one dollar. I always ask the students to make sure the bins are organized before they put them away. I noticed that if I do not enforce this expectation, the bins get disorganized and cluttered. Students can keep materials for the station in the bins and at the end of each week clean them out for the next group.

If feasible, provide an extra table for students to work at, depending on the number and type of stations available. Each station should have a designated area where students work. The listening center could be stored in the classroom library and the students can sit on the carpet area or floor by the

144

Chapter
Nine
Using Literacy
Workstations
to Provide
Scaffolded
Learning

Using labeled bins is a good way of organizing literacy station materials. Students can take the bins to their tables and put them back on the shelf when they finish.

library as they follow along with the story. When students know exactly where to go, they do not argue over who gets to sit where or cause distractions during transition times. With routines in place, students know where to go immediately.

I have a large class of thirty-one students in a relatively small classroom. It was hard enough for me to find room for the students to work independently, let alone with groups and an abundance of materials. When student desks are in groups, it creates a lot more space in the classroom. I created five different groups of desks with six students in each (and one with seven). I also have a round table off to the side. I have students work at four of the five groups of desks and at the round table. The computers are positioned against a wall, not requiring students in this station to need any desk space. The students at the listening station sit on the floor (or on bean bag chairs) in the library. When I work with students on PRC2, I come to them and have them stay where they are working. However, the computer station comes to me (because it would be difficult to do PRC2 at the computers) and we sit at the extra group of desks that is not being used. Figure 9.1 shows the general layout of my classroom.

**Figure 9.1** Classroom Layout

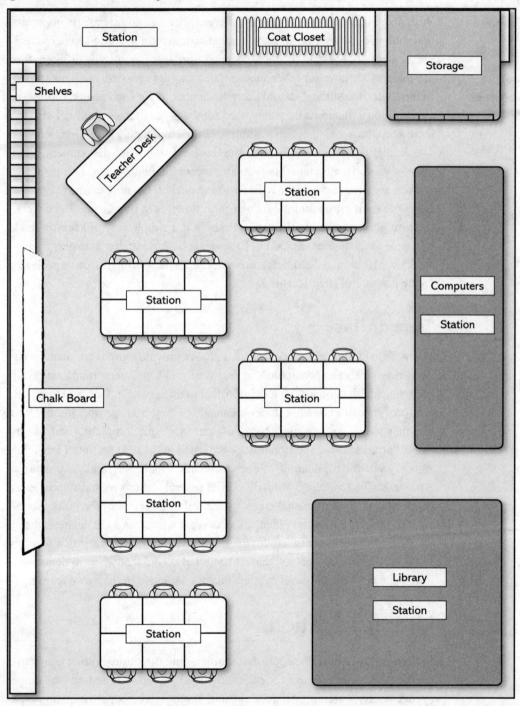

146

Chapter
Nine
Using Literacy
Workstations
to Provide
Scaffolded
Learning

## Organization

With many materials available and different activities going on, it is important that students stay organized. Each student should have a colored folder to use for all literacy workstations. I always make sure that this color is different from the folders they have for other subjects; this way, it is easy for students to find. In the folder, the student should keep the directions for each center, rubrics, and any additional materials they may need for the given literacy station. I also have them keep the books they are reading for PRC2 and their PRC2 direction sheets.

Sometimes it is easy for even the teacher to confuse what student is at a given station. To alleviate this problem, create a bulletin board or a poster with pockets that has each center written on the pocket. On note cards, the teacher can write each group and the name of the students in that group. Each week, the card gets switched to the next pocket; it is a simple way of keeping track of where each student should be. In several stations, students display their work on trifold boards. It helps them organize their information as well as create a visual of their learning.

### Time on Task

When planning literacy workstations, I always provide more work than the students may be able to accomplish in the time available. Some groups may work more quickly than others, so it is important to differentiate. One way to do this is to provide extra tasks the students can add to their literacy workstation. It may also help to incorporate an incentive of extra credit for completing additional work. Some ideas for additional work are listed in the next section. I label this work "Academic Challenge," "Super Academic Challenge," and "Ultimate Academic Challenge." As you will notice, several stations have different levels of challenges. I vary the challenges by the difficulty levels of the tasks. Not all stations include all levels. When students see it written as a challenge, rather than as extra work or extra credit, they are more likely to be intrinsically motivated to take their project to the next level. I also find that when students are allowed choice in a given activity, they take the initiative in their own learning.

## Literacy Stations

In this section, I describe each station, including directions, rubrics, and any supplementary items I use for each individual station. The stations are current events, poetry, listening, readers' theater, homophone, jeopardy, computer, and morphology.

# Current Events Station

At the current events station, students summarize three to five articles they find interesting from various newspapers, magazines, or Internet sources. An excellent resource to use for this station is *Scholastic News* or *Weekly Reader* magazine. These materials are usually at the students' reading level and provide meaningful articles that the students find interesting. Once the students have summarized their articles, each individual picks one of the current events to present. Then the four to six students work together to present each of their articles as a newscast to the class. They can work together or individually to create a visual of each of their articles. As a way to add additional work for this station, students can include a creative component, such as an interview, a debate, a skit, or a weather report. You can see the rubric I used to assess students in the current events station in Table 9.1.

On one occasion, an insightful group staged a "live" protest about their teacher not providing current enough articles for their newscast. It is amazing what students will come up with when allowed enough flexibility for them to have ownership in what they are producing. Often the students will ask critical-thinking questions to the class and their presentation turns into a lively discussion. You will find many teachable moments when the students participate in the current events station.

I always encourage students with higher reading levels to try using the actual newspaper. Students who read at a lower level can use the *Weekly Reader* magazine and *Scholastic News*. Students might also create a newscast as if they were living in ancient Egypt or any civilization that they are learning about in PRC2 or in social studies. This would be a way to make the station more thematic and cross-curricular.

## Materials for the Current Events Station
- Newspapers, magazines, *Scholastic News*, *Weekly Reader* magazine
- Markers, colored pencils, crayons
- Construction paper
- Poster board (optional)
- Lined paper (for individual summaries).

## Directions for the Current Events Station
Here is your chance to create your very own newscast!

1. Find at least three different current events from three different sections in the newspaper.

**Table 9.1** Rubric for the Current Events Station

| | 1 | 2 | 3 | 4 | +1 |
|---|---|---|---|---|---|
| **Participation** | Student had to be reminded two or more times to stay on task. He or she did not put forth as much effort as other group members. | Student had to be reminded at least once to stay on task. He or she did not put forth as much effort as the rest of the group. | Student worked well with others on the project and put forth a good effort. | Student put forth an outstanding effort and worked well with others. | Creative component was added. |
| **Visual** | Visual is sloppy. It is missing either the picture or summary. | Visual is missing either the text or picture. It is hard for the audience to see the visual. | Visual is sufficient. It meets all criteria. | Visual is out-standing and creative in some way. It is neat and easy for the audience to see. | Student works with group to create a large visual of all the articles. |
| **Summaries** | One or more summaries are not turned in. | Student turned in three summaries, but one or more do not show understanding of article. | Student turned in three adequate summaries. Student seems to understand most of the articles. | Student shows thorough understanding of articles in the summaries. | |
| **Presentation** | Student was hard to hear and said very little. Student completely relied on note cards or visual and made no eye contact with the audience. | Student was somewhat hard to hear but shared important information. Student relied on note cards and visual too often while speaking. Student made little eye contact with audience. | Student was easy to hear and did not rely on visual or note cards too often. Student included relevant information. | Student was clear and articulate with his or her voice and did not rely on note cards or a visual. The information presented was clear and relevant. | The presentation was creative or unusual in some way. |

(Kristina Utley)                                                                 **Total Points:**_____

2. Summarize each article you have chosen.

3. Choose one article to share with the class and create a visual to go along with it. The visual must include a picture and summary big enough for

Students are reading through different resources and collaborating to create a newscast.

the audience to be able to see it. You may also create a larger visual with your group.

4. Create a newscast to present to the class on Friday. Everyone in the group needs to have a role, and all members must participate in creating the presentation.

5. You must practice with your group at least *three* times before Friday. Remember to think about eye contact and fluency. It is important that you entertain your audience!

ACADEMIC CHALLENGE Include a weather report, an interview, music, or another creative piece.

SUPER ACADEMIC CHALLENGE Memorize your presentation.

ULTIMATE ACADEMIC CHALLENGE Create a newscast based on the ancient civilization you are reading about in PRC2. Pretend you are in that time period. What kinds of issues would come up? Is there a war you could report on? What about the weather? Be creative, and good luck!

150

Chapter
Nine
Using Literacy
Workstations
to Provide
Scaffolded
Learning

## Poetry Station

Prior to introducing this literacy station, it is important to review poetry style, elements, and techniques. You should also review the writing process.

At the poetry station, students browse through different poetry books and poems. Next, they can fill out a Poetry Interpretation Guide (Figure 9.2). The Poetry Interpretation Guide serves as a tool to help students interpret the poem they read. It makes them think about inferences, assumptions about the author, questions they may still have, techniques of the poem, and poetry style. After students have read and interpreted one poem through the guide, they can create their own guide using a similar style or technique. Students will use the writing process to create their poem (plan, write a rough draft, revise, edit, and publish), asking their group members for help with revision and editing. Students also have the option of publishing their poem on the computer. On the last day at the station, they present their poems to the class.

For extra credit or as an academic challenge, students may write more than one poem and choose their favorite to present. See Figure 9.3 for an example of Eduardo's poetry. Students could also give their poem a beat and turn it into a song. In addition, they can memorize the poem they wrote or a poem they read that they enjoyed. Figure 9.4 is a poem created by a small group after reading *Miss Nelson Is Missing*. See Table 9.2 on page 154 for the rubric for the poetry station.

### Materials for the Poetry Station
- Poetry books and different poems
- Poetry Interpretation Guide
- Lined paper
- Packet explaining different elements of poems (optional)

### Directions for the Poetry Station
1. Browse through the different poems in the different books in the poetry bin. Pick one poem to interpret.
2. Answer the questions on the Poetry Interpretation Guide.
3. Write a poem that uses the same style or technique as one of your chosen poems.
4. Work with a partner and go through the writing process to ensure quality in your poetry.
5. Practice your poem to share it on Friday.

*(text continues on page 155)*

**Figure 9.2** Poetry Interpretation Guide

151

Literacy
Stations

## Poetry Interpretation Guide

Name: _____

Date: _____

1. Title: _____

2. Author: _____

3. What can you infer about the poem? (What is the overall message?) _____

_____

_____

_____

4. What can you assume about the author based on the poem? (Is the author old, young, lonely, sad, happy, in love, and so on?) _____

_____

_____

_____

5. What questions do you still have for the author? _____

_____

_____

_____

6. What do you notice about the techniques used in this poem? (Does the poet use short sentences, long sentences, rhyming, flow, and so on?) _____

_____

_____

_____

7. Would you want to read more poems by the same author or on the same subject? Why or why not? _____

_____

_____

_____

(Kristina Utley)

152

Chapter
Nine
Using Literacy
Workstations
to Provide
Scaffolded
Learning

**Figure 9.3 Creative Poems by Eduardo**

*Great! 10/10*

## Family
Forgiving
Amazing
Mischievous
Interesting
Loving
Yells

## Stupid Steve
Stupid
Stupid
Stupid
Steve
Wants To See Time Fly
So he
Climbs
and
Climbs
And
Falls
With his watch

## Pants
If you are a liar
Whose pants are on fire
Or
You dance like you have ants in your pants

Wear shorts

*by Eduardo*

Figure **9.4** A Group Poem Created from *Miss Nelson Is Missing*

## Characters:

**Miss Nelson/Ms. Faviola Swamp:** Faviola

**Kid 1:** Araceli

**Kid 2:** Eddy

**Kid 3:** Eduardo T

**Mouse:** Eduardo L

**Narrator:** Araceli

**Narrator:** There once was a wonderful loving teacher named Miss Nelson.

**Miss Nelson:** Good morning children, it's a wonderful day. Let's read a story!

**Kid 1:** Shut up Miss Nelson!

**Kid 2:** I don't want to!

Kid 3 throws a paper airplane.

**Miss Nelson:** Then let's do an art project.

**Narrator:** So Miss Nelson's students do an art project, but they make a giant mess.

**Miss Nelson:** Clean up time!

**Kid 1:** You clean up!

Kids 2 and 3 throw papers at Miss Nelson.

**Narrator:** So Miss Nelson cleans up while the kids make paper airplanes. After school, Miss Nelson sees Kid 3

acting suspicious. When he's not looking she checks his desk and sees a mouse eating a piece of cheese.

**Miss Nelson** screams.

**Miss Nelson:** What is a mouse doing at school?!

**Kid 3:** I brought him. You got a problem with that? And now he wants a cookie.

Kid 3 takes a cookie out of his pocket.

**Miss Nelson:** Put that back in your pocket, if not I'll give you a detention.

**Mouse:** I want a cookie!

Kid 3 ignores Miss Nelson and gives the mouse a cookie. The next day, Miss Nelson doesn't show up at school.

**Kid 1:** Yay!

**Kid 2:** Maybe she died!

**Kid 3:** Now I can play with my mouse! But then a tall, ugly lady named Ms. Faviola Swamp appears and yells at them.

**Kid 1:** You're not Miss Nelson!

**Kid 2:** Where's Miss Nelson?!

**Kid 3:** Who are you?

**Ms. Faviola Swamp:** I'm Ms. Faviola Swamp! You'll do what I say or else!

**Kid 2:** Or else what?

**Narrator:** Says Kid 2, giving her attitude.

Ms. Faviola Swamp hits him with a ruler and he runs away.

**Ms. Faviola Swamp:** Are you gonna give me attitude too?

**Kid 1:** No, Ms. Faviola Swamp. Sorry, Ms. Faviola Swamp.

**Narrator:** Kid 1 is scared of Ms. Faviola Swamp, but Kid 3 was prepared.

**Kid 3:** Attack Ms. Faviola Swamp!!!

**Mouse:** I want a cookie!

The mouse attacks Ms. Faviola Swamp. Then Kid 3 gives his mouse a cookie. At that moment Miss Nelson enters the room.

**Miss Nelson:** Hi kids, did you miss me?

**Kid 1 and Kid 3:** No way!

**Mouse:** I want a cookie!

The End

## Epilogue:

**Kid 2:** Five years later Kid 3 aka "El mouse-kateer" made his famous speech "I have a dream that one day mice will be able to go to school with milk and cookies."

153

Table **9.2**  Rubric for the Poetry Station

| | 1 | 2 | 3 | 4 | +1 |
|---|---|---|---|---|---|
| **Participation** | Student had to be reminded two or more times to stay on task. His or her work is inadequate for the time allotted. He or she has failed to turn in certain components. | Student had to be reminded at least once to stay on task. He or she did not follow all the directions correctly. | Student did not have to be reminded to stay on task. He or she put forth adequate effort throughout the week. He or she worked well with group members. | Student put forth his or her best effort throughout the week. He or she worked well with group members. | Student put forth outstanding effort and went above and beyond expectations. |
| **Poetry Interpretation Guide** | Student did not thoroughly answer most questions on the guide. He or she did not write in complete sentences. | Student did not thoroughly answer all questions on the guide. He or she failed to put some answers in complete sentences. | Student answered all questions on the guide in complete sentences. He or she showed some thoughtful answers and insight. | Student answered all questions thoughtfully with complete sentences on the guide. He or she shows a deep understanding of the poem. | |
| **Poem** | Student did not complete the poem or follow directions for writing the poem. Many spelling errors are present. | Student wrote the poem, but did not follow the writing cycle. Some spelling errors are present. | Student wrote a poem that reflects the style of what he or she interpreted. Student followed all the components of the writing cycle to produce poem with few spelling errors. | Student wrote a very meaningful poem. It reflects the style of the poem he or she interpreted. Student followed all the components of the writing cycle. There are no spelling errors. | Student wrote more than one poem. |
| **Presentation** | Audience could not hear student. | Student made little eye contact. He or she was hard to hear. | Student made eye contact and spoke with fluency. | Student made eye contact and spoke with fluency and articulation. | Student memorized the poem. Student added a beat and made the poem into a song. |

(Kristina Utley) **Total Points:**___

ACADEMIC CHALLENGE Give your poem a beat and turn it into a song!!!

SUPER ACADEMIC CHALLENGE Memorize your poem.

## Listening Station

The listening station requires the use of headphones and a tape recorder or a CD player. Students work in a group to read along with a novel on tape or CD. As an assessment piece, students could have the choice of doing one of several things. They may write a book report, answer comprehension questions, create an epilogue, or take notes on their discussions.

If they choose to do a book report, students can select from a list of book-report formats, including a brochure, a character tree, a letter to the author, a poster advertising the book, or an interview with a character in the book. To create a brochure, the students fold the paper into three sections. In each section, they describe a different part of the book (for example, setting, characters, events, problem, solution). To make a character tree, they create a trunk with five leaf. On the trunk they write the name of the character and on each leaf a different trait that describes the character. To write a letter to the author, the student writes to the author and asks questions he or she might still have about the book. To create a poster, students advertise the book in some way. To interview one of the characters in the book, the student prepares a list of questions and then works with a partner and has the partner answer the questions from the point of view of the depicted character.

A standard literature book can also be used at the listening center if the book comes with a CD. The students can then answer comprehension questions at the end of the book, which is an easy way to keep students accountable for what they are reading.

Students who are more independent may stop the audiotape or CD every day for the last five to seven minutes and discuss what they just read. One student could be assigned to record key components of the conversation and, at the end of the week, turn in the audiotape. Another option is for students to work as a group and create an epilogue to the story.

Sometimes students do not finish the story, but this is okay. If they find the story interesting, they may choose to read the rest of it on their own or to listen to it during independent reading time.

### Materials for the Listening Station

- Book or story to listen to
- Listening Station Response Options (Figure 9.5)
- Lined paper

**Figure 9.5** Listening Station Response Options

| Listening Station Response Options |
| --- |

Now that you have finished your story, you can choose to create your book report using any of the following options.

**Brochure**

1. Fold your paper into three parts (so that it looks like a brochure).

2. On the front cover, write the title and the author, and illustrate a major event from the story.

3. On the first page (or back of the cover), write about the main characters and their character traits (what their personalities were like).

4. On the next section (middle), write a summary of the story and illustrate another major event from the book.

5. On the next page (far right), write the main problem in and resolution of the story.

6. On the back of the far-right page, pick three of your favorite quotations and explain what they mean. (Be sure to include the page numbers where you found these quotes).

7. On the back middle page, write your name, date, and whether you would recommend this book to someone. Tell why you would or would not recommend this book.

**Character Tree**

1. Choose a character to analyze.

2. List all the traits this character possesses.

3. Cut out a trunk of a tree and then five or six leaves.

4. Write the name of the character on the trunk and a different trait on each leaf.

5. Finally, write an explanation on notebook paper as to why you chose these traits. Use evidence from the text to support your answers.

**Letter to the Author**

1. Write a letter to the author about the book.

2. Please make sure it is in letter format (include the date, Dear, Sincerely, and so on).

3. Include any questions you may still have.

4. Your letter must be at least one page handwritten.

5. If computers are available, use the Internet to find the author's address.

6. Address the envelope and place your letter inside the envelope before turning it in.

**Poster Advertising the Book**

1. Create a poster that advertises the book.

2. Include a book review that entices the reader. (Be sure not to give away the ending.)

3. Illustrate an event or a character from the book.

4. Advertise the book in some way. Be creative!

**Interview with a Character**

What if you had the chance to interview one of the characters?

1. Create seven to ten thoughtful questions to ask your character.

2. Have a partner in your group pretend to be that character and answer the questions the way he or she thinks the character would.

3. Write the "character's" responses down.

| Other Options |
| --- |

**Questions**

If you are using the literature book, you may answer the follow-up questions in the back. Please make sure you answer them thoroughly, using complete sentences for full credit.

OR

Think of five discussion questions to ask a member of your group. Write down your questions and notes from the discussion.

**Epilogue**

An epilogue comes at the end of the story and usually tells the reader what happened after the story. This is your chance to create your own ending. Remember to include as many details as possible. Your epilogue must be at least a page long.

**Discussion**

Stop listening to the story for the last five minutes. Discuss with your group the events that have occurred. Choose one person to jot down notes or create a summary of the discussion. Be sure to include the date of the discussion and several key points. You should have between four to five notes or summaries of your discussions turned in by the end of the week.

## Directions for the Listening Station

1. Place the tape into the recorder or the CD into the CD player and put headphones on; when everyone is ready, relax and listen to the tape or CD while you read along.

2. When you finish, choose from the Listening Station Response Options in the list provided. You may also choose to do another activity. However, the entire group must agree to this, as everyone needs to participate.

3. If you choose to do a book report, make sure it shows your understanding of the book, as you will be graded mainly on how well you seem to understand it.

4. If you do not finish the book, that is okay; just create a book report on what you read or complete an optional activity from where you left off.

ACADEMIC CHALLENGE Work with your group to create a role play of the epilogue to the story.

Table 9.3 shows the rubric I use with the listening station.

**Table 9.3** Rubric for the Book Report

|  | 1 | 2 | 3 | 4 | +1 |
|---|---|---|---|---|---|
| **Participation** | Student did not put forth the needed effort. Student had to be reminded two or more times to stay on task. | Student put forth minimal effort. Student had to be reminded one or more times to stay on task. | Student put forth required effort to complete the assignment. He or she did not need to be reminded to stay on task. | Student put forth outstanding effort. He or she worked well with members of the group. | Student went above and beyond required expectations of the assignment. |
| **Book Report** | Student does not show understanding and is missing many components of the book report. | Student shows minimal understanding and is missing some components of the book report. | Student shows he or she understands what was read in the listening center. All components of the book report are present. | Student shows deep understanding of what happened in the story through his or her book report. Student presented the information in a creative way. | Student did a book report and another activity. |

(Kristina Utley)                                                      **Total Points:** _____

# Readers' Theater Station

Chapter
Nine
Using Literacy
Workstations
to Provide
Scaffolded
Learning

In this station, students work together to act out a play already written, look through various picture books and create a play based on the story, or create their own play. Because students work at varying levels, allowing this elasticity of choices provides the opportunity to meet the specific needs of each student. Usually I include in the bin different plays that are already written, and the students know that they can take picture books from the library for guidance. Often the literature book or basal series has a section of plays, so the students also have the option of using this resource.

While introducing this station, it is important to point out how dialogue in plays is written. Students seemed to really enjoy creating their own plays and became very involved in the writing aspect. One problem I ran into midyear was the appropriateness of some of the scripts. Although the plays were creative and entertaining, the students were starting to incorporate a lot of violence. We had to backtrack and talk about the importance of gearing writing toward the given audience. I mentioned that the plays should fit a G or PG rating. After this discussion, we had no other problems. You may want to address this issue initially.

Before they begin writing, students plan their script on a story map (where they include the setting, problem, events, solution, and so on) so that the play will have a plot. Students are better able to stay on task when each student writes the script down, rather than having just one person as the recorder. Students are required to create actions to go along with their writings. In addition, I require that the students practice their play at least five times; if they memorize it, I give extra credit. Students can also create props to go along with the play. The rubric I developed for this station is shown in Table 9.4.

Another method students use to create their play is the mysterious brown bag activity. Students receive a brown bag with various items in it (for example, a paper clip, string, a glue stick, a pencil, and a piece of candy). The students create a script incorporating these items. The items I listed are just an example; really, anything can be used. This encourages a lot of creativity in their thinking and writing, and the results can be humorous. One group wrote a love story. A girl in the story had a heart like a paper clip; it was always bending back and forth from each boy that she fell in love with. The group flattened the paper clip when her heart was empty, and then bent it back together again when her heart was full. At one point, a boy broke her heart (the paper clip broke). Later, a new suitor came and glued it back together (glue stick). As many middle-school teachers know, with

**Table 9.4**  Rubric for the Readers' Theater

| | 1 | 2 | 3 | 4 | +1 |
|---|---|---|---|---|---|
| **Participation** | Student had to be reminded two or more times to stay on task. Student did not cooperate well with group. | Student had to be reminded at least once to stay on task. Student put forth minimal effort with group. | Student did not have to be reminded to stay on task. He or she worked well with group to produce play. | Student put forth an outstanding effort. He or she collaborated well with group. | Student went above and beyond and was a leader in the group. |
| **Script** | Student did not turn in or use a completed script. The script is not written in the correct form. | Student is missing the story web to the script. Script is lacking some key details. Story is somewhat confusing. | Script and story web are complete. Script is clear and makes sense. | Script is very creative and well written. | |
| **Presentation** | Student did not have a part in the play. Student acted inappropriately. Audience could not hear student. | Student did not play a sufficient role in the play and did not help with scene changes or key parts. He or she did not speak clearly enough for the audience to hear. Some parts lacked action that was needed for understanding. | Student had a sufficient role in the play, spoke clearly, and acted out parts. His or her character role was believable. He or she used actions needed for understanding. | Student had a sufficient role in the play and spoke clearly with articulation. Student spoke loudly and his or her role was believable. Student's actions were appropriate and correlated to the story parts. The student used props. | Play was memorized or unique in some creative way. |

(Kristina Utley)

**Total Points:**_____

students going through the adolescent years, a lot of the scripts may incorporate some sort of love story.

On the presentation day, I give every student in the class an audience critique sheet to evaluate their peers (Figure 9.6). The critique sheet uses the 3-2-1 strategy. Before I do this, we talk about constructive criticism and appropriate ways of responding. The class then gives the groups their sheets to help them improve on future performances.

160

Chapter
Nine
Using Literacy
Workstations
to Provide
Scaffolded
Learning

**Figure 9.6** Audience Critique Sheet for Readers' Theater

Please provide feedback to the members in the Readers' Theater group. Remember when evaluating to think about their clarity of voice (articulation—words are clear and easy to understand), voice projection (loudness—could you hear it at the back of the room?), voice inflection (voices go up and down, as they do in real life), believability of the character, and timing (parts were read smoothly without unscripted pauses).

**3 things I liked about your presentation**

1. _____

2. _____

3. _____

**2 things I wonder about**

1. _____

2. _____

**1 way you can improve**

1. _____

(Kristina Utley)

## Materials for the Readers' Theater Station

- Plays or books with plays
- Literature book
- Story maps
- Brown bag with mysterious items
- Picture books

## Directions for the Readers' Theater Station

Choose one of these options and then complete the steps that follow.

1. Create a play based on picture books that are in the classroom library.

2. Act out one of the plays featured in your literature book.

3. Create a play from one of the stories in your literature book.

4. Create a play using mysterious items from the brown bag. You must include these items as part of the story of your play. They can be symbolic representations or actual props; you choose.

5. Write your own creative play. Please make sure it is appropriate for your audience.

### What You Need to Do for Each Option

1. Fill out a story map. (It must have a plot.)

2. Create a script if you are making up the play on your own. Everyone must have a copy of this script.

3. Practice. You must practice the play *at least five times*.

4. Create props for the play.

ACADEMIC CHALLENGE  Memorize the play.

## Homophone Station

Many students have trouble when it comes to spelling homophones. In this station, students can practice and internalize different homophone spelling in engaging ways. Prior to assigning students to this center, the teacher writes various pairs (or groups) of homophones on index cards. Each student picks one card (homophone pair or group) to work with. See Figure 9.7 for an example of these cards.

The students then create a comic strip depicting their homophones. Students can create the format for their comic strip by folding their paper so that there are six boxes. At the top, they write the title, which contains the

### Figure 9.7  Homophone Pairs on Index Cards

162

Chapter
Nine
Using Literacy
Workstations
to Provide
Scaffolded
Learning

homophone pair or group. Next, they create a story in their comic strip, depicting the word pairs or groups in the correct context (Figures 9.8 and 9.9).

After creating their comic strip, students choose a partner in their group. These students work together to act out and teach the homophones to the class on presentation day. During the skit, they can speak but cannot say the name of the homophone. The goal is to act out the skit so that students in the class can guess correctly. After the skit, the students write the two words on the board and explain their definitions and differences to the class.

For an extra challenge, students can write sentences using other homophones that their group is working on or from the cards provided in the center. They can also create an electronic version on the Comic Creator at www.readwritethink.org/materials/comic/. This can be added as an Academic Challenge. See Table 9.5 for the rubric for this station.

## Materials for the Homophone Station

- Note cards with pairs or groups of homophones
- Homophone reference list
- White paper
- Crayons, markers, colored pencils
- Lined paper
- White paper

## Directions for the Homophone Station

You must complete two assignments at this station by the end of the week.

### First

1. Pick out a card with a pair or group of homophones listed on it.
2. Create a comic strip depicting the homophones on your card. The homophones need to be written in the comic strip.
3. Fold a white sheet of paper so that there are at least six boxes. You should create at least six different pictures for your comic strip.
4. Make it creative, color it, and do your best quality work.

### Second

1. Choose *one* partner from your group. You may pick two only if there is an odd number of group members.
2. Work with your partner to come up with a short skit for your homophone and one for his or her homophone. By presentation day, you need to be

Figure **9.8** Comic Strip Depicting *Hire* and *Higher*

Figure **9.9** This Student Shows the Difference between *Threw* and *Through* in Her Comic Strip

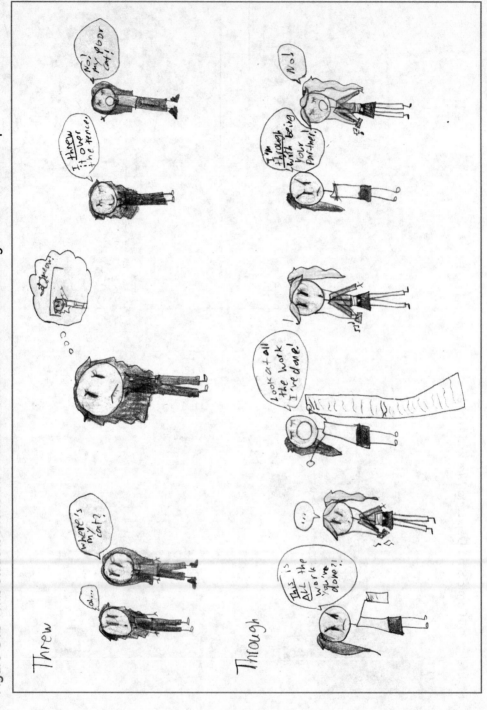

prepared to present *both* skits to the class. *Note:* If you are working with two partners, you will be required to take part in *three* skits.

3. Remember that you can speak during the skit, but you cannot say the name of your homophone. The goal is to get the class to guess your homophone.

4. If you still have time, write different sentences for different homophones that your group is working on.

**Table 9.5** Rubric for the Homophone Comic

| | 1 | 2 | 3 | 4 | +1 |
|---|---|---|---|---|---|
| **Participation** | Student had to be reminded two or more times to stay on task. Student did not cooperate well with partner(s). | Student had to be reminded at least once to stay on task. Student put forth minimal effort with partner(s). | Student did not have to be reminded to stay on task. He or she worked with the partner to produce a quality script. | Student put forth an outstanding effort. Student collaborated well with his or her partner to produce a creative script. | Student went above and beyond the expectations of the assignment. |
| **Illustrations** | Student did not provide at least six illustrations. The illustrations do not match the homophones that the student is trying to convey. | Some illustrations are not appropriate to the homophone. Student created pictures, but they show minimal effort. | There are at least six illustrations that appropriately depict the homophone and are colored in. Student has put forth quality work. | There are six or more illustrations that appropriately depict the homophone. The illustrations are creative and show quality work. | Student used Comic Creator on the computer to publish his or her work. |
| **Text** | Homophones were not spelled correctly. Homophones were not used in a complete sentence. Student does not show understanding of the homophone. | Student spelled the homophones correctly. Student did not put homophones into complete sentences. | The assigned homophones are spelled correctly throughout the comic strip. Complete sentences are given with the homophones used correctly. | Homophones are spelled correctly throughout the comic strip and complete sentences are given with the homophones used correctly. Student's understanding of the homophones is evident. | |

Continued

Table 9.5 Rubric for the Homophone Comic (Continued)

| | 1 | 2 | 3 | 4 | +1 |
|---|---|---|---|---|---|
| **Skit** | Students did not seem to have a skit prepared ahead of time. Audience could not hear student. Skit does not appropriately depict meaning of the homophones. | Skit was well done, but student said the name of the homophone. Student was hard to hear. Skit appropriately depicts meaning of homophone. | Skit was well done. Student's voice was clear and audible. Student did not say the name of the homophone. Skit was appropriate to the homophone, but the class could not guess the homophone. | Skit was creative and student's voice was clear and audible. Student did not say the name of the homophone. The class was able to guess what the homophone was based on the skit. | Skit provided a unique component that added humor or originality. |

(Kristina Utley)

Total Points:_____

ACADEMIC CHALLENGE Use the Comic Creator at www.readwritethink.org/materials/comic/ to publish your comic strip.

## Jeopardy Station

The jeopardy game station is usually the most popular station. Here students create a jeopardy game, either related to material they are studying in other content areas or with word parts (see Chapter 12). The students create a jeopardy game on a trifold poster board and share it with the class on presentation day. The group is responsible for coming up with rules and managing the classroom at this time. The group also needs to provide resources from the classroom (such as books, articles, charts, and so on) so that the class can try to find the answers as they participate in the game. The students can find their answers using the Internet, textbooks, books in the classroom library, or encyclopedias as long as they provide the reading material to their classmates on presentation day. Students who are studying word parts can pass out a dictionary or thesaurus to each person as a way of using a resource. The students can use (3″ × 5″) sticky notes (placing three on top of each other) to write the answer, question, and number of points the question is worth. I ask students not to write directly on the board so that it can be reused by the next group.

In games in which students use content area as their theme, they must come up with at least four categories about the particular topic. For example, if a group decides to use the solar system as a theme, categories could be

Mercury, Venus, Earth, and Mars. Under each category, the students need to include the point total, question, and answer. The points are placed on top, the question underneath, and then the answer. If the students are doing word parts, they could do prefixes. For example, for the top categories they may choose *peri*, *ex*, *re*, and *deci*. In each category, they will provide a clue as to what the word is, such as, "This word means to measure around something." The answer would be, "What is *perimeter*?"

## Materials for the Jeopardy Station

- Resource books for content area games
- Dictionary and thesaurus
- Package of 3″ × 5″ sticky notes
- Construction paper
- Markers, crayons, colored pencils

## Directions for the Jeopardy Station

1. Either I will assign you a topic or you can choose your topic based on something we are learning or have learned this year. Please make sure you get the topic approved by me first.

2. Obtain resources from the classroom library about your topic (for example, a science text, content area books, magazines, a dictionary, or a thesaurus).

3. PLEASE DO NOT WRITE ON THE ACTUAL BOARD. Place the sticky notes on the board so that we can use the board again.

4. Put the title at the top of the board.

5. Find at least four different subjects from your topic that you can ask at least five questions about.

6. Create questions. (You may want to write the questions down on a separate sheet of paper first, as you have a limited number of sticky notes).

7. Write the answers, questions, and point totals on the sticky notes.

The rubric I created for the game is in Table 9.6.

## Computer Station

Both the teacher and students like the computer station. Teachers are fond of this station because students are very quiet. Students enjoy this station because they like working with technology, especially in today's world of

**Table 9.6** Rubric for the Jeopardy Station

| | 1 | 2 | 3 | 4 | +1 |
|---|---|---|---|---|---|
| **Participation** | Student had to be reminded two or more times to stay on task. Student did not cooperate well with group. | Student had to be reminded to stay on task. Student put forth minimal effort with group. | Student did not have to be reminded to stay on task. He or she worked with group to produce the game. | Student put forth an outstanding effort. He or she collaborated well. | Student went above and beyond the expectations and was a leader in the group. |
| **Game Board** | Game is incomplete or contained incorrect information. | Game is complete but did not show all components of quality work. Specific rules were included on the game board. | The game is complete and it is evident that the student put forth quality work. Specific and clear rules were included on the game board. | The game is complete and is unique or creative in some way. Specific and clear rules were included on the game board. | |
| **Presentation** | Student did not present any of the material on the jeopardy game board. | Student did not play a sufficient role while presenting the jeopardy information. He or she was hard to understand. Resources were provided for other members of the class to use as a tool during the game. | Student had a sufficient role in the presentation, spoke clearly, and acted out parts. Resources were provided for other members of the class to use as a tool during the game. | Student had a sufficient role in the presentation and spoke clearly. He or she acted as a game show host and made the presentation entertaining in some way. Resources were provided for other members of the class to use as a tool during the game. | The presentation included a unique or creative component. |

(Kristina Utley)                                                        **Total Points:**_____

video games. I use several different activities for this workstation, three of which are listed here, followed by their directions. I always incorporate vocabulary into computer station work. The students at the computer station usually do not make a presentation, as their assessment is turned in to the teacher.

**Learning Vocabulary Can Be Fun Website.** The Learning Vocabulary Can Be Fun website at www.vocabulary.co.il/ provides vocabulary exploration through word searches, crosswords, hangman, quizzes, match games, and unscrambling words. Originally, I allowed students to go onto this website and choose what they wanted to do. However, I realized they would stay only on hangman or the match game. I found that if I provided structured guidelines, they tried all the vocabulary exercises. At the end of the week, they have to put ten words that they learned into complete sentences and turn the assignment in to me. Table 9.7 has the rubric I used to evaluate their work.

Table **9.7** Rubric for the Computer Station

| | 1 | 2 | 3 | 4 | +1 |
|---|---|---|---|---|---|
| **Participation** | Student had to be reminded two or more times to stay on task. Student was not on appropriate page for assignment one or more times. | Student had to be reminded at least once to stay on task. Student did not put forth enough effort needed to complete the final product. | Student was on task and put forth an adequate effort. | Student was always on task and put forth a lot of effort. | Student went above and beyond expectations. He or she helped others as well. |
| **Quality of Work** | Student is missing one or more of the components that are required for the assignment. | Student finished all components but did not show that he or she put forth his or her best work. | Student finished all components and provided quality work. | Student exceeded expectations for the assignment. | Student completed the academic challenges correctly. |
| **Accuracy of Definitions** | Student had three or more definitions that were inaccurate. The definitions are not in his or her own words. | Student had one or two definitions that were inaccurate. The definitions are in his or her own words. | Student defined all words accurately and in his or her own words. | Student explicitly defined all words accurately and in his or her own words. He or she showed a deep meaning of each word through the definitions. | |
| **Vocabulary Notebook** | Student's vocabulary notebook is missing more than two items. | Student's vocabulary notebook is missing one or two items. | Student's vocabulary notebook is complete and adequately done. | Student's vocabulary notebook is complete and thoughtfully done. | |

(Kristina Utley)                                                                 **Total Points:**____

170

Chapter
Nine
Using Literacy
Workstations
to Provide
Scaffolded
Learning

## Directions for the Computer Station "Learning Vocabulary Can Be Fun"

You may use any science books or resources that will help you at this center.

**Day 1:** Go to www.vocabulary.co.il/ or *Learning Vocabulary Can Be Fun* under favorites. Click on *Word Search* and then *Astronomy*. Try level 2 or challenge yourself on level 3.

**Day 2:** Go to the website again and click on *Crosswords*. Click under topics on *Earth* and play level 1. If you finish, challenge yourself and try level 2.

**Day 3:** Today, on the same website, click on *Quizzes*. Play level 1, 60 seconds, 10 questions. Click on *World of Science*. Complete the quiz to the best of your ability. Continue retaking the quiz until you get all the answers correct. Challenge yourself by trying more difficult levels and different topics.

**Day 4:** Using the same website, click on *Hangman*. Next click on *English Grammar*. Play the game. Once you complete this you can continue playing hangman with topics of your choice.

**Day 5:** Today click on *Learning Vocabulary Can Be Fun* and then click on *Jumble*. Next, click on *Astronomy*. Start with an easier level and then try harder levels to challenge yourself. Once you have completed all the exercises, you may choose what games to play.

ACADEMIC CHALLENGE  Find another website that would be useful for this center and type up reasons why it would be useful.

**Dictionary.com or Wikipedia.**  For this activity, I give students vocabulary terms from the book they read at the listening station and have them use the websites www.dictionary.com or www.wikipedia.com to find the meanings of the words. The students have to put the definitions into their own words and draw a picture of the words in their vocabulary notebooks. Next, they have to type each word in a sentence. Then the students go to a website to practice using these vocabulary words. The website www.quia.com has free shared vocabulary games that teachers have created to go along with a multitude of books. Teachers can search a particular book, and a list of online activities related to that book will come up. The website also allows teachers to create their own activities. To create activities, the teacher can subscribe to a free thirty-day trial but eventually will have to pay for the service. However, the shared activities are free; just click on the link.

Computers are a convenient station as students are usually engaged and quiet, and they can learn independently while working.

### Directions for the Computer Station Dictionary.com and Wikipedia

1. Use your vocabulary notebook and www.dictionary.com or www .wikipedia.com to write out the meanings of and draw a picture to illustrate these words from the book that you will be reading in the listening center. The book is *The Outsiders*.

   a. Nonchalant

   b. Abiding

   c. Gallantly

   d. Premonition

   e. Fierce

   f. Incredulous

   g. Sarcasm

   h. Gingerly

   i. Submissively

   j. Indignantly

2. Type ten sentences using these words. Make sure you print out your sentences and hand them in!

172

Chapter
Nine
Using Literacy
Workstations
to Provide
Scaffolded
Learning

3. When you finish, you can go to www.quia.com/jg/775571.html and use what you learned about your vocabulary words to play matching, flash-cards, concentration, or word-search games.

ACADEMIC CHALLENGE Create a story using all the vocabulary words.

**Illustrated Approach to Bigger and Better Vocabulary.** For this activity, go to www.wordinfo.info/ and then click *An Illustrated Approach to Bigger and Better Vocabulary*. This website explains the meanings of numerous Latin and Greek terms. I allow the students to explore the website for a while and then choose at least ten words for which they must find meanings. The students have to fill in a Word Morphology sheet (Figure 9.10), defining the Latin or Greek root and the prefix or suffix meanings. Students then write the actual definition of the word. When the students have done this for ten words, they type these words into ten sentences. If students complete this activity, they can go to various quizzes provided on this website or they can go to www .vocabulary.co.il/ and play various games. I did not introduce this station until the spring. It is important to build a strong foundation of word parts by teaching affixes explicitly in order for the students to succeed at this station.

**Directions for the Computer Station "Illustrated Approach to Bigger and Better Vocabulary"**

1. Go to www.wordinfo.info/, scroll down, and click on the link *An Illustrated Approach to Bigger and Better Vocabulary* (or just click *Favorites—An Illustrated Approach to Bigger and Better Vocabulary*).

2. Choose ten words to learn.

3. Fill out the Word Morphology sheet, paying attention to how the parts of the word affect the meaning.

4. Write each of these words in your vocabulary notebook. Make sure you define each term in your own words. After defining the term, draw a picture to go along with it.

5. Type ten sentences with one vocabulary word in each sentence.

6. If you have extra time, you may play games on www.vocabulary.co.il/.

ACADEMIC CHALLENGE Make up your own words that may make sense and write a letter to *Webster's* dictionary explaining why your new word should be included in the English language.

SUPER ACADEMIC CHALLENGE Create a story using the new words that you learned.

Figure **9.10** Word Morphology Sheet

| Word Morphology | | | | |
|---|---|---|---|---|
| Name _____ | | | Date _____ | |
| Word | Latin/Greek root and definition | Prefix with definition | Suffix with definition | Actual definition of word in my own words |
| 1. | | | | |
| 2. | | | | |
| 3. | | | | |
| 4. | | | | |
| 5. | | | | |
| 6. | | | | |
| 7. | | | | |
| 8. | | | | |
| 9. | | | | |
| 10. | | | | |

(Kristina Utley)

174

Chapter
Nine
Using Literacy
Workstations
to Provide
Scaffolded
Learning

ULTIMATE ACADEMIC CHALLENGE Go to Comic Creator at www .readwritethink.org/materials/comic/ and create a comic strip using some of your vocabulary words.

## Morphology (Reading Rods) Station

In the word morphology station, students work with reading rods to complete word morphology activities involving affixes. These reading rods are manipulatives with word parts on cubes that can be joined to form words. In my classroom, we used reading rods from ETA/Cuisenaire®. There are many different types of reading rods available through ETA/Cuisenaire® (including phonemic awareness, word building, silly sentences, etc.), but to work on word morphology, we used the rods for affixes and root words. The students completed different activities provided by a student booklet that comes with the kit, and they put together the different word parts to create new words. The booklet provides many activities to do with these words, which makes it easy for the teacher, who does not have to create his or her own. The activities are engaging; for example, one activity has the students create a riddle using one of the words they make. They then read the riddle to their partner. The partner has to guess the word. In order to hold students accountable, I had them write the words they came up with or anything the activity asked of them and had them turn the assignment in at the end of the week. Usually students can complete one activity each day. By the end of the week, they should hand in four completed assignments. Students do not prepare a presentation.

I always have dictionaries and thesauruses available at this station. Students can look up a word in the dictionary, but they do not always understand the definition. The use of a thesaurus provides synonyms and may be easier for students to understand. I also provide note cards because they make flashcards for one of the activities.

These reading rods can be purchased online at www.etacuisenaire.com/; click on the reading tab, then click on *Reading Rods*. This station is easy to set up if you are fortunate enough to have your school purchase these manipulatives. However, I have seen other teachers use beans (see Chapter 12): teachers write the affixes and root words on raw lima beans, and the students can place these together to form words. Another option is to use flashcards. The teacher can write the different word parts on flashcards, and students can use these to create different words. Students can also create their own word parts and then have partners place them together. The rubric for this station is shown in Table 9.8. This station can be adapted in many different ways, and I encourage you to try what works best for your students.

## Morphology Station Materials
- Reading rod container
- Reading rod booklet
- Looseleaf paper
- Dictionaries
- Thesauruses
- Note cards
- Highlighters

## Directions for the Morphology Station
1. You may work with a partner at this station.
2. Take a reading rod container and empty out all the reading rods. (Be careful not to mix them in with those of another group!)

Table 9.8   Rubric for the Morphology Station

| | 1 | 2 | 3 | 4 | +1 |
|---|---|---|---|---|---|
| **Participation** | Student had to be reminded two or more times to stay on task. He or she did not put forth as much effort as other group members. | Student had to be reminded at least once to stay on task. He or she did not seem to put forth as much effort as other group members. | Student worked well with others on the project and put forth a good effort. | Student put forth an outstanding effort and worked well with others. | Creative component was added. |
| **Activities** | Student completed three or fewer activities. He or she did not show quality work. | Student completed three or fewer activities, but all activities showed quality work. | Student completed at least four activities. All four activities showed quality work. | Student completed four or more activities. He or she went beyond required expectations. | Student completed a letter to *Webster's* or one of the Academic Challenges for this activity. |
| **Accuracy** | Four or more words were inaccurate. Student does not show a clear understanding of the word parts. | Two or three words were inaccurate. Student shows a limited under-standing of the word parts. | One or two words were inaccurate. | All words listed were accurate. Student shows a solid understanding of word parts. | |

(Kristina Utley)

**Total Points:**_____

176

Chapter
Nine
Using Literacy
Workstations
to Provide
Scaffolded
Learning

3. Open the booklet to lesson 1.

4. Write down all the words you come up with on looseleaf notebook paper.

5. Also write the "writing" part of the directions in your looseleaf note-book, unless you are instructed to write it somewhere else. Note cards should be in the bin for day 3's lesson. If not, let me know.

6. You should be able to complete one or more lessons each day.

7. Make sure you return all the reading rods to the container; please be careful to make sure you have all the reading rods. There is a booklet in the container that tells you how many you should have of each color.

ACADEMIC CHALLENGE Create your own word(s) and write a persuasive letter to *Webster's* explaining why you think the word(s) should be added to the English language. We will send this letter out. How cool would it be to have founded a word in the English language?

SUPER ACADEMIC CHALLENGE Write some of the new words you learned in complete sentences or create a story.

## Conclusion

Some of the most powerful learning happens when students are able to make discoveries through interactive activities and discussion. For years, we have designed stations (or centers) for primary students and little has been done for the middle grades. The stations I have included are for you to try with your class. They can easily be adapted to fit the needs of your students.

Once the stations are in place, it is easy for you to sit with small groups and have meaningful discussions centered on the book the students are reading. Many teachers worry that students will be off task if they are not continuously monitored. However, if students are engaged and held accountable, they will produce. This does not mean students will never be off task or misbehave; if stations are handled effectively, though, these pro-jected concerns are minimized.

Students need time during the day to investigate and learn with one another, eventually becoming independent learn-ers. Stations allow students to educate themselves without the crutch of a teacher, which is our overarching goal as educators. Keep in mind that learn-ing is socially mediated and students need to interact and use discourse as much as possible in order for the most significant learning to take place.

# Understanding External Text Features

? How can I help students to understand and use text features to read more strategically?

In this chapter, **Renee Mackin**, a Literacy Lead Teacher and now Office of Literacy Coordinator for Striving Readers, addresses the challenge of teaching text features in informational text.

Renee worked as a Literacy Lead Teacher at Pablo Casals Elementary School in Chicago's west Humboldt Park area. She has designed some hands-on activities to support the explicit instruction of text features. The examples and activities described in this chapter came directly from her work with the sixth-grade students from Pablo Casals and the ancient Egypt text set they used.

178

Chapter
Ten
Understanding
External Text
Features

I never realized that my students didn't know how to use text features to help them when they are reading.

—Genevieve Tueros, Pablo Casals School, Chicago

Over the last few years, I have had the opportunity to present the work that I have done with text features to teachers throughout Illinois, and more often than not I hear comments similar to Genevieve's.

A valuable yet often overlooked part of reading instruction is the explicit teaching of the various elements that informational books incorporate. Indexes, glossaries, text boxes, photographs, illustrations, charts, graphs, maps, captions, print styles, headings, and subheadings are all features that good readers use when navigating informational text. Although we as experienced readers know the importance of these features in aiding comprehension, our students often neglect or don't understand how to use some of these elements. Through shared reading experiences, modeling, hands-on activities, and independent practice, students can better understand the use, purpose, and importance of informational text features.

## Hands-On Activities for Teaching Text Features

A few years ago, I was asked to develop some hands-on activities that would introduce the features of nonfiction text and that would help students practice what they learned about text features. As a teacher, I know how important it is to find activities that are easy to make and simple and convenient to put into use in a classroom. Card stock, overhead transparency film, adhesive magnet strips, and sticky notes are all the items needed to create any of the activities that I use. Plastic sandwich bags are a great way to keep all of the materials together and ready for an instant center or a reinforcement activity.

Before beginning partner reading with the students, we took the time to introduce the various elements of informational text using a variety of shared and hands-on activities. The following lessons and activities were designed to explicitly instruct students on the process of navigating informational text and to provide practice using the features. Because our goals were to maximize student engagement and to promote purposeful discussion, all of the activities were framed to be done with a partner.

# Introducing the Table of Contents

The table of contents is a powerful feature of informational text. By sharing with students an overhead transparency of a table of contents from one of the books you are using, you can explore the importance of this feature. Based on the chapter titles, students can make predictions about the book as well as activate prior knowledge. They can determine the topic or topics that the book supports or decide if the topic is something that they are interested in reading more about.

For a hands-on activity that enables students to bring academic language into their partner conversation, make copies on card stock of a table of contents from one of the books that you will be using. Remove the page numbers, cut the chapter titles into strips, and shuffle them into a random order. Students can then work in pairs to determine a logical order for the titles. You will hear discussions about why they should put the introduction first or why the glossary should be near the end of the list. As students order the titles, they negotiate a rationale, allowing for rich conversation between partners.

This conversation took place in a sixth-grade classroom between two students working on the ordering task:

*José:* I think the table of contents goes first because it always goes first in books.

*Carla:* Always? O.K. that works, but put the "Contributions" last because that is what the people who wrote the book each did to help.

*José:* No. That is not right. That's supposed to be the contributions that the Egyptians made to the world. The index is always last, just like the table of contents is always first.

*Carla:* Isn't the glossary last?

*José:* No, and I can prove it if you want. Go get another book and I'll show you.

This conversation showed me that José was applying what he knows about how nonfiction books are set up to this particular task. It also produced rich and purposeful discussion. I love that he wanted to offer Carla proof!

Here is the table of contents from National Geographic's *Civilizations Past to Present: Egypt* (Supples, 2002), the book that was used for instruction in José and Carla's classroom.

**Contents**

Introduction

Egypt: Then and Now

Life Along the Nile River

180

Chapter
Ten
Understanding
External Text
Features

Farming

An Egyptian Community

The Pharaohs

Mummies and Tombs

Hieroglyphs and Papyrus

Contributions

Glossary

Index

The students then worked in pairs to change the chapter titles into focus questions.

The following is a list created by a pair of sixth graders using the same sample table of contents:

- What will this book tell us?
- How has Egypt changed?
- What was life like near the Nile?
- How is the land farmed?
- What was the Egyptian community?
- What was the government like in Egypt?
- Why did Egyptians preserve the dead?
- How did Egyptians write?
- What things are the Egyptians famous for?
- What are the definitions for the words in bold print?
- Where are the topics mentioned in this book?

By creating questions such as these, the students set a purpose for reading, create a focus when previewing the book, and learn that chapter titles are an important tool for locating answers.

## Introducing the Index

It was shocking to me to realize that many of the students in our partner-reading classrooms were not aware that books don't have to be read from cover to cover. An index, as well as a table of contents, can help students make decisions about where to go in a book or whether the book is appropriate for their purpose. To tackle this problem, we made a transparency of the index from the previously mentioned National Geographic book for explicit instruction. Remember to draw attention to the fact that entries are in alphabetical order (students are not always aware of this fact) and the numbers indicate pages. It was truly an eye-opener when one seventh-grade student asked me what the difference was between "91–93" and "91, 93." Activities might include adding additional entries to the index using sticky notes, creating an index for a trade book that might not have one, or preparing an index for a nonfiction book that the student has written.

**Practice Using the Table of Contents and the Index.** An activity that I refer to as "Will This Book Work for Me?" is an engaging way to provide practice using the table of contents and index for a nonfiction book in your text set. Using the chapter-title strips that you created for the table of contents sorting activity and an overhead transparency of the index of the same book (samples below), partners will answer questions about whether the book is appropriate for what they need.

| Index | |
|---|---|
| Aswan Dam 7, 9 | mummies 18–19, 22 |
| Cairo 7, 12 | Nile River 4, 8–9, 11, 17, 19, 21, 22 |
| clothes 13 | Nubia 16 |
| education 14 | papyrus 21, 22 |
| farming 8–9 | pharaohs 4, 16–17, 19, 22 |
| food 15 | pyramids 4, 6, 19, 22 |
| Giza 6 | Rosetta Stone 20 |
| Hatshepsut 16 | temples 6, 14, 17 |
| hieroglyphs 20–21 | tombs 16, 18–19, 20 |
| homes 12 | Tutankhamen 18 |
| Luxor 6, 18 | |

(From Supples, K. (2002). *Civilizations Past to Present: Egypt*. Washington, DC: National Geographic Education.)

**Create Question Cards.** Print the questions onto card stock and then cut the questions apart. We used the following questions for this assignment:

- Will this book help me find information about the weather in Egypt?
- I want to find out about the sports teams that they have in Egypt today. Will I be able to find anything about that in this book?
- I want to find out about Egyptian gods and goddesses. Is this book for me?

182

Chapter
Ten
Understanding
External Text
Features

- I need to find out about the early settlers in the United States. Will this book be useful?

- I need to locate information about mummies for a report. Should I use this book?

- I am looking for information on King Tutankhamen. Would this book help me?

- I love to read about pyramids. Will this book have any pyramid information?

- Will this book give me information about the Nile River?

- I heard about the Rosetta Stone on television last night. Can I find information about it in this book?

The following are examples of question cards:

Will this book help me find information about the weather in Egypt?

I want to find out about Egyptian gods and goddesses. Will this book help me?

Student sorting words for glossary.

## Introducing the Glossary

Most of our students are quite familiar with how to use a dictionary; however, a few don't realize that there is a mini-dictionary located in the back of some informational texts. When first introducing the glossary through a shared reading experience, create an overhead transparency of a page from the glossary. Make sure to draw attention to the boldface words within the text and discuss how they can be located, much like a dictionary, in the glossary. Invite some of your ELs to the overhead to share translations of the words or to identify cognates. Have a variety of colored overhead markers available for the artists in your classroom and encourage volunteers to come forward and draw a visual representation of a word from the glossary. Working with partners, students can select new words that might not be bolded within the text and add them to the glossary using sticky notes. They can create their own graphic representations—pictures or diagrams—for words on sticky notes and add those to the glossary as well. Students can create a glossary for a book that might not have one or create a glossary for a nonfiction book that they might have written.

**Practice Using the Glossary.**  Print the words from a glossary on card stock. Students can work with partners to create topic headings and sort the words into categories. Definitions and visual representations can also be copied, and students can match the glossary words with pictures or definitions. By playing with the words from the glossary before reading the book, partners are both activating and sharing background knowledge.

## Modeling with Shared Text

A preview map is a way to introduce your students to the function of the graphic features that authors include in nonfiction text (see Figure 10.1). These graphic maps prompt students to react to headings, pictures, illustrations, print variations, and important terms. To create a graphic preview map, select a page from one of the books in your text set and replicate the format replacing the text features with boxes, ovals, lines, blocks, or circles. Create an overhead transparency and then provide questions to direct students to the features that you want them to notice. For example, looking at the large rectangle along the top of a sample, help students to see that a heading would most likely be in that spot. Have students make predictions about what might be placed in other areas of the preview map and discuss why an author might have chosen that particular format.

Copying a page or two from one of the books in your text set is a wonderful way to model how good readers use the various text features to help them understand what they are reading. Have your students count the text features or make predictions based on the headings alone. Partners can turn the headings into questions to help with comprehension, or they can cover and guess the heading based on what is written below. They can also explore internal text structure by using a piece of shared text. In our sample text, the authors incorporated a compare-contrast method to discuss the ancient Egyptians from past to present. Other examples might include cause-effect, problem-solution, or argument-persuasion. By taking the time to point out signal words that authors use when writing expository text, you are helping them to identify the structure that is being used.

184

Chapter
Ten
Understanding
External Text
Features

Figure **10.1** Sample Preview Map

```
┌─────────────────────────────────────────────────────────┐
│   ╭─────────────────────────────────────────────────╮   │
│   │          Preview Map—Ancient Egypt               │   │
│   ╰─────────────────────────────────────────────────╯   │
│                                                          │
│   Name: _____  Date: _____      │
│                                                          │
│   ┌──────────────────────────────────────────────────┐  │
│   │  ┌─────────────────┐                              │  │
│   │  │ Before Tut's Reign │   Turn this heading into  │  │
│   │  └─────────────────┘     a question.              │  │
│   │                          _____       │  │
│   │                          _____       │  │
│   │                                                    │  │
│   │        What is the time period shown on the        │  │
│   │        timeline?                                   │  │
│   │        _____            │  │
│   │        _____            │  │
│   │                                                    │  │
│   │  ┌────────────────────────────────┐               │  │
│   │  │ Understanding Egyptian History │               │  │
│   │  └────────────────────────────────┘               │  │
│   │                                                    │  │
│   │              Turn this heading into a question.    │  │
│   │              _____      │  │
│   │              _____      │  │
│   │                                                    │  │
│   │          Place King Tut's reign on the timeline.   │  │
│   └──────────────────────────────────────────────────┘  │
│                                                          │
└─────────────────────────────────────────────────────────┘
```

## Exploring Illustrations, Photographs, and Captions

Writing captions for pictures or illustrations that might not have them or creating new captions for pictures or diagrams within a piece of text is a way not only to draw attention to this particular text feature but also to explore the importance of noticing captions within text. Share with students on the overhead a picture from your book that does not have a caption. We used a picture of an Egyptian cat statue on page 6 of our sample book that did not have a caption and had partners brainstorm potential captions.

Paris and Jonquell wrote: *This statue of a cat was a valuable artifact found in ancient Egypt.*

Jonathon and Veatrice wrote: *A very interesting statue found by archaeologists in Egypt—probably a god or goddess.*

The captions indicated to me that the students did have some background knowledge about ancient Egypt by their use of the words *archaeologists*, *god*, *goddess*, and *artifact*.

The size of a text box, an illustration, or a photograph often indicates importance, or value, of the object or statement. Having partners locate and chart these features based on size and then discussing why specific illustrations or photographs were larger or smaller than others can lead to rich conversation about features and concepts. I created the following record sheet for students to use when analyzing the size and frequency of features in a text (from S = small to XL = extra-large). After looking through the text, students then tally the range and size of the features.

| Text Boxes | S | |
| | M | 3 |
| | L | |
| | XL | |
| Illustrations | S | 1 |
| | M | 1 |
| | L | |
| | XL | |
| Photographs | S | 1 |
| | M | 1 |
| | L | 1 |
| | XL | |

(From Supples, K. (2002). *Civilizations Past to Present: Egypt* (pp. 12–15). Washington, DC: National Geographic Education).

The following conversation is typical of the discourse that takes place during this type of activity:

**Dantrell:** The picture of this pyramid takes almost all of the two pages. I think that pyramids must be important in this book or to the ancient Egyptians because it is given so much space.

**Maurice:** I think so, too. Why would the writer give so much space for the picture if it wasn't special to the Egyptians?

Also encourage students to notice the relationship of space between captions and illustrations. Students can chart how many captions are located above, below, beside, or over photographs or illustrations. Consider copying a couple of pages from the text onto card stock and cutting them out to make a puzzle. Students can work in partners to place pictures, illustrations, captions, text boxes, headings, and paragraphs. This activity will also lead to wonderful

# 186

Chapter
Ten
Understanding
External Text
Features

discussions about how the pages have been structured to fit the text and the various features within.

# Practice Application and Assessment

## Students Can Practice Using Text Features in Several Activities

**Sorts.**  Sorts are wonderful ways for students to work together and apply new academic vocabulary. Using a sort, in which students match the name of a text feature with a visual representation and description of the feature, allows for practice and application of the new vocabulary and brings content language into the discussion. In this sort, definitions, pictures, and terms are copied from our sample book onto card stock. Students work with partners to match text features with their visual representations and descriptions.

A larger version can be created with small stick-on magnets and placed on a file cabinet, chalkboard, or whiteboard for an instant reinforcement center.

**Discussion Cards.**  Discussion cards can be used to assess students' knowledge of text features. The questions can be copied onto card stock and cut out for partner discussion or a center activity.

Students matching text features and examples.

- Why might an author use an illustration instead of a picture?
- The best thing about a table of contents is _____.
- I like to use the index because _____.
- Why might you change a heading into a question before reading a section?
- Captions help me when I am reading because _____.
- I want to find out if the book I have has any information about _____. Where do I look first?
- Authors include diagrams and graphs because _____.
- I come across a word in bold print that I do not understand. Where should I go to find out more?
- An author probably puts an index in alphabetical order because _____.

The following are examples of discussion cards:

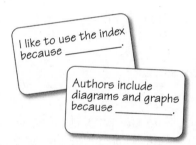

The value of students' attention to the text features is clear in comments students make, such as following:

**Callie:** I like to use the index because I can tell right away if the book is what I need.

**Joseph:** An author might use an illustration instead of a picture if the book is about things from long ago—like before cameras.

**Scavenger Hunt.** A scavenger hunt can be used to offer additional practice or for assessment purposes as well. Students work with partners, or independently if assessment is desired, to identify features within a book and discuss how it can help the reader better understand the topic. Prepare a scavenger hunt form for the students to fill in (Figure 10.2).

188

Chapter
Ten
Understanding
External Text
Features

Figure **10.2** Scavenger Hunt Form

| Text Feature Scavenger Hunt |||
| --- | --- | --- |
| Name: _____     Partner: _____ |||
| **Directions:** Work with your partner to find examples of the text features that we have talked about. Give the page number and tell what the feature is used for. For example, if you find an illustration, tell why the author might have used it and how it can help you to better understand what you are reading. |||
| **Feature** | **Page number** | **Why is it used and how can it help you to better understand what you are reading?** |
|  |  |  |

Flip book.

**Flip Book.** A flip book is a creative way for students to demonstrate their knowledge of text features through writing and pictures. Students discuss each of the features within the eight-page flip book, noting the importance, usefulness, and characteristics of each feature. Students can comment on how each feature meets their needs as readers or in what cases the feature might help them to better understand the concepts.

A pre-test and post-test assessment form was created to evaluate the work being done with text features (Figure 10.3). Administer the assessment before the hands-on activities take place and then again following the lessons to see the amount of growth your students have made in their knowledge of text features. Following the post-test, you will see how, by using just one book from your

**Figure 10.3** Pre-Test and Post-Test Text Features Assessment Form

## Pre-Test and Post-Test Text Features Assessment

Name: _____ Date: _____

Use the words in the box to answer the questions about nonfiction text features.

| | | | | |
|---|---|---|---|---|
| Table of Contents | Glossary | Index | Pictures | Boldface Print |
| Illustrations | Text Box | Captions | Titles | Heading |

1. A list at the back of a book that gives definitions for new or difficult words.

   _____

2. A title or short explanation that goes along with a picture or an illustration.

   _____

3. A list of chapters and the pages on which they start.

   _____

4. Photographs that are used to clarify, decorate, or explain what is in a book.

   _____

5. The name of a chapter or of a book.

   _____

6. Drawings that are created to explain or clarify what is written in a book.

   _____

7. An alphabetic list of names, topics, or places from a book and the pages on which they are found.

   _____

8. This provides extra information about the topic or subject.

   _____

9. The title or topic that stands at the top of a paragraph.

   _____

10. The letters in the word or words are darker than the rest. It is usually a new or an important word.

   _____

(Renee Mackin)

190

Chapter
Ten
Understanding
External Text
Features

text set to model and explicitly instruct your students on the features that can be found in informational text, you are providing an anchor experience for students to relate to throughout the year.

## Conclusion

As I reflect back on the activities that were created and presentations that were given over the course of the last few years, I can't help but return to Genevieve's quote at the beginning of this chapter that it never occurred to her that her students really needed instruction on the use of text features. In the past, I took for granted that all readers did the same things that I did when reading nonfiction. It wasn't until I began working with PRC2 and incorporating more nonfiction into my classroom routines that I realized the importance of taking the time to show my students how to navigate nonfiction.

## Reference

Supples, K. (2002). *Civilizations past to present: Egypt.* Washington, DC: National Geographic Education.

# Developing Academic Vocabulary

**?** How do I plan for vocabulary instruction?

This is one literacy coach's journey with Partner Reading and Content, Too, which focuses on the classroom and student experience with academic vocabulary.

In this chapter, **Margaret McGregor** talks about points to consider when selecting vocabulary words, assessing students' vocabulary knowledge, and providing student-friendly visuals and definitions. She also discusses how to plan for teaching vocabulary and developing word consciousness—an awareness of and an interest in words and their meanings—in order to maximize student engagement.

Margaret, a Literacy Coach in the Chicago Public Schools, has documented the development of word study in several Chicago public school upper-grade classrooms within the framework of PRC2.

She has focused on the student experience with academic vocabulary in the classroom.

One goal of the PRC2 Literacy Project was to develop academic vocabulary, the language of content area subjects. Marzano (2004) makes a point of preciseness when he defines *academic vocabulary* as vocabulary critical to understanding the concepts of the content being taught. Content area subjects and themes often contain a spectrum of vocabulary, ranging from critically important to useful but not essential to interesting but not helpful to understanding the text. This span makes careful consideration of the words essential, especially given the time limitations, number of words to be learned, and need for deep understanding. It was within this framework that we took on the challenge to become more systematic and reflective with our selection and teaching of academic vocabulary. We felt that if we carefully chose the words to teach, the structure of the PRC2 process would facilitate multiple interactions with these important words and concepts. We also wanted to develop student interest in the structure, meaning, and relationship among words.

Confirming the importance, influence, and long-term implications of vocabulary knowledge is the prominent place of vocabulary in discussions about reading (Pearson, Hiebert, & Kamil, 2007). Although evidence suggests that vocabulary knowledge strongly influences reading comprehension (Beck, McKeown, & Omanson, 1987), this essential relationship is even more significant for content texts because of the numerous and often unfamiliar technical words students need to understand (Harmon, Hedrick, & Wood, 2005; RAND Reading Study Group, 2002). Learning English vocabulary is one of the most crucial tasks English learners will undertake (Folse, 2004; Nation, 2001); and comprehension of textbooks is one of the most cognitively demanding tasks ELs will encounter (Cummings, 1994). It is anticipated that the number of students with this challenge will continue to increase, as the percentages of ELs in our nation's schools increased dramatically during the last ten years (Genesee, Lindholm-Leary, Saunders, & Christian, 2005). As August and Hakuta (1997) point out, an increasing number of ELs are born in the United States of immigrant parents. These students often lack the English vocabulary needed to understand difficult texts (August, Carlo, Dressler, & Snow, 2005). Kieffer and Lesaux (2007) found that by fourth grade many ELs born in the United States have developed interpersonal English but not the academic English vocabulary needed to comprehend content area text.

Finding time for direct and systematic instruction of large numbers of content area words is challenging (Anderson & Nagy, 1991; Stahl & Fairbanks,

1986). The majority of upper-elementary teachers spent less than 2 percent of instructional time on developing vocabulary knowledge in their core academic subject area, and the majority of instruction was mentioning and assigning rather than explicit teaching (Scott, Jamieson-Noel, & Asselin, 2003). In addition, Walsh (2003) found there was little follow-up with selected words. These factors encourage short-term learning, but they decrease the likelihood that students will develop a deep enough relationship with words to facilitate entry into their own speaking and writing vocabularies (Buehl, 2008). Students need to interact with individual words and concepts on many occasions and in different ways in order to internalize meaning. McKeown, Beck, Omanson, and Pople (1985) found that although four encounters with a word did not reliably improve reading comprehension, twelve encounters did. Blachowicz and Ogle (2001) recommend between fifteen and twenty exposures to a word in order for students to know it. See Chapter 12 for examples of different ways students can interact with vocabulary using games.

Graves's comparison of the average sixth-grade student's knowledge of 25,000 words and the average high school graduate's knowledge of about 50,000 words suggests a 3,000-word-a-year pace for learning vocabulary (Graves, 2006); a possibility only if vocabulary was the sole subject taught all day long, suggests Adams (1990). Although the consensus is that it is impossible to teach all words, the process of selecting words is often less than strategic; McKeown (2008) found the prevalent criteria for selection was "words judged unfamiliar."

# Choosing Words as a Starting Point

Choosing the appropriate words for vocabulary study is important and can be approached thoughtfully and strategically. This section describes the process, challenges, and strategies used to select words for the PRC2 project. We hope that teachers can use this process as a guide to focus vocabulary instruction in their classrooms.

## Introduction to Choosing Words

Within the PRC2 project, teachers developed various social studies and science units that include Human Body Systems, Solar System, Ancient Egypt, Industrial Revolution, Weather and Climate, Decimals and Fractions, Ancient Rome, Illinois, American Revolution, Civil War, Simple Machines, Native Americans, and China. Each unit's text sets contain approximately fifteen different books and magazines at different reading levels, spanning below,

194

Chapter
Eleven
Developing
Academic
Vocabulary

on, and above grade level. The unit vocabulary was extracted from this collection of books and magazines, using several different criteria. For every text in each unit, teachers compiled a list of words that were considered prominent—words that were listed in the glossary or words that were bold, italicized, or underlined within the text. In most instances, these prominent words seemed essential to understanding the text, an important consideration in compiling the list (Beck, McKeown, & Kucan, 2002; Boynton & Blevens, 2004; Marzano, 2004). As we expected, many words were tier-three words, which are often domain specific and usually learned in a content area (Beck, McKeown, & Kucan, 2002). Examples of tier-three words are *isotope*, *lathe*, and *revolutionary*. Texts were also scanned to identify tier-two words, high utility words, which support the content area and have potential to add depth and richness to an individual's oral and written language (Beck, McKeown, & Kucan, 2002). Examples of tier-two words are *emerging*, *occurrence*, and *establish*.

Another consideration for selecting vocabulary words included thinking about a word's usefulness beyond the text in which it was contained. Could this word potentially appear with some frequency in other domains? Does the word connect to other words and concepts in the unit? Does the word have multiple meanings?

## Roots and Affixes

Morphemic analysis and study of derivations and origins can expand and deepen content vocabulary knowledge (Bear, Invernizzi, Templeton, & Johnston, 2004; Marzano, 2004). Anderson and Nagy (1991) found that students' application of word-part knowledge increased vocabulary growth in the elementary and middle grades, a time when developing word-learning strategies impacts metalinguistic knowledge (Nagy & Scott, 2000). In keeping with this research, we took into consideration several important structural components of words: prefixes, suffixes, roots, and base words. A *prefix* is an affix added to the beginning of a root or base word to create a new word—for example, rewrite and disengage. A *suffix* is an affix added to the end of a root or base word to create a new word—for example, richest and singing. A *root word* is one or more morphemes to which affixes or other bases may be added—for example, transportation and spectator. A *base word* is a word that can stand alone without any affixes—for example, readability and disengagement.

An analysis of each word's morphological structure and potential for application was considered by examining the relationship of the considered word with the most commonly occurring roots and affixes. We used the Illinois

State Board of Education *Illinois Assessment Framework*, which provides a specific list of roots and affixes for each grade from third through eighth (Illinois Reading Assessment Framework, 2007), and identified the occurrence of the most common prefixes and suffixes by White, Sowell, and Yanagihara (1999) to determine essential prefixes, suffixes, roots, and bases to highlight for each grade level. See Appendixes 11.1–11.7 for common prefixes, suffixes, and roots.

## Importance of Choosing Generative Words

The analysis of common roots was considered important, as Templeton (2008) concurred with the early research of Dale, O'Rourke, and Bamman (1971), which found that students do not naturally make associations between related words—such as *reduce, reduction, reductionism*, and *reductionist*—even though the first five letters, *reduc*, are the same in each word. This supports the importance of considering morphological families in order to develop generative word knowledge (Hiebert, 2008). Knowledge of word families and word structure can help unlock the meaning of related words as students connect meaning when they study, compare, and contrast similar words. For example, students' knowledge that *poly* means "many" can help them unlock the meanings of and understand words in different content areas, such as the meaning of *polygon, polysyllabic, polyphony*, and *polychromatic*. Students learn through analysis that word sets like *revolt, revolution*, and *revolutionary* are related, as are *patriot, patriotic*, and *patriotism*. Learning related terms instead of a series of unrelated terms is much more beneficial for students' learning and internalization of words and their meanings (Bear, 2008; Blachowicz & Fisher, 2000; Templeton, 2008). We used the website www.onelook.com to generate related words, from which we selected the most relevant. For example, a search with words containing the root *aud* generated *auditory, audition, auditorium, audit*, and *audible*. This simple process generated morphologically related words for word-study activities.

## Marzano Academic Word List

We also searched the Academic Word List (Marzano, 2004) to see if the unit vocabulary words were included in the list of 7,923 terms, which were extracted from standards documents from twenty-eight states. The terms were identified using a linguistic analysis process, as described in Marzano (2002) and are arranged in seventeen content areas—English language arts, math, science, general history, U.S. history, world history, geography, civics, economics,

196

Chapter
Eleven
Developing
Academic
Vocabulary

health, physical education, general arts, dance, music, visual arts, technology, and theater—and in four grade-level bands—K–2, 3–5, 6–8, and 9–12.

## English–Spanish Cognates

We also considered English–Spanish cognates because of the high percentage of ELs in our classrooms. English–Spanish cognates can be rich points for discussions about word origins and connective meanings, and they often provide an entry point for Spanish ELs as they can use their knowledge about one language to unlock word meanings in another language. A *cognate* is a word in one language that shares a similar look, refers to the same thing, and shares the same source as a word in a different language (Montelongo, 2004). Some examples of English–Spanish cognates are *acid* and *acido*, *discrimination* and *discriminación*, and *hemoglobin* and *hemoglobina*.

Cognates were selected for study in three ways. A Spanish-speaking colleague scanned the text sets and word lists and indicated possible cognates. Monolingual teachers looked up possible cognates on various Internet sites and double-checked each content area word in an English–Spanish dictionary. Teachers added related English–Spanish cognates that were found during subsequent searches, as well as words that students discovered during their reading of the text sets. These related and incidental words were recorded, as we knew they might be used as part of the development of games. Cognates will be discussed in more detail later in the chapter.

## Volume of Words Generated

The numbers of possible words generated for each of the units ranged from a total of 239 words or concepts for the text sets in the American Revolution unit to 110 words or concepts for the text sets in the Human Body unit, with about 150 words in each of the other units. In addition, each unit had at least twenty related English–Spanish cognates. Within each of the leveled books, we looked

**Some useful websites for cognates**

www.spanishstudies.com/spanish_cognates.htm

http://kellyjones.netfirms.com/spanish/cognatedoublets.shtml#list

www5.esc13.net/science/docs/Span_Eng_Science_Cognates_Jan_2008 .pdf at our generated list and decided on the most essential words. We reviewed all the bold, italicized, or underlined words and narrowed down the list by retaining only one form of a word (for example, we listed *communicate* over *communication*, *communicates*, and *communicating*). We decided if the term was essential to understanding the text and if the content area words were generative and connected to other big ideas. For example, the word *revolution* has a common prefix *re-* and the suffix *-tion*, and it evolved from the Latin *volvere*, "to roll." *Revolution* is a prominent word in the Industrial Revolution and American Revolution units, as well as in astronomy and math units. For example, the following is a list of essential words for the Industrial Revolution unit:

| | |
|---|---|
| agricultural | mass production |
| child labor | monopoly |
| Civil War | revolution |
| communication | strike |
| congress | technology |
| constitution | telegraph |
| depression | textile |
| factories | transcontinental |
| immigrant | transportation |
| industrialization | unemployed |
| inventions | union |
| manufacturers | |

Usually ten to fifteen words and concepts were common to all of the unit selections, so instruction was planned for the whole group with words common to or essential within the theme. Text-specific words were integrated throughout the instructional time with students who were reading in their paired groupings. Teaching common vocabulary encouraged a sense of classroom community, and discussing and learning text-dependent words within their pairings gave students a sense of freedom and independence during their partner reading time, something that tied into our goals for students to become independent learners, able and willing to monitor their own learning and achievement.

## Student-Friendly Definitions and Descriptions

As teachers, we were well aware that many dictionary definitions are dense, often introduce more unfamiliar words to the reader, and are generally not

198

Chapter
Eleven
Developing
Academic
Vocabulary

helpful in defining new words for the reader. We felt it was essential that teachers have an option to create their own definitions, and we searched for one easy-to-use, accurate source for supplying student-friendly definitions or for serving as a resource for teachers to create their own student-friendly definitions. Take, for example, the dictionary definition of *astronomy* from three online dictionaries. The Encarta® World English Dictionary (2009) defines *astronomy*: "The scientific study of the universe, especially of the motions, positions, sizes, composition, and behavior of astronomical objects. These objects are studied and interpreted from the radiation they emit and from data gathered by interplanetary probes." This is a rather dense definition as unit-related words that students may not immediately know—like *motions*, *astronomical*, and *interplanetary*—are contained within the definition. Dictionary.com (2009) has a slightly more understandable definition of *astronomy* as "the study of objects and matter outside the earth's atmosphere and of their physical and chemical properties." Finally, the Longman Dictionary of Contemporary English Online (2009) defines *astronomy* as "the scientific study of the stars and planets." This dictionary contains student-friendly definitions, simple, useful, and easily changed by the teacher from a definition to a description. Beck, McKeown, and Kucan (2002) found presenting meanings in everyday language and in descriptive terms, rather than definitions, helps students with their initial understanding of new words.

Other dictionary definitions used difficult words such as *celestial*, *magnitudes*, *astronomical*, *interplanetary*, *eclipses*, *constitution*, and *phenomena*, all important, related words, but we thought it counterproductive to have to look up definition-contained words that may needlessly increase the number of words students need to learn to figure out the original word *astronomy*. The "scientific study of the stars and planets" is a student-friendly definition that, when combined with context and supporting examples, will provide students with a basic level of understanding and set the stage for exploring words on a deeper level as they read and discuss their leveled text sets. This echoes the suggestion of Stahl (1999), that vocabulary knowledge is a gradual process moving from "the first meaningful exposure to a word to full and flexible knowledge" (p. 16).

An interesting and useful aspect of the Longman Dictionary of Contemporary English Online is the word focus and list of related words it provides. For example: "**space** vehicles used in space: *spaceship, spacecraft, rocket, (space) shuttle, probe, satellite, space station*; someone who travels in space: *astronaut, cosmonaut, Russian*; parts of a rocket's journey: *countdown, launch, blast-off/take-off/lift-off, leaving the earth's atmosphere, going into* *orbit, re-entering the earth's atmosphere, splashdown/touchdown*; places and things in space: *planet, moon, star, sun, satellite, solar system, constellation, galaxy, universe, the cosmos, black hole, quasar, comet, meteor, asteroid*."

## Visual Support

The leveled text sets were carefully selected to include a range of reading levels and to provide colorful, interesting, and informative visuals and graphic images. Other visual supports for vocabulary were generated, as research has shown that information about words is "dual-coded" and is stored in both linguistic and nonlinguistic forms in memory. The linguistic form includes print and meaning, while the use of pictures, photographs, and diagrams are the nonlinguistic form, or sensory images, that enhance the linguistic form and provide an additional entry point for students to access word meaning (Paivio, 1990).

## Word Management

In terms of word management, we type the list of words into an Excel® document, referring to the text source and using font type bold, italics, and color—to associate the word with each individual text source. This file served as an

---

**Some useful websites for visuals**

*Google Images*

http://images.google.com/

*Yahoo! Images*

http://images.search.yahoo.com/

*Ask.com Images*

www.ask.com/

*Pics4Learning*

www.pics4learning.com/

*The Library of Congress American Memory*

http://memory.loc.gov/ammem/index.html

---

200

Chapter
Eleven
Developing
Academic
Vocabulary

ongoing reference, and, as the units progressed, teachers added other related information, such as word parts, morphology, picture links, and teacher-friendly definitions and descriptions for the unit vocabulary. These Excel® documents are useful for many instructional activities that are described in Chapter 12.

## Assessment of Students' Vocabulary Knowledge

Before teaching the projected academic vocabulary, teachers assessed students at three levels. To assess students' familiarity with key concepts and terms associated with them, students clustered twenty to twenty-two related content words into three concepts. For example, in the Human Body unit, students were asked to cluster the words *aorta, artery, biceps, blood, bones, capillary, fibers, fracture, heart, involuntary, joint, platelet, red blood cells, ribs, skull, spine, tibia, triceps, vein, vertebrae,* and *voluntary* into one of the three concepts of *skeletal system, circulatory system,* or *muscular system.* The results of this assessment allowed teachers some insight into the students' knowledge of words and concepts and their relationship with connected concepts.

In a connected assessment, students indicated their familiarity with selected vocabulary words using a Knowledge Rating Chart (Blachowicz, 1986) on which they indicate if they don't know the word, have seen or heard it, or know it well enough to use it in a sentence and sketch a representation. Figure 11.1 shows a portion of the chart. Generally, there are eight to twelve words for students' analysis.

In each classroom, students exhibited a wide range of knowledge with the vocabulary words, and further analysis showed useful patterns. In one example, Alejandra indicated that she knew three of the ten words: *archaeologist, claustrophobic, decomposing, dehydrate, Egyptologist, embalmer, hieroglyphs, mummify, pictogram,* and *surveyors.* With the three words she knew, she had different levels of understanding.

Alejandra indicated that she knew the word *Egyptologist,* gave the accurate but limited definition of "a person who studies about Egypt," and provided a sketch of a pyramid. For the word *archaeologist,* she provided the less accurate and limiting definition of "a person who studies fossils" and used a sketch of a faint line drawing to represent fossils (see Figure 11.1). Her definition of *mummify* touches on the concept of the wrapping of a dead person; however, her specific definition of *mummify* is "a person who wraps up a dead body," which seemingly contradicts her knowledge of the suffix of *ologist,* referring to a person. Alejandra indicated a person with her definition of

*Egyptologist* and *archaeologist*, but she did not seem to apply the knowledge of *ologist* as a person when constructing her definition of *mummify*. This type of analysis suggested that students are somewhat fragmented in their understanding and inconsistent in their application of morphological knowledge and gave teachers a starting point with their classroom word study.

We examined students' knowledge of how words are formed and how affixes and roots from Greek and Latin can be used to determine the meaning of new words. Students divided words into morphological units, explained the meaning of each unit, and supplied a probable meaning for the entire word. For example, the word *imported* probably means that something was carried into someplace, as the prefix *im* means "into"; the root *port* means "to carry"; and the suffix *ed* means "it happened in the past." The words in the Ancient Egypt assessment included *dehydrate, decomposing, mummify, embalmer, pictogram, hieroglyphs, surveyors, Egyptologist, archaeologist,* and

**Figure 11.1** Pre- and Post-Assessments (Vocabulary)

## Knowledge Rating Chart

Name: Alejandra Garcia                                          Date: _____

Reflect on the following words. Which ones don't you know at all, which ones have you seen or heard, and which ones do you know well? For the ones you know well, write a sentence and/or provide a sketch.

| Word | Don't Know It | Seen or Heard It | Know It Well | Use it in a sentence. | Draw a picture of it. |
|---|---|---|---|---|---|
| archaeologist | | | X | An archaeologist is a person who studies fossils. | |
| claustrophobic | X | | | | |
| decomposing | | | X | The food is decomposing in the fridge. | |

202

Chapter
Eleven
Developing
Academic
Vocabulary

*claustrophobic*. In one example, Arturo provided some tangential definitions that were related to the deeper and more detailed meaning of the words. He divided *mummify* correctly with *mumm-ify* and in his definition provided the phrase "rapt [wrapped] up" but did not define the *ify* suffix as "to make." Arturo knew *embalmer* had "something to do with bodies," but he could not divide the word into meaningful morphological parts. He indicated that an *archaeologist* was "someone who studies the past" and an *Egyptologist* was "someone who looked at Egypt," but in both definitions he did not indicate the meaning of the *ologist* ending when segmenting the words. In *Egyptologist* he indicated the ending morphological part as *ogist*, and in the word *archaeologist* he indicated the ending morphological part as *gist*. Although he did not divide the words showing the prefix of *de* in *dehydrate* and *decomposing*, he did indicate the correct division of *claustrophobic* and *pictogram* and gave a definition of "scared of something" and "picture," respectively.

Spanish speakers can often access unfamiliar academic terms in English by associating them with the Spanish equivalents. These words are called *cognates* and are defined as two words in different languages that have a common origin, look identical or similar, and share the same meaning (Montelongo, 2004). A simple assessment was to ask students to write the equivalent English cognates for each of ten Spanish words. In many ways, this assessment served as a discovery experience for some Spanish-speaking students as they seemed to connect their knowledge of Spanish and English in an "aha!" moment while completing this informal assessment.

An analysis of the initial classroom assessments indicated several trends. Many students had at least three or four words for which they could provide a related or partially correct definition. These students exhibit what Nagy (1988) refers to in the initial stages of learning words as "partial word knowledge." Another observation was that not all students seemed to draw on their prior knowledge to apply word-analysis strategies to figure out word meaning. The analysis of the morphology assessment indicated that many students were not aware of how to segment words based on meaningful parts, as they tended to use syllable boundaries when dividing words. The research of Garcia and Nagy (1993) was reinforced, as some Spanish ELs did not seem to use their knowledge of Spanish to unlock or connect to the meaning of cognates. These assessments encouraged students to self-evaluate their own knowledge of the words as a starting point and, by thinking about their understanding, activated prior knowledge; and, as students interacted with the words while reading their leveled text and doing follow-up activities, they gained a deeper understanding of the academic vocabulary.

# After Assessment: Planning for Teaching Vocabulary

The principles for vocabulary instruction in PRC2 are based on suggestions from the National Reading Panel (2000) as well as Blachowicz and Fisher's analysis of twenty years of vocabulary instruction (Blachowicz & Fisher, 2000). Students were encouraged to develop their own understanding of words and ways to learn them. This active participation in gaining knowledge of words was supported with general classroom word study and class-specific lessons that encouraged and supported the exploration of words, their structure, and their meaning.

The classrooms were language-rich environments that immersed students in words; as a result, student interest and research of words was a thread that helped students sustain and connect words across content. Students personalized word learning through activities like Vocabulary Self-Selection Strategy (Haggard, 1982), individual word-study books, and partner discussion about important words in the leveled books. Students built on multiple sources of information and learned new words through repeated exposures through classroom, paired, and small-group discussions and activities and kinesthetic and electronic games.

Students benefited from explicit instruction with student-friendly definitions and explanations for learning content terms. Marzano (2004) stresses the importance of students having the academic background knowledge to understand content as well as associative activities that assisted students in making connections between known and unknown words.

A word-rich environment was created in classrooms that developed and supported the concept of word consciousness, a cognitive and an affective disposition toward words (Anderson & Nagy, 1992; Graves & Watts-Taffe, 2008). An awareness of and an interest in words and their meanings inevitably assists students in developing how they think about vocabulary and language and increases their motivation for, interest in, and enjoyment of reading (Graves & Watts-Taffe, 2008).

Teachers modeled and provided multiple opportunities to interact with, manipulate, and use new words, as well as to ponder, reflect, and wonder about words and their relationship to other words, known and new. In addition, students engaged in isolated analysis of words in terms of structure and more open thought about multiple word meanings, while all the time attempting to use these words in authentic and relevant ways. Greenwood (2004) suggests that an environment in which teachers talk passionately about words and

204

Chapter
Eleven
Developing
Academic
Vocabulary

language and students are immersed in language, combined with direct, thoughtful, varied, and intentional instruction is essential in order to develop lifelong learners.

# After Assessment: Planning for Vocabulary Instruction

Several of the lessons used in the PRC2 classrooms are presented in this section: Beginning Morphology Mini-Lesson; Introducing the unit key content vocabulary Mini-Lesson; and Cognates Mini-Lesson.

We constructed lessons based on Word Web Vocabulary (Miller, 1997) in order to provide whole-class instruction on important Greek and Latin combining forms and roots. One new word part is introduced each week, and students are encouraged to use words built from this part and to explore content vocabulary. This short morphology warm-up consists of the teacher writing a combining form or an affix on an overhead and asking students to generate as many words as possible for that affix or combining form within a one-minute time frame. We wanted to establish routines, build interest, and collect more information about students' knowledge of morphology, as well as focus students' attention on how morphemes work and develop students' curiosity and interest in word parts.

## Beginning Morphology Mini-Lesson

**Topic:** Generating and Discussing Prefixes

**Goal:** Students will focus on prefixes and generate multiple words with the same prefix. The teacher will explain that identifying prefixes can help unlock meanings of words. The same prefix may occur on many words; in general, the prefix retains the same or related meaning.

### Whole-Class Lesson

*Supplies:*

- overhead projector, transparency, marker, board, chart paper
- pens, paper, vocabulary notebook (regular lined-paper notebook)

- if possible, computer, Internet connection, and LCD projector
- familiarity with words beginning with the prefixes *pre* and *re*
- word-origins dictionary or word-origins websites, such as the Online Etymology Dictionary at www.etymonline.com

This lesson is important as it activates prior knowledge as well as providing a scaffold for students in their analysis and interpretation of words constructed of common morphological parts. The study of morphemes, the smallest units of meaning in words, is important because the meanings of 60 percent of multisyllabic words can be inferred by analyzing word parts (Nagy & Scott, 2000). In addition, prefixes are the most frequent morphemes, and if students know twenty-five they have access to thousands of words.

This lesson could be the first of several that will connect to the study of morphologically rich words within the nonfiction units. In this lesson, students will generate words starting with a specific prefix. Students, under teacher guidance, will create an anchor learning chart, which will serve as a scaffold for subsequent word analysis as well as a record of collective learning throughout the year.

Use the morphology assessment from the PRC2 unit (Figure 6.5) to measure students' knowledge of morphological parts. The results from the pre-assessment, listening to students read orally and decode words, and analysis of the results from the oral-reading classroom Fluency Snapshot are all good sources of data. To be familiar with the most common morphological parts, teachers can refer to Appendixes 11.1–11.7, which list the most common prefixes, suffixes, roots, and base words.

Students will be generating words, starting with the prefix *re* for this lesson. The prefix *re* typically means "again," or "back," and is a commonly occurring prefix for which instruction usually occurs in the middle-elementary grades. The structure for this lesson is a whole-group mini-lesson and modeling, individual generation of words, and teacher-led discussion about the generated list of words.

## Teacher Model

The teacher will model how to think about and generate words with another common prefix, *pre*, within a specific time frame (twenty seconds). Next, students will replicate the same process, with each student generating as many words as they can that begin with the prefix *re* within a one-minute time frame.

206

Chapter
Eleven
Developing
Academic
Vocabulary

Create a Visual Anchor Chart for Word Parts or Morphemes. After this mini-lesson, students will share their generated words, starting with the prefix *re*, and those should be made into a posted anchor chart, which will be referred to, added to, and adjusted as students internalize the meanings of specific affixes and roots. A series of similar mini-lessons can connect students to other morphological concepts, and the students will be able to apply their knowledge of word parts when reading independently. The students will be able to think about the meaning of word parts, to view the anchor chart, and to apply their thoughts and the knowledge learned to determine the meaning of content words.

The following is a sample transcript of a teacher-led lesson. This is provided to serve as a model for teachers to construct their own lessons.

> **Say** *italicized words.* **Do** nonitalicized words.
>
> *Over the course of the semester, we will be studying many words, parts of words, and the word origins. Today we are going to start with an activity to get your minds thinking about words and the parts they are made of.*
>
> *A word can be made up of several parts. A "prefix" is an affix added to the beginning of a root or base word to create a new word.* (Write the word *"preview"* on the overhead or board.) *For example, the word "preview" is made up of the word "view"* (underline *view*) *and the prefix "pre"* (underline *pre*). *Now I know that the prefix "pre" means "before" and "view" means "to see," so "preview" means "to see before," just like a preview when you go to the movies. You get to see parts of movies before they come out; they give you a "preview."* (Reiterate the word parts.)
>
> *I can think of many other words that start with the prefix "pre," even the word "prefix." See, I've already thought of another one! Now I am going to take twenty seconds to generate other words with the prefix "pre." I'm not going to stop and think about what they mean, though, I'm going to brainstorm and see how many words I can write down. I'll think about the meaning after I get them all written down. Now I am also going to think aloud so that you will be able to hear what I am thinking because whatever I am thinking I will say out loud. Join me in thinking of words you know; write your words in your notebook.*
>
> Assign one student to look at the clock, put on a timer, or be the timekeeper.
>
> Think aloud and generate words with the prefix *pre* and write them on the board or overhead, underlining the prefix.

207

After
Assessment:
Planning for
Vocabulary
Instruction

*Hmm. Okay prefix . . . predict . . . prepare . . . (look around the room) . . . oh "predict" made me think of other things we do in this class . . . pre-assessment, oh, and associated with social studies, preamble . . . and weather, precipitation . . . okay, there are a lot more . . . ah . . . preface . . .*

Step back from the board/overhead.

*How did I do?*

*I came up with prefix, predict, prepare, pre-assessment, preamble, precipitation, and preface.*

*Okay, I came up with seven words starting with the prefix "pre" in twenty seconds. Now it's your turn. See if you can do just what I did, but there will be two differences. First, you will have sixty seconds and, second, you will have a different prefix.*

Write the following example on an overhead transparency or on the board: rewrite

*Now I want you to turn to your neighbor and decide what part of the word "rewrite" is the prefix.*

Wait five seconds and confirm with students that the prefix in "rewrite" is "re."

*The word "rewrite" has a prefix "re," which means "again," or "back to the original." (Underline "re.") And "write" is what we do every day in writing workshop. (Underline "write.") So to rewrite means "to write again," just like when you rewrite your drafts.*

Check to make sure students have pens and their vocabulary notebooks.

*Do you remember how I didn't stop to think about what the words meant? I was brainstorming and I wrote down as many words as I could think of quickly. Sometimes the words that start alike may not all have prefixes, so don't worry about that. Do you remember how I was thinking by remembering things we had done? I want you to do the same thing if you get stuck when you are brainstorming.*

*You have one minute for this activity. You have your vocabulary notebooks and a pen. I want you to brainstorm and write down as quickly as you can all the words you can think of that have the prefix "re." If you get stuck, check with your partner and together you may have an even longer list of words. Go!*

After one minute, have students put down their pens. Elicit student responses and write them on an overhead. You may want to collect the notebooks and analyze each student's responses, but for the whole-class

208

Chapter
Eleven
Developing
Academic
Vocabulary

activity have students call out words, which should be placed on the overhead, on the board, or on a chart. After listing the words students generated, model how you can separate the base words from the prefixes. Make a chart with two columns: prefix and root/base words. Create the chart with your students. When you are done, chances are your chart will contain similar responses to the one shown in Table 11.1. You have choices here because you may not want to address all of the words the students listed as there are various points of conversation, which will occur frequently as the students work through different affixes and roots.

Encourage students to use their dictionaries to locate more words and also to start exploring how prefixes work in various words. This is when a laptop and an LCD projector would be useful for visual and nonauditory learners, as students can follow as you facilitate the conversation.

Table 11.1 Morphology Analysis

| Prefix | Root/Base |
|--------|-----------|
| re | assure |
| re | plant |
| re | dial |
| re | group |
| re | produce |
| re | consider |
| re | shuffle |
| re | cycle |
| re | bound |
| re | sign |
| re | volution |
| re | solve |
| re | sort |
| re | build |
| re | unite |
| re | read |
| re | play |
| re | locate |
| re | do |

See Chapter 12 for games and other activities that help students reinforce and internalize the meaning of the morphological parts. In the game Borrowed, Before, Base and Beyond, students work with the meaning of roots, prefixes, base words, and suffixes. In Ology of Morph, students analyze the meaning of the morphological parts or words in order to make meaning.

## Learning Key Content Vocabulary Mini-Lesson

**Topic:** Introducing the Unit Key Content Vocabulary

**Goal:** Students will focus on the unit's key vocabulary terms. Students will learn the meaning of the vocabulary, engage in activities to draw attention to the vocabulary, and create with the teacher a classroom chart for the key content vocabulary terms. The teacher will explain each key term and ask students to create a vocabulary entry in their vocabulary notebooks. The teacher will also pronounce each word with the students and then do one of several activities to highlight the terms.

Other ways to highlight the words is for the teacher to read a short passage containing some key vocabulary terms and ask students to raise their hands whenever they hear one of the terms. This strategy will connect the print term with the sounds of the language. An activity for visual learners and ELs is to draw or sketch the image in the vocabulary notebook or to locate an appropriate image online using Google images.

Students can interact with the vocabulary words by being word detectives, trying to find the vocabulary words, either in their PRC2 books or in their content area textbooks. Students can add examples of sentences when they find the words in print. They can also work with a partner to locate meanings and diagrams of the words.

As a class, students can work together to create a key content vocabulary chart for any of the content terms. This visual can support the learner throughout the science, math, and social studies content areas, as well as provide opportunities to use cross-subject vocabulary knowledge. For example, if students know the meaning of *archaeologist* in social studies, they can be encouraged to make the connection to the word *musicologist* by being a word detective and noticing the structure of the word's ending.

### Whole-Class Lesson

*Supplies:*

- overhead projector, transparency, marker, board, chart paper
- pens, paper, vocabulary notebook (regular lined-paper notebook)

210

Chapter
Eleven
Developing
Academic
Vocabulary

- if possible, computer, Internet connection, and LCD projector
- familiarity with words beginning with the unit's key content vocabulary
- access to a dictionary or the Longman Dictionary of Contemporary English Online at www.ldoceonline.com

This lesson is important as it introduces the students to the key vocabulary and provides opportunities for students to become familiar and comfortable with the words. The teacher will explain the meaning of the key vocabulary words using student-friendly definitions. The key content area vocabulary was selected as the words related to important ideas and concepts that were used in many of the PRC2 books. Knowing these important words increases students' ability to make and articulate clearer distinctions among important concepts within the units.

Under teacher guidance, students create an anchor learning chart, which serves as a resource for the current unit of study and also as a tool for continued word analysis.

Teachers should use Rate Your Knowledge assessment (Blachowicz, 1986) to measure students' knowledge of the key content terms. The results from the Rate Your Knowledge assessment provide a window on students' familiarity of the key vocabulary. In order to be familiar with the key vocabulary and to be able to look up simple student-friendly definitions, teachers can access the Longman Dictionary of Contemporary English Online at www .ldoceonline.com.

The structure for this lesson is a whole-group mini-lesson and small-group extension activities.

**Teacher Model**

The teacher will present the list of key vocabulary words for the unit of study and provide students with simple, student-friendly definitions.

The following is a sample transcript of a teacher-led lesson. This is provided to serve as a model for teachers to construct their own lessons.

> **Say** *italicized words*. **Do** nonitalicized words.
>
> *So far this semester we have started studying many words, parts of words, and the word origins. Today we are going to study our key unit vocabulary. These are the vocabulary words that are likely to appear in ALL your books, as they are the most important words and concepts related to the unit, the Industrial Revolution. I am going to tell you the words, we will practice saying them because a lot of them you might never have said*

211

After
Assessment:
Planning for
Vocabulary
Instruction

*out loud, and then I am going to give you a simple definition to help you remember what the word means. We have words connected with three concepts: inventions/improvements, working people, and business.*

*Let's look at some of the words under inventions/improvements. Let's look at an invention. An "invention" is something new that a person makes for the first time. Or it is a new, useful process, machine, improvement, and so on, that did not exist previously. Hmm. Let's see; some useful inventions that have been made in the past few years are the iPod and the thumb drive, which was quite recent as well. Inventions that were made during the Industrial Revolution were quite different; we will talk about that later.*

*Let's look at the word "telegraph." A telegraph is an old-fashioned method of sending messages using radio or electrical signals. Well, this definition is not all that useful; I can't quite get a picture of this. Now, because it is also a noun, I am betting there is a picture of a telegraph. Let's go to Google.com and search Images for a picture of a telegraph.* Check Google.com and select an image to show students.

*After I explain each word, create a vocabulary entry in your vocabulary notebook.* The teacher will also pronounce the vocabulary word with the students and then do one of several activities to highlight the terms.

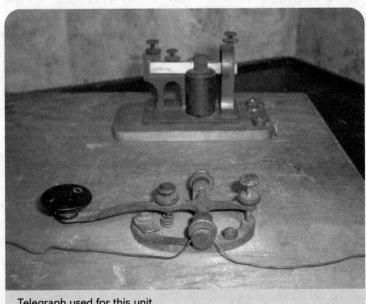

Telegraph used for this unit.

212

Chapter
Eleven
Developing
Academic
Vocabulary

Students can follow Marzano's six-step process to build academic vocabulary (2004). After the teacher explains the new word by providing a student-friendly definition, students must restate the explanation in their own words. This step assists students in storing the meaning in their long-term memory. Next, the students create a nonlinguistic representation of the term. This representation can be a picture, graphic organizer, or pictograph. Students must be exposed to the words, so any type of activity where students are comparing, classifying, or using the words will deepen their knowledge of those words. Discussion is an important part of vocabulary development, and teachers should periodically organize students into groups and ask them to discuss the words listed in their vocabulary notebooks. To stimulate group discussion and encourage word consciousness, teachers might ask questions such as the following: What terms do you find interesting? What issues or questions do you have about certain words? What new information do you have that has made you understand this word better? The final step is to encourage students to play games that allow them to work with the key vocabulary terms. Some games and suggestions for the creation of games can be found in Chapter 12.

Other ways to highlight the words is for the teacher to read a short passage containing some key vocabulary terms and ask students to raise their hands whenever they hear one of the terms. This strategy will connect the print term with the sounds of the language. An activity for visual learners and ELs is to draw or sketch the image in the vocabulary notebook or to locate an appropriate image online using Google images.

Students can interact with the vocabulary words by being word detectives, trying to find the vocabulary words, either in their PRC2 books or in their content area textbooks. Students can add examples of sentences when they find the words in print. They can also work with a partner to locate meanings and diagrams of the words.

As a class, students can work together to create a key content vocabulary chart for any of the content terms. This visual can support the learner throughout the science, math, and social studies content areas, as well as provide opportunities to use cross-subject vocabulary knowledge. For example, if students know the meaning of *archaeologist* in social studies, they can be encouraged to make the connection to the word *musicologist* by being a word detective and noticing the structure of the word's ending.

See Chapter 12 for games and other activities that help students reinforce and internalize the meaning of the morphological parts. In the game Six

Degrees of Connection students sort various concepts into a semantic gradient. Teachers can make unit-relevant games using the concept of Six Degrees of Connection.

## Cognates Mini-Lesson

**Topic:** Discovering Patterns

Small-Group Instruction

**Goal:** Students will focus their attention on English–Spanish cognates. Students, in pairs, will look at individual cognate tiles in order to match up the corresponding cognates, the English word with the Spanish word. Students will discuss what patterns and similarities they notice in the English and Spanish cognates. After partners talk, there will be a whole-class share.

*Supplies:*

- overhead projector, marker
- transparency with printed words cut up into word tiles
- paper copies of printed words, each set cut and placed in an envelope, one for every two students
- pens, paper, vocabulary notebook (regular lined-paper notebook)
- if possible, computer, Internet connection, and LCD projector
- familiarity with English–Spanish cognates in the PRC2 units

This lesson is important as it activates prior knowledge and provides a scaffold for students in their knowledge of English–Spanish cognates. Bilingual students whose first language is a Romance language can use their knowledge of cognates in their native language to determine the meanings of the words in their second language. Explicit instruction is important, as not all second-language learners automatically recognize and use cognates (Garcia & Nagy, 1993).

In this sample lesson addressing English–Spanish cognates, students will look at English and Spanish cognates from various PRC2 units, think about the cognates, and discuss what they observe. Each word tile should contain one word, and each word should have a corresponding cognate. For example, the eleven word pairs would be typed, copied onto a transparency, and cut into twenty-two tiles prior to the cognate lesson (Table 11.2).

214

Chapter
Eleven
Developing
Academic
Vocabulary

Table 11.2 Cognate Pairs

| English | Spanish |
| --- | --- |
| technology | technología |
| denominator | denominador |
| depression | depresión |
| mineral | mineral |
| photosynthesis | fotosíntesis |
| plankton | plancton |
| labor unions | uniones laborales |
| monopoly | monopolio |
| cartilage | cartílago |
| pyramids | pirámides |
| cardiac | cardíaco |

As students learn about cognates, they can write them in their vocabulary notebooks and contribute to a class learning chart, which can serve as a scaffold for subsequent cognates as well as a differentiation tool for other students.

Use a pre-assessment to measure students' knowledge of cognates. Students can jot down any cognate pairs that they know or they can write down cognates drawn from content words within the unit, which are both sources of data. Regardless of the assessment used, the teacher should be familiar with the most common cognates.

Because this is a small-group lesson, have the students work with partners. As students discuss words, keep anecdotal notes of their conversation and interaction.

The cognate pairs shown in Table 11.2 represent the characteristics of many cognate pairs. When comparing *depression* and *depresión*, students may note the double consonant *ss* in *depression* and the single consonant *s* in *depresión*. They may note that some words look the same, such as *mineral* and *mineral*. When comparing *cartilage* and *cartílago*, students may notice that the words are identical except for the ending vowel, *e* in *cartilage* and *o* in *cartílago*. They may also notice the difference in the letter *i*, with the Spanish having an accent instead of a dot. The changing of a *y* in English to an *i* in Spanish is seen in *pyramids* and *pirámides*, as well as in *photosynthesis* and *fotosíntesis*.

The structure for this lesson is small-group mini-lesson and modeling, with pairs talking about and matching up English and Spanish cognates.

215

After
Assessment:
Planning for
Vocabulary
Instruction

## Teacher Model

The teacher will model how to read the word tiles and think about similarities of words. Next, students will pair up and replicate the same process with the envelope containing the eleven cognate sets, the twenty-two word tiles.

After this mini-lesson, students will share their matched-up English–Spanish cognates and be able to articulate something they found that was interesting. Relevant cognate pairs can be placed on a posted anchor chart, which will be referred to, added to, and adjusted as students internalize the connections of English and Spanish cognates. A series of similar mini-lessons can connect students to other structures of English–Spanish cognates and students will be able to apply this knowledge when reading independently. The students will be able to think about the meaning of the cognate, to view the anchor chart, and to apply their thoughts and the knowledge learned to determine the meaning of the content words.

The following is a sample transcript of a teacher-led lesson and some student conversation. This is provided to serve as a model for teachers to construct their own lesson.

> **Say** *italicized words.* **Do** nonitalicized words.
>
> *Over the course of each of our PRC2 units, we will be studying many words, parts of words, and the word origins. We are also going to study something called* cognates. *Today we are going to start with an activity to get your minds thinking about cognates. You will be working with your PRC2 partner or your center partner for this activity.*
>
> Place the word tiles on the overhead so that most can be seen. They do not have to be in rows, as you will be searching around.
>
> *Hmm. Okay, I have all these words that I am going to sort in some way. I am going to say each word, look at the tile and see if I can make any connection to any of the other words, then I am going to say what I noticed. Let's see, I have* (point to each word as you say it) *depresión, technology, denominador, monopolio, pirámides, depression* (stop when you have said out loud a matching English and Spanish cognate or, depending on your group, continue on with the words). [Note that the other words are fotosíntesis, cartílago, tecnología, cardíaco, labor unions, denominator, mineral, photosynthesis, plankton, plancton, uniones laborales, monopoly, mineral, cartilage, pyramids, *and* cardiac.]

216

Chapter
Eleven
Developing
Academic
Vocabulary

*I notice that I have found two words that look almost the same. (Move the word tiles for "depresión" and "depression" side by side on the overhead.) The words "depresión" and "depression" look almost the same. One is shorter than the other because it has only one "s," and the one with only one "s" has an accent, a mark over the "o" at the end of the word, and the one with the double "s" doesn't have the accent. I think I have seen the one with the accent and one "s" before. The word can mean different things. I think it can mean like an imprint, like it is lower than the surrounding part. It can also mean when you are feeling really bad for a long time.*

*Did you see what I saw? I looked at these words and decided on two that I thought were connected and said what I noticed and what I thought. Now I want you and your partner to do the same thing with the rest of these words. Open your envelope, read through the words together, and talk to your partner about what you notice. Ready . . . get all your words out, face side up . . . you will have three minutes. Go!*

As you keep track of time, listen to what students are saying and take notes on how they are discussing the English–Spanish cognates. Occasionally some students may make general comments and sort words into English and Spanish without making the connection that there are two words that look similar and have the same meaning. However, it has been my experience that students will discover the connection and figure out that an English and a Spanish word are connected by structure and meaning. Having said that, there may be different levels of understanding. For example, some students may make general comments about the visuals of the words, allude to the same meaning, or make the connection of English and Spanish, but they may not actually talk about meaning.

*Hey, here are some science words.*

*What about "monopoly," isn't that a game?*

*Yeah. I think so.*

*Oh, look, some of them are in Spanish.*

*Look at "photosynthesis" and "fotosíntesis," aren't those the same thing? Do they sound the same?*

*I don't know.*

*Some are in English and some are in Spanish.*

*These are the Spanish and these are the English ones.*

Other students may make it clear they know what a cognate is, how cognates work, how the pronunciation works, and how the cognates are connected by meaning.

217

After
Assessment:
Planning for
Vocabulary
Instruction

> *There are Spanish words and English words.*
>
> *I think we can match them all up; there is an even number of cards.*
>
> *There are eleven Spanish words and eleven English words.*
>
> *Oh, I know the cognate for "cardiac," it is "cardíaco." It is the same thing, but you pronounce it differently because it is Spanish, not English.*
>
> *They both mean something about the heart. They mean the same thing, but the words look different and you say them differently. Like, look at "mineral" and "mineral." Those look like the same word and they mean the same thing, but in English you say min-er-uhl and in Spanish you say mi-ne-ral.*
>
> *The rest are easy; they are all cognates.*

Other students focus mainly on the structure of the words.

> *Let's put together the ones that look the same.*
>
> *Here, let's divide them by Spanish and English and then match them up.*
>
> *Here is one that is the same, "mineral."*
>
> *Maybe it is a mistake. Let's sort the rest and see what is left.*
>
> *I think they all match, just like the teacher's. There is one Spanish word and one English word.*

After three minutes, have students stop their conversations. Elicit student responses about the matching words, taking care to weave in the concept of a cognate, explaining that cognates are words in more than one language that look similar and mean the same.

Move the overhead word tiles around as students talk about the cognates. Encourage students to record these cognates in their vocabulary notebooks. English–Spanish cognates are connected to the different PRC2 units, and words from these units can be made into games. See Chapter 12 for games and other activities that students can participate in to reinforce

218

Chapter
Eleven
Developing
Academic
Vocabulary

Figure **11.2**   **Sample of Word Study through the Week**

| | Monday | Tuesday | Wednesday | Thursday | Friday |
|---|---|---|---|---|---|
| 8:20–8:40 | Whole-Class Morphology Warm-up | Whole-Class Morphology Warm-up | Whole-Class Morphology Warm-up | Whole-Class Morphology Warm-up | Whole-Class Morphology Warm-up |
| 12:20–12:40 | Small-Group English–Spanish Cognates | PRC2 Essential Word Study | Small-Group English–Spanish Cognates | PRC2 Essential Word Study | Small-Group English–Spanish Cognates |
| 1:00–1:20 | | Independent Word Study | | Independent Word Study | |

and internalize the meaning of English–Spanish cognates. Cognados-Cognates-Connect is a game in which students work with English–Spanish cognates.

It is often helpful to plan out the word study throughout the week. A sample plan is shown in Figure 11.2.

# Developing Word Consciousness

In a typical classroom, vocabulary instruction may consist of the teacher, in front of the room, writing down words on the overhead transparency, asking students if they know the definition of each word, if they can infer the meaning, and if the word looks like any other words they know. More than likely, there will be limited discussion before the teacher writes the definition next to the word. If the word is *desolate*, the definition could be "lonely, solitary, uninhabited." This defining of the words is often followed by a whole-group assignment, usually using the word in a sentence. Students will comply and dutifully write sentences. Those sentences will range from "The immigrants often came to settle in *desolate* places" to "Our apartment was *desolate* while we were at school." The second example propelled us to try to develop student interest in words instead of teaching, or telling, the definition to students and hoping they would remember.

Teachers used various activities for introducing the concepts of word consciousness and of morphological awareness and analysis. During the initial discussions about Greek and Latin roots, some classrooms had students generate their own unique words. Analysis of these words led to a rich classroom discussion and demonstration that made it clear that the student knowledge was connected and aligned to the morphological language of etymology. An example was a teacher-led discussion of the word *pneumonoultramicroscopicsilicovolcanoconiosis.* Our purpose was to examine this engineered word to learn how morphological units combine to create meaning. Students and teacher looked at the word and looked at the chunks they recognized, talked about possible meanings, made connections to similar words, and engaged their background knowledge in constructing meaning. Students figured out that *pneumono* has something to do with lungs; *ultra* means going above what is normal; *microscopic* means very small; *silico* is like the word *silica,* which are those little rocklike things found in shoes; a *volcano* is where molten ash, lava, and gas come out of; and *coniosis* refers to a disease or condition caused by dust. According to the *Oxford English Dictionary* (1989), *pneumonoultramicroscopicsilicovolcanoconiosis* is a factitious (created by humans, artificial) word alleged to mean a lung disease caused by the inhalation of very fine silica dust, causing inflammation in the lungs. It was coined to serve as the longest English word ever to appear in an English language dictionary (http://en.wikipedia.org).

## Go with the Flow

The conversation in the classroom made it apparent that students were connecting not only to all they knew but also to things they knew but did not think were important. A natural follow-up to this activity was a discussion about the morphological unit *phobia*, as one student, apparently intent on manufacturing a longer word, jumped up from his chair, looked stricken, and announced he had a severe case of "pneumonoultramicroscopicsilicovolcanoconiosis*phobia.*" This generated discussion about different phobias, and students then talked in groups and generated their own list of phobias based on their knowledge of the world. A few were accurate, such as *aquaphobia, microphobia,* and *claustrophobia*; other generated phobias tended to be common words with either *phobia* or *ophobia* attached. Examples of other generated words are *soundophobia, dieophobia, dirtyophobia, uglyophobia, birdophobia, alienphobia, obeseophobia, sunophobia*, and the more fanciful concepts of *bigwritingphobia* and *homeworkphobia*.

220

Chapter
Eleven
Developing
Academic
Vocabulary

**Some useful websites**

*The Phobia List*

http://phobialist.com/index.html

*Phobia List A–Z*

http://psychology.about.com/od/phobias/a/phobialist.htm

## Tie into Student-Related Responses

Students and teachers researched their generated list to explore a more scientific way to express phobias with Latin and Greek roots. Students then made the connection between *soundophobia* and *acoustophobia*, *dieophobia* and *thanatophobia*, *dirtyophobia* and *misophobia*, *sunophobia* and *heliophobia*, *uglyophobia* and *cacophobia*, *writingphobia* and *graphophobia*, *foreignerphobia* and *xenophobia*, *dentistophobia* and *odontophobia*, and *bookophobia* and *bibliophobia*. This activity used the student-generated responses as an opportunity to extend students' interest and openness toward the meanings of words, word parts, and connected meaning in words.

## Analysis and Connecting Work to the Curriculum

An analysis of students' responses made it clear that these were some concerns that they had as teenagers and this activity was not only incorporating learning about morphology but also giving them voice and vocabulary for themselves. This is an example of a simple lesson that has the potential to plant the seeds for a shared learning experience. As students generated morphologically accurate phobias, many common roots such as *cardio*, *photo*, *micro*, *astro*, *biblio*, *graph*, and *hydro* were "discovered." This initial activity with student-generated words facilitated students making connections to both the current content and created the potential for students to connect with other words. It is more beneficial when students learn related terms instead of a series of unrelated terms (Bear, 2008; Blachowicz & Fisher, 2000; Templeton, 2008). Students can make associations that connect the new with the unknown when they are manipulating and categorizing related words

(Bromley, 2007). In addition, as students link new information to their existing schemata, or network of organized information, there is a better chance the new word will be remembered later (Rupley, Logan, & Nichols, 1999). Chapter 12 outlines many games and activities that can help to build vocabulary knowledge in the classroom.

## Conclusion

While implementing these PRC2 units, we felt we established not only time for direct and systematic instruction of content area words but also a sense of word consciousness within the classroom community. The students developed a deeper relationship with words, and it was apparent that students interacted with individual words, and concepts on many occasions and in different ways in order to internalize meaning during the units. McKeown, Beck, Omanson, and Pople (1985) found that four encounters with a word did not reliably improve reading comprehension, but between fifteen and twenty exposures did have an effect (Blachowicz & Ogle, 2001). In addition, the process of selecting words was more strategic than "words judged unfamiliar," a finding of McKeown (2008). When students chose their own words, they tended to choose them in conjunction with the current or previous morphology study. Students took the initiative to develop their word awareness, took responsibility for choosing new words, and connected them with their growing knowledge and their interest.

## References

Adams, M. J. (1990). *Beginning to read: Thinking and learning about print.* Cambridge, MA: MIT Press.

Anderson, R. C., & Nagy, W. E. (1991). Word meanings. In R. Barr, M. L. Kamil, P. B. Mosenthal, & P. D. Pearson (Eds.), *Handbook of reading research* (Vol. 2, pp. 690–724). New York: Longman.

Anderson, R. C., & Nagy, W. E. (1992). The vocabulary conundrum. *American Educator, 16*(4), 14–18.

August, D., Carlo, M., Dressler, C., & Snow, C. (2005). The critical role of vocabulary development for English language learners. *Learning Disabilities Research and Practice, 20*, 50–57.

222

Chapter
Eleven
Developing
Academic
Vocabulary

August, D., & Hakuta, K. (1997). *Improving schooling for language-minority children: A research agenda*. Washington, DC: National Academy Press.

Bear, D. (2008, February 21). Word study. Skokie, IL: National–Louis University.

Bear, D., Invernizzi, M., Templeton, S., & Johnston, F. (2004). *Words their way: Word study for phonics, vocabulary, and spelling instruction*. Upper Saddle River, NJ: Prentice Hall.

Beck, I., McKeown, M., & Kucan, L. (2002). *Bringing words to life*. New York: Guilford.

Beck, I. L., McKeown, M. G., & Omanson, R. C. (1987). The effects and uses of diverse vocabulary instruction techniques. In M. G. McKeown & M. E. Curtis (Eds.), *The Nature of Vocabulary Acquisition* (pp. 147–163). Hillsdale, NJ: Erlbaum.

Blachowicz, C., & Fisher, P. (2000). Vocabulary instruction. In R. L. Kamil, P. B. Mosenthal, P. D. Pearson, & R. Barr (Eds.). *Handbook of reading research* (Vol. 3, pp. 503–523). Mahwah, NJ: Erlbaum.

Blachowicz, C., and Ogle, D. (2001). *Reading comprehension*. New York: Guilford.

Blachowicz, C. L. Z. (1986). Making connections: Alternatives to the vocabulary notebook. *Journal of Reading*, *29*, 643–649.

Boynton, A., & Blevens, W. (2004). Keys to reading nonfiction: The art of teaching. [Special Issue] *Instructor*, pp. 4–5.

Bromley, K. (2007). Nine ideas about vocabulary instruction. *Journal of Adolescent and Adult Literacy*, *50*(7), 528–537.

Buehl, D. (2008, March 3). Generative vocabulary instruction helps students find meaning. In *Reading room*. Retrieved from Wisconsin Education Association Council: http://www.weac.org/news/2007-08/march08/readingroom.htm.

Cummings, J. (1994). Knowledge, power, and identity in teaching ESL. In F. Genesee (Ed.), *Educating second language children: The whole child, the whole curriculum, the whole community*. New York: Cambridge University Press.

Dale, E., O'Rourke, J., & Bamman, H. (1971). *Techniques of teaching vocabulary*. Palo Alto, CA: Field Education Enterprises.

Dictionary.com. Retrieved January, 12, 2009 from http://www.dictionary.com

Encarta® World English Dictionary, The, North American Edition. Retrieved July 2009 from http://encarta.msn.com/encnet/features/dictionary/DictionaryResults.aspx?refid=1861587402

Folse, K. S. (2004). *Vocabulary myths: Applying second language research to classroom teaching*. Ann Arbor: University of Michigan Press.

García, G. E., & Nagy, W. E. (1993). Latino students' concept of cognates. In D. J. Leu and C. K. Kinzer (Eds.), *Examining central issues in literacy research, theory, and practice*. Chicago: National Reading Conference.

Genesee, F., Lindholm-Leary, K., Saunders, W., & Christian, D. (2005). English language learners in U.S. schools: An overview of research findings. *Journal of Education for Students Placed at Risk, 10*(4), 363–385.

Graves, M. F. (2006). *The vocabulary book: Learning and instruction*. Champaign, IL: National Council of Teachers of English.

Graves, M. F., & Watts-Taffe, S. M. (2008, May 4). Word consciousness comes of age. Inernational Reading Association 53rd annual conference Atlanta, GA.

Greenwood, S. (2004). Content matters: Building vocabulary and conceptual understanding in the subject areas. *Middle School Journal, 35*(3), 27–34.

Haggard, M. R. (1982). The vocabulary self-selection strategy: An active approach to word learning. *Journal of Reading, 26*, 203–207.

Harmon, J. M., Hedrick, W. B., & Wood, K. D. (2005). Research on vocabulary instruction in the content areas: Implications for struggling readers. *Reading and Writing Quarterly, 21*, 261–280.

Hiebert, E. (2008, May 4). *Promoting vocabulary development in grades 4 through 12: A comprehensive approach, panel discussion*. International Reading Association 53rd annual conference, Atlanta, GA.

Kieffer, M. J., & Lesaux, N. L. (2007). Breaking down words to build meaning: Morphology, vocabulary, and reading comprehension in the urban classroom. *The Reading Teacher, 61*(2), 134–144.

Illinois Reading Assessment Framework. (2007). *Roots and affixes*. Springfield: Illinois State Board of Education.

Longman Dictionary of Contemporary English Online, The. Retrieved July 2009 from http://www.ldoceonline.com

Marzano, R. (2002). *Identifying the primary instructional concepts in mathematics: A linguistic approach*. Englewood, CO: Marzano & Associates.

Marzano, R. J. (2004). *Building background knowledge for academic achievement*. Alexandria, VA: Association for Supervision and Curriculum Development.

224

Chapter
Eleven
Developing
Academic
Vocabulary

McKeown, M. (2008, May 4). *Rev up vocabulary in the middle grades: Presentation.* International Reading Association 53rd annual conference, Atlanta, GA.

McKeown, M. G., Beck, I. L., Omanson, R. C., & Pople, M. T. (1985). Some effects of the nature and frequency of vocabulary instruction on the knowledge of use of words. *Reading Research Quarterly, 20,* 522–535.

Miller, E. (1997). *Word web vocabulary.* Cummaquid, MA: Sage.

Montelongo, J. (2004). *Concept learning and memory for Spanish–English cognates.* Unpublished doctoral dissertation, New Mexico State Univ., Las Cruces.

Nagy, W., & Scott, J. (2000). Vocabulary processes. In M. L. Kamil, P. B. Mosenthal, P. D. Pearson, & R. Barr (Eds.), *Handbook of reading research* (Vol. 3, pp. 269–284). Mahwah, NJ: Erlbaum.

Nagy, W. E. (1988). *Teaching vocabulary to improve reading comprehension.* Urbana, IL: National Council of Teachers of English.

Nation, I. S. P. (2001). *Learning vocabulary in another language.* Cambridge: Cambridge University Press.

National Reading Panel. (2000). *Teaching children to read: An evidence-based assessment of the scientific research literature on reading and its implications for reading instruction.* Washington, DC: National Institute of Child Health and Human Development.

*Oxford English Dictionary* (2nd ed.). (1989). Oxford: Oxford University Press.

Paivio, A. (1990). *Mental representations: A dual coding approach.* New York: Oxford University Press.

Pearson, P. D., Hiebert, E. H., & Kamil, M. L. (2007). Vocabulary assessment: What we know and what we need to learn. *Reading Research Quarterly, 42,* 282–296.

RAND Reading Study Group. (2002). *Reading for understanding: Toward an R&D program in reading comprehension.* Santa Monica, CA: RAND.

Rupley, W. H., Logan, J. W., & Nichols, W. D. (1999). Vocabulary instruction in a balanced reading program. *The Reading Teacher, 52,* 338–346.

Scott, J. A., Jamieson-Noel, D., & Asselin, M. (2003). Vocabulary instruction throughout the day in twenty-three Canadian upper elementary classrooms. *The Elementary School Journal, 103,* 269–286.

Stahl, S., & Fairbanks, M. (1986). The effects of vocabulary instruction: A model-based meta-analysis. *Review of Educational Research, 56,* 72–110.

Stahl, S. A. (1999). *Vocabulary Development*. Cambridge, MA: Brookline Books.

Templeton, S. (2008, April 24). Exploring and developing morphological knowledge. Skokie, IL: National–Louis University. Presentation lecture.

Walsh, K. (2003). Basal readers: The lost opportunity to build knowledge that propels comprehension. *American Educator*, *27*, 24–27.

White, T. G., Sowell, V., & Yanagihara, A. (1999). Teaching elementary students to use word-part clues. *The Reading Teacher*, *42*, 302–308.

## Appendix 11.1 The Twenty Most Common Prefixes

| Prefix | % | Grade Level in the IAF | Meaning | Examples |
|---|---|---|---|---|
| un- | 26 | 3 | not, opposite of | unhappy, unable, unfinished |
| re- | 14 | 3 | again, back | return, redo, rebuild, rewrite |
| in-, im-, il-, -ir (not) | 11 | 4 | not, opposite of | indirect, indigestion, immature, illegal, irregular |
| dis- | 7 | 3 | not, opposite of | discover, disobey, disappear |
| en-,* em- | 4 | 5* | cause to be, make | enjoy, encourage |
| non- | 4 | 4 | not, opposite of | nonfiction, nonsense, nonstop |
| in-, im-, (in) | 4 | — | in or into | inside |
| over- | 3 | 4 | too much, above | overgrown, overdone |
| mis- | 3 | 5 | wrongly, not | mistake, misinterpret, misguide |
| sub- | 3 | 5 | under, lower, or below | submarine |
| pre- | 3 | 4 | before | prepared, preview, precooked |
| inter- | 3 | 5 | between, among | international, interstate |
| fore- | 3 | 6 | before | foresee, foreshadow, foreword |
| de- | 2 | 6 | opposite of, down | descend, deform |
| trans- | 2 | 5 | across | transport, transcontinental |
| super- | 1 | 6 | above, beyond | supermarket, superman, superintendent |
| semi- | 1 | 7 | half | semicircle, semimonthly |
| anti- | 1 | 7 | against | antiwar, antiperspirant |
| mid- | 1 | 8 | middle | midbrain, midnight, midwife |
| under- (too little) | 1 | 8 | too little, below | underfed, underdone, underarm |
| all others combined | 3 | | | |

*Indicates the prefix that is noted in the Illinois Assessment Framework.

Based on the Illinois Assessment Framework for Grades 3–8, Illinois State Board of Education and White, T. G., Sowell, V., & Yanagihara, A. (1999). Teaching elementary students to use word-part clues. *The Reading Teacher, 42*, 302–308.

## Appendix 11.2 The Twenty Most Common Suffixes

| Suffix | % | Grade Level in the IAF | Meaning | Examples |
|---|---|---|---|---|
| -s, -es | 31 | 3 | plurals | boys, lunches |
| -ed | 20 | 3 | past-tense verb | wanted, talked, helped |
| -ing | 14 | 3 | verb form/past participle | playing, walking, barking |
| -ly | 7 | 3 | characteristic of, manner of | friendly, slowly |
| -er, -or, (plus -ar)* | 4 | 3 | person connected with | teacher, inspector, (liar) |
| -ion,* -tion, -ation, -ition | 4 | 5* | act, process | action |
| -able, -ible | 2 | 4 | can be done | likeable, edible, dependable |
| -al,* -ial | 1 | 4* | having characteristics of | final, rental, natural |
| -y | 1 | 3 | characterized by, to be | funny, sleepy |
| -ness | 1 | 8 | state of, condition of | happiness, lightness, kindness |
| -ity,* -ty | 1 | 5* | state of | activity |
| -ment | 1 | 5 | action or process, act or state of | enjoyment, contentment |
| -ic | 1 | 4 | having characteristics of | comic, heroic, realistic |
| -ous,* -eous, -ious | 1 | 5* | possessing the qualities of | serious, humorous |
| -en | 1 | 3 | form adjectives from nouns, made of, or to make | golden, ashen |
| -er | 1 | 3 | means more (not one who) | bigger, brighter, faster |
| -ive,* -ative, -tive | 1 | 8* | adjective form of a noun | attentive, derivative |
| -ful | 1 | 3 | full of | sorrowful, beautiful, thankful |
| -less | 1 | 3 | without | hopeless, careless |
| -est | 1 | 3 | comparative, superlative, most | biggest, brightest, fastest |
| all others combined | 7 | | | |

*Indicates the suffix that is noted in the Illinois Assessment Framework.

Based on the Illinois Assessment Framework for Grades 3–8, Illinois State Board of Education and White, T. G., Sowell, V., & Yanagihara, A. (1999). Teaching elementary students to use word-part clues. *The Reading Teacher, 42,* 302–308.

## Appendix 11.3 Common Greek and Latin Roots

| Root | Origin | Grade Level in the IAF | Meaning | Examples |
|------|--------|------------------------|---------|----------|
| aud | Latin | 8 | hear | audiophile, auditorium, audition, audible |
| astro | Greek | 7 | star | astrology, astronaut, asteroid, astrophysics |
| bio | Greek | 6 | life | biology, biography, biosphere |
| dict | Latin | 5 | speak, tell | dictate, predict, dictator, dictionary |
| geo | Greek | 4 | earth | geology, geography |
| meter/metr | Greek | 5 | measure | thermometer, barometer, metronome |
| min | Latin | — | small, little | miniscule, minimum, miniskirt |
| mit, mis | Latin | — | send | mission, transmit, remit, missile |
| ped | Latin | — | foot | pedestrian, pedal, pedometer |
| phon | Greek | — | sound | phonograph, microphone |
| port | Latin | 4 | carry | transport, portable, import |
| scrib, script | Latin | — | write | scribble, manuscript, inscription |
| struct | Latin | 4 | build, form | construction, destruction, instruct |

Based on the Illinois Assessment Framework for Grades 3–8, Illinois State Board of Education and White, T. G., Sowell, V., & Yanagihara, A. (1999). Teaching elementary students to use word-part clues. *The Reading Teacher, 42*, 302–308.

# Appendix 11.4 Other Common Roots and Affixes/Prefixes

| Common Prefix | Grade Level in the IAF | Meaning | Examples |
|---|---|---|---|
| bi- | 4 | two | bicycle, bivalve, bivariate |
| ex- | 4 | out, from | exclude, expel |
| co-, con-, com-, coll- | 5 | with | coincide, congregate, combine, collision |
| multi- | 5 | many | multimillionaire, multitude |
| pro- | 5 | for, or in favor of | production, proceed |
| ambi- | 6 | both sides | ambidextrous, ambivalent |
| di- | 6 | to give or place | divide, divorce |
| ex- | 6 | out | excel, excite |
| para- | 6 | similar | parameter |
| sym-, syn-, sys- | 6 | with, together | symmetry, synonym, system |
| ultra- | 6 | beyond, or excessive | ultraviolet, ultrasonic |
| eu- | 7 | well, good | eulogy, eureka, euphemism |
| macro- | 7 | large | macroeconomics, macrocosm |
| micro- | 7 | small | microcosm, microscope |
| mono- | 7 | one | monomania, monograph |
| peri- | 7 | around | periscope, periodic |
| pseudo- | 7 | false | pseudonym, pseudoscience |
| semi- | 7 | half | semimonthly, semicircle |
| ad- | 8 | to, toward | addict, advise, adhere |
| bin- | 8 | two | binary, binomial |
| cata- | 8 | down | catacombs, catatonic |
| mal- | 8 | bad | malady, malaria, malpractice |
| mid- | 8 | middle | midnight, midwife |
| ob- | 8 | against | obituary, obese |

Based on the Illinois Assessment Framework for Grades 3–8, Illinois State Board of Education and White, T. G., Sowell, V., & Yanagihara, A. (1999). Teaching elementary students to use word-part clues. *The Reading Teacher, 42,* 302–308.

## Appendix 11.5 Other Common Roots and Affixes/Suffixes

| Common Suffix | Grade Level in the IAF | Meaning | Examples |
|---|---|---|---|
| -al | 4 | relating to | natural, rental, renal, final |
| -ance | 4 | act of, state of, condition of | reluctance, tolerance |
| -ish | 4 | resembling, or origin | childish, babyish, churlish |
| -age | 5 | state of, rank, place | package, usage |
| -ate | 5 | state or function | generate, dictate |
| -ion, -ian* | 5 | act, result, or state of | location, celebration, guardian |
| -ize | 5 | to cause | economize, homogenize |
| -ual | 5 | a state of | usual, gradual |
| -ous | 6 | full of, or having the quality of | famous, various, humorous |
| -ship | 6 | state of | friendship, relationship |
| -cide | 7 | killing | fratricide, suicide, pesticide |
| -ure | 7 | action or process | puncture, lecture |
| -ary | 8 | relating to | dictionary, dietary |
| -ive | 8 | inclined to | definitive, derivative |
| -ness | 8 | state or quality of | kindness, lightness |

*Indicates the suffix that is noted in the Illinois Assessment Framework.

Based on the Illinois Assessment Framework for Grades 3–8, Illinois State Board of Education and White, T. G., Sowell, V., and Yanagihara, A. (1999). Teaching elementary students to use word-part clues. *The Reading Teacher, 42*, 302–308.

# Appendix 11.6  Other Common Roots and Affixes/Roots/Base

| Common Root/Base | Grade Level in the IAF | Meaning | Examples |
|---|---|---|---|
| fact | 4 | done, to do | factory, manufacture |
| tri | 4 | three | tricycle, triangle |
| auto | 5 | self | automobile, automatic |
| demo | 5 | people | democratic, demographic |
| graph | 5 | write or record | graphic, photograph |
| human | 5 | man or earth | humanity, inhuman |
| sphere | 5 | round or ball | spherical, hemisphere |
| arch | 6 | first, or leader | archenemy, archbishop |
| bene | 6 | well or favorable | benefactor, beneficial |
| cycle | 6 | wheel or circular | bicycle, cyclone |
| duct | 6 | to lead | introduction, deduct |
| tempo | 6 | time | temporal, contemporary |
| vale, vali | 6 | strength or worth | validity, valor |
| calor | 7 | heat | caloric, calorific, calorie |
| corp | 7 | body | corporal, corporation |
| cred | 7 | believe | credibility, incredible, credential |
| dorm | 7 | sleep | dormitory, dormant |
| epi | 7 | on, outer | epicenter, episode |
| flex | 7 | bend | flexible, reflex |
| mar, mari | 7 | sea | marine, mariner |
| acid, acri | 8 | sour, sharp | acidic, acrimonious |
| anthrop | 8 | man, mankind | anthropoid, anthropology |
| circ, circum- | 8 | around | circumference, circumstance |
| helio | 8 | sun | heliotherapy, heliocentric |
| hydra, hydro | 8 | water | hydrate, hydraulic |
| omni | 8 | all | omnipotent, omnipresent |
| pater, part | 8 | father | paternal, patrimony |
| spect | 8 | see, look | spectacular, inspect |
| theo | 8 | god | theocracy, theologian |

Based on the Illinois Assessment Framework for Grades 3–8, Illinois State Board of Education and White, T. G., Sowell, V., and Yanagihara, A. (1999). Teaching elementary students to use word-part clues. *The Reading Teacher*, *42*, 302–308.

## Appendix 11.7 Number–Related Word Parts

| Prefixes of Numbers | Meaning | Examples |
| --- | --- | --- |
| uni | one | uniform |
| mono | one | monologue, monocle, monorail |
| du, duo | two | duet |
| bi | two | biped |
| giga | billion | gigawatt, gigabyte, gigahertz |
| tri | three | triangle, triplet, triumvariate |
| tetra | four | tetrameter |
| quad | four | quadruplets |
| penta | five | pentagon |
| quint | five | quintet, quintuplet |
| sex | six | sexagenarian |
| hex | six | hexagon, hexagram, hexadecimal |
| hept | seven | heptagon, heptameter, heptarchy |
| sept | seven | septuple, septuagenarian |
| oct | eight | octopus |
| nov | nine | novena |
| dec | ten | decade |
| cent(i) | hundred | percent, centimeter |
| hect | hundred | hectogram |
| mill | thousand | millimeter, millennium, millipede |
| kil(o) | thousand | kilometer, kilogram, kilobyte |
| semi | half | semicircle, semiconscious |
| hemi | half | hemisphere, hemistich, hemiplegia |
| demi | half | demitasse |
| mega | large, million | megawatt, megahertz |
| quadr | four | quadrant, quadruple, quadriplegic |
| deci | tenth | decimeter |
| quint | five | quintuplet, quintet, quintessential |

Based on the Illinois Assessment Framework for Grades 3–8, Illinois State Board of Education and White, T. G. Sowell, V., and Yanagihara, A. (1999). Teaching elementary students to use word-part clues. *The Reading Teacher*, *42*, 302–308.

# Activities to Reinforce Vocabulary Learning

**12**

**?** How can I incorporate content vocabulary into my teaching?

In this chapter, **Carol Schmitz**, a Literacy Lead Teacher, and **Margaret McGregor**, a Literacy Coach, address the challenge of teaching vocabulary in the content areas.

Carol works as a Literacy Lead Teacher in several sixth-grade classrooms, including special education, ELs, general education, and gifted classrooms. She also has worked as a co-teacher and coach in implementing PRC2.

Margaret works as a Literacy Coach, helping other teachers implement PRC2 in their classrooms.

234

Chapter
Twelve
Activities to
Reinforce
Vocabulary
Learning

Vocabulary has been the black hole that many schools fall into every spring when the state assessment results are in. When we analyzed the scores at my school, the Bateman School, nothing had changed when we focused on the flat vocabulary scores, with the exception of one grade level. Upon further analysis, we realized that this was the grade level that had participated in the PRC2 project. A component of our state assessment, ISAT (Illinois Standards Achievement Test), covers Greek and Latin roots and affixes. This was a major focus of PRC2.

Renowned researchers such as Camille Blachowicz, Peter Fisher, Timothy Rasinski, and Robert Marzano have conducted numerous studies on vocabulary and have arrived at similar conclusions to those stated by Richek (2005, p. 414), "Vocabulary knowledge is among the best predictors of reading achievement." One aspect of their work focuses on the need for repeated exposure to words to facilitate students' comprehension of unknown words. Children need to manipulate words to make the words theirs. Research shows that students need multiple exposures to words to fully grasp their meaning. Blachowicz and Fisher (2000) have prescribed specific procedures for teaching vocabulary in order for teachers to be effective in their vocabulary instruction. Students must be active learners who know how to make personal connections to words. This enables students to think critically and use their schema to help them construct meaning. A necessary component to vocabulary instruction is an immersion in words. Blachowicz and Fisher conclude by stating, "Children should have multiple meaning sources to help determine meaning" (p. 13). Students must encounter words in context more than once to learn them. Opportunities to manipulate words and word morphological units supply students with strategies that can be called on when new words are encountered.

Vocabulary games, often played in literacy centers, provide the students with an avenue for learning these words within a fun and an exciting context. This repetitious and sometimes competitive atmosphere aids children in their acquisition of the meaning of the terms. The study of words varies by age. The activities presented in this chapter are geared to the upper grades (6–8), although many of the activities can be adapted for younger students. Research and our own experiences indicate that students do, indeed, perform better with repeated, multiple exposures and hands-on experiences with words.

Much of the emphasis of PRC2 at the middle-grade level was on Latin and Greek root words, concentrating on the meaning of parts, or morphology. The importance of this is realized when one considers that 90 percent of English words with more than one syllable are Latin based and most of the remaining words are Greek based (Rasinski, 2008). Knowledge of a single root can aid in understanding five to twenty related English words. Some of the suggestions that Rasinski and others compiled will be discussed later in this chapter. Participants in PRC2 attended a seminar at which Dr. Tom Estes spoke on morphology. He offered many fun and clever ideas that he later developed into a program. His close connection to Dr. Donna Ogle enabled participants to realize the benefits of the meaning parts of words and how much fun learning vocabulary can be made to be. The students think they are playing games when they are really cementing words and meanings into their memory bank to call upon when needed. They are depositing into their schema.

This chapter describes some of the vocabulary activities that we have used in the PRC2 content units. The activities include those that use the morphology (meaning parts or words), concept categorization, English–Spanish cognates, word families, and other vocabulary activities. Most of these activities are described so that teachers can easily and inexpensively make the games. The last section of this chapter describes how teachers can use the Excel® spreadsheet to create computer-based games and activities that reinforce the same concepts. Classroom computers should all have Vocabulary University (www.vocabulary.com) bookmarked as a favorite. This website is full of puzzles and other activities based on Greek and Latin roots. The puzzles change frequently, so students may visit without doing the same ones over and over.

# Morphology

This section describes two activities in the area of morphology that address the meaning of word parts.

## Vocabulary Beans

This activity provides the student with opportunities to physically manipulate the units within a word. These parts are often affixes (prefixes and suffixes) and Greek or Latin roots, although not specifically limited to these. (See also Chapter 9.)

### Materials for Vocabulary Beans
- lima beans
- permanent ultrafine markers
- resealable plastic bags, small tins or margarine cups with covers

236

Chapter
Twelve
Activities to
Reinforce
Vocabulary
Learning

## Preparation

The teacher (or students when they are ready to scaffold what they have learned) selects words from a unit of study or word lists such as those found on the ISBE (Illinois State Board of Education) website or that are grade- or subject-specific root and affixes. These words are then divided by the teacher into their morphological (meaning) units—for example, *trans port tion* (*transportation*).

Next the teacher writes each morphological part on one side of a lima bean in permanent marker and its meaning in a different color on the reverse side. For example:

| Morphological Side | Meaning Side |
| --- | --- |
| trans | across |
| port | to carry |
| tion | act of |

This activity also provides the teacher with the opportunity to teach a mini-lesson on grammar—for example, dropping letters. Sometimes the creators of these vocabulary beans need to consult additional sources, such as etomology.com, dictionary.com, dictionaries, thesauruses, and other materials, to clarify meaning or to simplify. The inaugural set of vocabulary beans should be constructed and modeled by the teacher, but subsequent sets can be easily student generated for center activities. All student-made vocabulary should be checked by the teacher for appropriateness and accuracy. Class sets may be constructed for whole-class activities. Each set should be placed in a used mint or gum tin or in a plastic resealable bag. Sets for centers should consist of five or six sets of ten words. In centers, children should individually attempt to construct the word from its morphological parts and work collaboratively if assistance is needed. (See Chapter 9.) This activity was of particular benefit to our ELs because it afforded them the opportunity for academic conversation and listening—important elements included in the SIOP (Sheltered Instruction Observation Protocol) model (Echevarria, Vogt, & Short, 2007).

## To Play Vocabulary Beans

Students take a container with the morphological (meaning) parts written on the beans.

Turn all the beans to the word-part side (color 1).

Manipulate the beans to form new words.

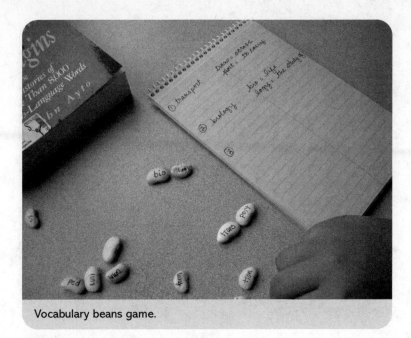

Vocabulary beans game.

Decipher the meanings of words by turning the beans over to the definition side (color 2).

Write the completed words and meanings derived on the recording sheet.

## Jeopardy

The purpose of this game is to help the students become familiar with Greek or Latin root words as well as other root words to make connections and call upon their prior knowledge of words and their meanings. This teacher/student-made game is an academic game based on the TV quiz show, *JEOPARDY!* It is aimed at establishing an awareness and a definition of words, using their morphological units. The goal is to have students say a word after reading the category it belongs within and its definition. (See also Chapter 9.)

### Materials for Jeopardy

- dictionaries
- thesauruses
- Internet
- trifold science boards
- colored paper

238

Chapter
Twelve
Activities to
Reinforce
Vocabulary
Learning

Jeopardy game.

## Preparation

Select Greek or Latin root words. Think of five words that contain these roots and that your students would benefit from having an understanding of. (These may be part of a current unit of study as in Project ALL, textbooks, words on the state lists, and so on.) Write the roots on colored paper and attach them across the top of a trifold board with the meaning of each root written beneath. Next, cut fifteen rectangles (8″ by 12″) of paper the same color (three for each of the five select words that contain the root word and definition on top). Write the word on one piece of paper—to be placed on the bottom of the pile. Write the definition of the word on another piece of paper—to be placed on top of the actual word. Last, assign a point or monetary value for each word, with increasing values.

**Example 1:** SPECT (to look)

Top sheet (point value)

Middle sheet (definition): looking around, watchful, prudent

Bottom sheet (word): circumspect

**Example 2:** FORM

Top sheet (point value)

Middle sheet (definition): disfigurement, spoiling the shape

Bottom sheet (word): deform

When the words, definitions, and point values are written, attach them to the board with double-sided tape in ascending order. This is your prototype board to model and explain to your students, the double-sided tape enables the students to create their own boards. Students may work in teams to create and play with these boards in centers. Helpful hint: You may wish to precut the paper in quantity to save time.

**To Play Jeopardy**

One student acts as host; at least two contestants are needed. The host asks, "What category and point value would you like?" Another student (contestant) selects a point value, "Form, for 300." The host flips up the first paper and reads the definition "to change the form of." The contestant states the answer in the form of a question, such as, "What is *deform*?"

# Categorization

The following activities provide an avenue to link vocabulary instruction to what students already know. They also provide a way to expand conceptual understanding of a unit of study. In Project ALL, they were often used as a review of the concepts found in the texts. Students maintain a better command of vocabulary when the words are grouped into related categories (similar to concept sorts); this has proven extremely beneficial within the PRC2 content units. These activities also benefit comprehension within informational text.

## Picture Frame

In this category word sort activity, students actually manipulate words by cutting them out and placing them beneath the correct category (or they can determine the category among the pictures for an advanced activity). Students are given a duplicate sheet of paper or card stock that has the title, categories, and words arranged in a mixed order. The outside border acts as the frame that the students or teacher can decorate with related drawings and pictures. The students cut all the words and categories and arrange them in the proper places.

The purpose of this concept sort is for students to sort words within a specific subcategory of a concept. Sorting words by concepts provides students with a method linking vocabulary instruction to what they already know. It expands their conceptual understanding of essential topic vocabulary. In Project ALL, the picture-frame strategy was used as a review after the

240

Chapter
Twelve
Activities to
Reinforce
Vocabulary
Learning

students completed the practice. Concept sorts may, however, be used to assess and provide background knowledge prior to beginning a new unit of study. The picture-frame activity is quick and inexpensive, and it enables the teacher to obtain a pulse on the classroom.

## Materials for Picture Frame

- templates
- paper or card stock and markers or pens
- scissors

## Preparation

Select three or four major subject categories and seven or eight related words for each category (the unit used here was from Ancient Egypt, sixth grade, Project ALL).

> **Example:** Ancient Egypt Main Concepts
>
> Mummification
>
> Places
>
> People

Fill in a blank template with the title across the top in the largest font, followed by the main concepts in a slightly smaller font and then the related words in a smaller font, mixed and not in order under the correct main concepts (Figure 12.1a).

These completed mixed-word picture frames are duplicated (card stock works best) and distributed to the students. The students cut out the mixed related words, being careful not to cut into the unit title or main category

Figure **12.1a** Words in Mixed Order

| Ancient Egypt | | |
|---|---|---|
| Mummification | Places | People |
| Hieroglyphics | Hatshepsut | Silt |
| Quarries | Archaeologist | Egypt |
| Valley of the Kings | Soft tissue | Desert |
| Embalmer | Architect | Tomb |
| Preserving | Astronomer | Scribe |
| Nile River | Decomposing | Pharaoh |
| Sarcophagus | Pyramid | Africa |

Figure **12.1b** Completed Template for Picture Frame

|  | Mummification | Places | People |
|---|---|---|---|
| **Related Words** | Hieroglyphics | Africa | Embalmer |
|  | Sarcophagus | Quarries | Archaeologist |
|  | Silt | Desert | Scribe |
|  | Soft tissue | Nile River | Architect |
|  | Decomposing | Egypt | Astronomer |
|  | Preserving | Pyramid | Pharaoh |
|  | Tomb | Valley of the Kings | Hatshepsut |

component. They then manipulate the words so that they are placed within the correct category. This activity allows for discussion if the students work in pairs or small groups. When the words are in the order the students think is correct, they glue the words in place or write them on a blank template. See Figure 12.1b.

## Pyramid Game

The purposes of the pyramid game are to encourage the students to recall what they know about a specific concept or category and to organize their thinking systematically. Students focus on the attributes of concepts represented by or associated with words as they try to determine what these words have in common. This activity is based on the popular TV quiz show *$100,000 Pyramid* and has many variations. It provides a good review for what students have learned in a unit of study and also what they have in their knowledge banks. Robert Marzano (2004) has renamed this game "Name This Category." There is also a copyrighted version available online. It is more beneficial for the students to actually construct the game categories because it gives them multiple exposures as well as tactile experiences that aid greatly in the acquisition of vocabulary.

### Materials for the Pyramid Game

- trifold presentation board
- colored paper
- template (or you may wish just to affix the shaped paper permanently on your board and use large index cards for the categories and words)
- markers
- double-sided tape

242

Chapter
Twelve
Activities to
Reinforce
Vocabulary
Learning

Pyramid game.

## Preparation

Select categories of words that are relevant to a unit of study (these are from units on the solar system and ancient Rome) and seven words related to each category.

**Example 1:** Main category: Things in Outer Space

Catchy title: "Fly Me Past the Moon"

Related words:

Sun

Mars

Venus

Saturn

Galaxy

Meteors

Orbits

**Example 2:** Main category: Things Found in Roman Baths

Catchy title: "Rub a Dub Dub"

Related words:

Thermae

Atrium

Unctorium

Gymnasium

Tepidarium

Caldarium

Frigidarium

## To Play the Pyramid Game

Write each word on the appropriately shaped paper (or on large index cards) in descending order of difficulty, with the most difficult at the top. Place the words on top of one another with double-sided tape, with the easiest on the bottom, affixed to the board. This game can be student created after specific modeling by the teacher.

One student selects a topic, the other student (the host) flips up the pages one by one and reads the words aloud, giving time for the first student to propose possible responses.

**Example:** *Student 1:* I'll take "Everyone in the Pool."

*Student 2:* "Frigidarium" [as the first card is flipped up]

*Student 1:* Other names for refrigerator?

*Student 2:* No, sorry.

"Caldarium."

*Student 1:* I have no idea.

*Student 2:* "Atrium."

*Student 1:* Things found in Roman Baths.

*Student 2:* Correct!

This example illustrates how vocabulary specific to a component within a unit of study can help students with meaning. The words were content specific, level-three words (Marzano, 2004). These students had finished a Cricket book titled *If I Were a Kid in Ancient Rome* and these words were presented and explained in the text. This activity enabled the students to connect the concepts that were just presented in a meaningful way. Another reason for the words chosen in this example is that many of them are cognates (words that are similar to words in other languages); they can be easily translated and connections can be made.

244

Chapter
Twelve
Activities to
Reinforce
Vocabulary
Learning

## What the Words Mean

In this activity, the children break the words into morphological units to help them determine the meaning of a word that may puzzle them. They select the meaning of each part and then try to put the morphological parts together to determine meaning. Figure 12.2 shows the form we use for this activity.

Here is an example using the word *claustrophobia*.

| Word in Parts | Meaning of Each Part |
| --- | --- |
| claus | shut |
| phobia | fear |

I think the word *claustrophobia* means *fear of being shut in*.

We have used all these activities, and our students showed great growth on the pre- and post-tests on the units.

## Additional Activities

I would also like to share some of the ideas and websites that Rasinski included in his book, *Greek and Latin Roots: Keys to Building Vocabulary* (2008), as well as others that my students have enjoyed. These activities have been used by many teachers and students throughout the history of education, but it is helpful to see them together and to have them organized in a user-friendly fashion. The majority would work well in centers, and many provide whole-class opportunities; some are based on TV quiz shows.

**Word Webs.** This activity has had numerous titles, but the main idea is that students work with the words and recognize their significance as they become familiar with the roots and affixes. It is useful for whole-group, small-group, and individual work.

### Preparation

Prepare blank templates, select words, and explain the activity to students. You will need to model this activity for the first time with the students. Write the root word in the middle of the web and leave spaces in the second (and third, if applicable to the word) columns as students may wish to add an additional column.

Figure **12.2** **What the Words Mean**

245

Categorization

**What the Words Mean**

1. _____

   Word in parts _____    Meaning of each part _____
   _____    _____
   _____    _____
   _____    _____

   I think the word means _____
   _____

2. _____

   Word in parts _____    Meaning of each part _____
   _____    _____
   _____    _____
   _____    _____

   I think the word means _____
   _____

3. _____

   Word in parts _____    Meaning of each part _____
   _____    _____
   _____    _____
   _____    _____

   I think the word means _____
   _____

4. _____

   Word in parts _____    Meaning of each part _____
   _____    _____
   _____    _____
   _____    _____

   I think the word means _____
   _____

5. _____

   Word in parts _____    Meaning of each part _____
   _____    _____
   _____    _____
   _____    _____

   I think the word means _____
   _____

246

Chapter
Twelve
Activities to
Reinforce
Vocabulary
Learning

Here is an example using the root word *port* (to carry).

| Prefixes | Root | Suffixes |
|----------|------|----------|
| re | port | ing |
| trans | | tion |
| im | | ed |
| pur | | ance |
| ex | | folio |
| | | ant |

This activity contains numerous applications. One would be students putting the morphological units together to make words and then looking them up in the dictionary to see if they are correct. Another would be students seeing how many words can they make.

**Word Theater.** This activity has the students thinking about the words and connecting to the words visually and physically. Word Theater is based on the game Charades (Hoyt, 1999). Its use of pantomime and oral language is particularly useful to ELs and is also included with the SIOP strategies. You will need a list of at least ten words that contain the root you wish the students to be exposed to and that can be dramatized easily. The children should conduct this activity after the words, roots, and affixes have been introduced.

**Vocabulary Cube.** In this activity, the students toss a cube to another student across the room or in a small group. The "catcher" must answer the prompt where his or her right thumb caught the cube.

**Preparation**

Cover the six sides of an empty tissue box with construction paper. On the sides write the following:

Side 1: Root word

Side 2: Affix

Side 3: Definition

Side 4: Use in a sentence

Side 5: Spelling

Side 6: Synonym/Antonym

**Example:** Word: BIOLOGY

Root word: bio (life)

Affix: ology (study of )

Definition: study of life

Use in a sentence: In biology, we did a simulated dissection of a frog.

Spelling: biology

Synonym/Antonym: study of death

This activity is suitable for whole-group, small-group, or partnering work. One student (or teacher) tosses the cube.

---

**Some useful websites**

*With resources for students (Rasinski, 2008)*

http://edhelper.com

www.vocabulary.co.il

www.lexfiles.info

www.surfnetkids.com/games

www.vocabulary.com

www.wordcentral.com

---

# Instructional Examples

## Vocabulary Activities with Cognates

Students developed an understanding and appreciation of English–Spanish cognates through collecting and sharing examples of environmental print (graphic symbols and print that are found in the physical environment such as street signs, billboards, and directions) illustrating cognates. Many examples were sketches of bilingual signs throughout the city. For example, on the Chicago Transit Authority trains various safety notices contained English–Spanish cognates, such as *operator* and *operador*, *permitted* and *permite*, *vehicle* and *vehiculo*, *cooperate* and *coopere*, *protection* and *proteccion*, and *person* and *persona*.

248

Chapter
Twelve
Activities to
Reinforce
Vocabulary
Learning

There are more than 20,000 English–Spanish cognates. The greater the number of syllables in the English word, the greater the chances of its being a cognate (Montelongo, 2004), which raises the probability of multisyllabic science and social studies words being cognates. Spanish words are often more sophisticated than the corresponding English word. Hiebert (2008) asserts that academic words are usual and customary for Spanish, as oftentimes the Spanish cognates for low-level English content words are commonly used words. Spanish speakers can use their knowledge of linguistically rich words to access content area words. An example of a high-level word being usual and customary for Spanish is the word *extraterrestrial*, which rivals the lower-level English word *alien*.

**Three Examples of Cognate Sorts and Rule Finding.** Students sorted the following cognate pairs: *abdicación/abdication, clasificación/classification, confederación/confederation, constelación/constellation, constitución/constitution, construcción/construction, desagregación/desegregation, discriminación/discrimination, excavación/excavation, inauguración/inauguration,* and *inscripción/inscription.* A possible rule students generated was that in pairs of cognates the English suffix *tion* corresponds to the Spanish suffix *ción.*

Students sorted the following cognate pairs: *anual/annual, canibal/cannibal, colateral/collateral, comercial/commercial, diferential/differential, intelectual/intellectual, ocasional/occasional, oficial/official,* and *profesional/professional.* One rule students generated was that in pairs of cognates in which the double consonants in English correspond to a single consonant in Spanish, double the second letter of the Spanish word to create the English cognate.

Students sorted the following cognate pairs: *independencia/independence, democracia/democracy, distancia/distance, experiencia/experience, importancia/importance, insistencia/insistence, inteligencia/intelligence, importancia/importance, noticia/notice, obediencia/obedience, paciencia/patience, permanencia/permanence,* and *tolerancia/tolerance.* A possible rule students generated was that in pairs of cognates the English suffix *ence* or *ance* corresponds to the Spanish suffix *encia* or *ancia.*

## Building and Studying Word Families

Traditional vocabulary instruction for many teachers is having students write or copy dictionary definitions and then use the words in an original sentence (Basurto, 2004). Using dictionary definitions to define words and writing a sentence to show understanding can result in student sentences that are "odd," a situation Miller and Gildea (1985) found in 63 percent of the students' sentences. The following example contains the definition for the word *midst* extracted from a selection about a Civil War battle. *Midst* is "the condition of being surrounded or beset by something." The obligatory sentence is, "My brother is in the midst of our family," which means the brother has an older sibling and a younger sibling. In addition, McKeown (1991, 1993) found 60 percent of students' responses unacceptable when students used dictionary definitions as a source, and Scott and Nagy (1989) found students frequently interpreted one or two words of the dictionary definition as the entire meaning.

Even though the English language is heavily influenced by Greek and Latin and the meanings of 60 percent of multisyllabic words can be inferred by analyzing word parts (Nagy & Scott, 2000), students need to be metacognitive in their awareness of this strategy in order to use it. For example, students' knowledge that *aud* means *to hear* can help them unlock and understand the meaning of *audience, auditorium, audition,* and *audible.* Studying word families helped unlock the meanings of related words as students connected meaning when they studied, compared, and contrasted similar words. Students learned through analysis that word sets like *revolt, revolution,* and *revolutionary* are related as are *patriot, patriotic,* and *patriotism.*

One strategy we used to build word families was at the website www.onelook.com, where we collected related words. A search of *legis* generated twenty-two connected words and phrases, eleven words that had direct and relevant potential for study; for example, *legislation, legislate, legislated, legislates, legislative, legislating, legislatively, legislator, legislatorial, legislators, legislature, legislatures,* and the related terms of *legislative act, legislative assembly, legislative branch,* and *legislative council.* We also used online resources, such as Online Etymology Dictionary at www.etymonline.com/index.php?l=e&p=12, to extract a simple definition. The definition of *legislator* is from the Latin and means "proposer of a law" and is from *legis,* "law" + *lator,* "proposer."

## Closing Gaps in Word Choice and Teaching

The vocabulary words presented different challenges in each unit. There were several interesting points about the words in the units. The more concrete terms, such as *cerebellum, hypothalamus, hippocampus, capillaries, chemotherapy, antibodies, cardiology, circulatory, epidemic, hemoglobin, meteoroid, weightlessness, atmosphere, constellation, microscopic,* and *transplant,* were taught using the support of illustrations and photographs.

250

Chapter
Twelve
Activities to
Reinforce
Vocabulary
Learning

The more abstract terms, such as *democracy*; *executive branch*; *judicial*; *legislative*; *life, liberty, and the pursuit of happiness*; *prejudice*; *liberalism*; *conservatism*; *populism*; *libertarianism*; *bicameral*; and *decentralization*, required more conversation, analysis of use of context, and wide connection.

Although there were morphologically rich words, with roots and affixes that could be used to unlock the meaning of many other words, not all of the most common prefixes, suffixes, and roots were contained in the unit vocabulary, and not many Marzano words were listed. While there were important far-reaching concepts such as *unconstitutional, unjust, injustice, prejudice, democracy*, and *revolutionary*, eight of the most common prefixes were not included within the unit vocabulary. There were many words with common prefixes, such as *immoral, unstable, involuntary, incline, indictment, inherit, interplanetary, interpreter, immigrant, reconciliation, discontented*, and *discharge*, but there were missing elements. We decided that it was imperative that the twenty specific prefixes that occur in 97 percent of all words that contain prefixes (White, Sowell, & Yanagihara, 1999) be studied in a connected way. Words were taught to students by linking the direct teaching of prefixes, suffixes, and roots of the unit words and then extending word study with structurally related words. We used *Word Web Vocabulary* (Miller, 1997) for teacher mini-lessons, and it provided opportunities to encourage, develop, and foster an interest in words, their meaning, and their structure. The sequence of presenting prefix, root, and suffix and then generating and discussing related words was used as an activity that, as the year progressed, showcased the investment in the initial word-conscious building activities.

## Extending Word Study

Often word-sorting activities were used to study the structural composition of words. An example was the study of the effect of a suffix on word meaning. Teachers modeled word sorts on overheads and assisted students in sorting words according to patterns. For example, students drew connections with *archaeologist, biologist*, and *cardiologist. Biology, biography*, and *biograph* were studied as a meaningful group of words. Students figured out that words with the *ist* suffix is a noun, as in *suffragist, loyalist*, and *audiologist*, and a suffix of *less* indicates an adjective, such as *powerless, hopeless, lifeless*, and *weightless*. After the teacher modeled these sorts, other related sorts were placed in the word study center.

Students also constructed words by combining paper tiles containing various prefixes, affixes, roots, and base words. This activity provided students an opportunity to extend their word knowledge while studying the internal structure of words, in particular the smallest units of meaning in words—morphemes—while creating meaning. When students gave attention to word parts, they often discovered patterns and connections, such as that the endings *ity* and *tion* can be used to change the part of speech. In addition, working with and paying attention to derivations and origins of words solidified the connection of the relationship of roots in word families.

## Electronic Vocabulary Games

Research suggests that one of the important differences between achieving and nonachieving students is their level of vocabulary development (Beck, McKeown, & Omanson, 1987; Hart & Risley, 1995). Although it is generally accepted that the number of exposures students need to internalize words is in the double digits (Blachowicz & Ogle, 2008; McKeown, Beck, Omanson, & Pople, 1985), the concept of playing with and manipulating vocabulary is often an undervalued and overlooked classroom activity (Graves & Watts-Taffe, 2002). The creation of electronic vocabulary games was influenced by research suggesting that playing with words will help foster awareness of and deep and lasting interest in words and their meanings (Blachowicz & Fisher, 2004; Graves & Watts-Taffe, 2002; Marzano, 2004).

This section illustrates how the Microsoft program Excel® (2003) was used to construct electronic vocabulary games connected to both the multi-level nonfiction book sets and general content. In addition, more information and visual support are available on the enclosed DVD. These games illustrate some of the game-making possibilities of Excel®, and I hope the results will encourage teachers to construct games that not only connect technology, students, and content but that also engage a sense of exploration and creativeness in capturing the flexibility and fluidity of Excel® technology.

The games will be presented in the following format. An outline of the game will be followed by a screenshot of the game, including an explanation of the process of how to play each of the four games. The enclosed DVD has a file called Making_Games, which shows the technology of making the games and provides guidance for creating new games. After reading a short explanation of each game, open the enclosed DVD to view and play a sample of each game. The technical foundation of each game is the conditional formatting function in the Excel® program, which is explained in detail on the enclosed DVD.

252

Chapter
Twelve
Activities to
Reinforce
Vocabulary
Learning

# Four Games

The following is a list of the four games presented in this section, their primary source and function, and their file name:

### Cognados-Cognates Connect

- A game built around English–Spanish cognates. The object of the game is to type in the English cognate that matches the Spanish cognate.
- File name: Cognados_Cognates_Connect

### Borrowed, Before, Base and Beyond

- A game in which students work with the meaning of roots, prefixes, base words, and suffixes.
- File name: Borrowed_Before_Base_Beyond

### Ology of Morph

- Students analyze the meaning of the morphological parts of words in order to make meaning.
- File name: Ology_of_Morph

### Six Degrees of Connection

- The players sort a related set of six words or concepts into a prescribed order.
- File name: Six_Degrees_of_Connection

## Cognados-Cognates Connect

The importance of multiple exposures to content vocabulary has been well documented, and Kamil (2004) suggests that collaborative, active tasks can be supported by the use of technology. Thoughtful, high-quality, collaborative vocabulary encounters will contribute to the development of the writing, speaking, listening, and reading domains (Pearson, Hiebert, & Kamil, 2007). Lubliner and Grisham (2008) found that cognate strategy instruction had a positive effect on Spanish-speaking students' motivation, and anecdotal evidence was found in classrooms where cognate games were used as an integral part of vocabulary instruction.

> *Two boys were making connections to math words and were confused about the cognate for* fraction, *as one student said it should be* fracción *and another was arguing that the Spanish cognate for* fraction *should be* fricción. *Well, they*

*eventually, thanks to an interloper from another group, figured out there were two similar words and they could actually generate two sets of English–Spanish cognates—fraction and fracción for math and friction and fricción for science.*

The interloper, obviously proud of his accomplishment stated, *"Me, I know both languages. I can speak both."*

Steps to play the game:

1. Put the DVD into your disc drive.
2. Open the file called Cognados_Cognates_Connect.
3. Click on the maximize icon to get the full screen.

You will see the following directions: "Welcome to *Cognados-Cognates Connect.*" We will work with the screen shot shown in Figure 12.3 as the process is explained.

The words in this sample game are associated with the Human Body unit. The objective of the Cognados-Cognates Connect game is to connect the English–Spanish cognate. The column on the left contains the Spanish cognates; on the right, the student types the corresponding English cognate.

In general, students will type their response into the corresponding cell and press "enter." A correct answer will turn the cell green, and an incorrect answer will turn the cell red. Participants must be precise, as extra spaces before or after the response will cause the response to be interpreted as being incorrect.

If you would like to practice, or práctica (hint), place your cursor in the cell opposite *práctica*, type in the English word, and press "enter."

If you typed *practice*, the cell should have turned green as *practice* is the correct English cognate for *práctica*.

## Figure 12.3  Cognados-Cognates Connect

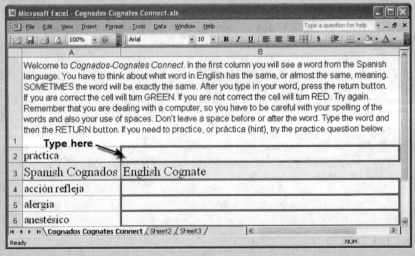

(Margaret McGregor)

Continued

254

Chapter
Twelve
Activities to
Reinforce
Vocabulary
Learning

Now try some of the other English–Spanish cognates. Try the next three: *acción refleja*, *alergia*, and *anestésico*.

Keep in mind that this game is an extension of students' learning. Students have been introduced to the words, talked about them, perhaps entered them into their vocabulary notebook, and possibly played games with them already. In addition, this form of the game is quite sophisticated, as students must generate the corresponding cognates with little support. However, differentiation possibilities are wide and varied with this game structure, as the number of words and level can be adjusted for students. See the enclosed DVD for more information.

## Borrowed, Before, Base and Beyond

Borrowed, Before, Base and Beyond concentrates on the meanings of prefixes, suffixes, base words, and root words. Students need to know how to access word meaning through knowledge of morphology, as Anderson and Nagy (1991) found that vocabulary growth in the elementary and middle grades was attributable to students' application of word-part knowledge. Developing independent word-learning strategies is important, as this metalinguistic knowledge develops during the upper elementary grades (Nagy & Scott, 2000), and students can use this morphemic analysis and study of derivations and origins to expand and deepen their knowledge of content vocabulary (Bear, Invernizzi, Templeton, & Johnston, 2004; Marzano, 2004).

Steps to play the game:
1. Put the DVD into your disc drive.
2. Open the file called Borrowed_Before_Base_Beyond.
3. Click on the maximize icon to get the full screen.

You will see the following directions: "Welcome to *Borrowed, Before, Base and Beyond.*" We will work with the screen shot shown in Figure 12.4 as the process is explained.

This example is not associated with any one particular unit, as the primary purpose is on the reinforcement of learning word parts with the expectation that knowledge will transfer to other words. This will assist students in making connections with other words that share common word parts.

In general, students will type their response into the corresponding cell and press "enter." A correct answer will turn the cell green, and an incorrect answer will turn the cell red. Participants must be precise, as extra spaces before or after the response will cause the response to be interpreted as being incorrect. See arrow A for samples of the answers *acid* and *omni*.

The third column provides the student with hints about the answer, and the fourth column provides additional words that use the same affix—prefix, suffix, base word, or root word. See arrow B in the screen shot. If students move their cursor over the small red triangle in the upper right corner of the cell (see arrow C), they can access these hints and words for the corresponding question. Three words— *audible, auditory, audition*—appear on the screen shot; they are samples of words that have a Latin-derived affix, base, or root that means *to hear*.

## Figure 12.4  Borrowed, Before, Base and Beyond

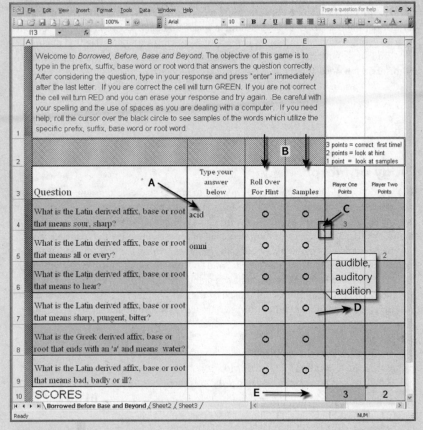

(Margaret McGregor)

> *This isn't a game. There are no points, no teams, and no winner. How can you call it a game without points, teams, and a winner?*

This comment, with which most of the students agreed, necessitated points and a team structure being added to the game (see arrow D). The game was made with a two-colored alternating sequence so that the question corresponds with the color. In addition, rules were constructed. Players get three points if they get the answer correct without having to look at the hint or sample column. Players get two points if they have to look at the hint column before getting the answer correct, and they get one point if they get the correct answer after looking at the hint and sample columns. Students then have to manually enter the points. Arrow E shows that Player One received three points for getting the correct answer, *acid*, and Player Two received two points for the word *omni*, after looking at the hint in order to get the answer.

Continued

256

Chapter
Twelve
Activities to
Reinforce
Vocabulary
Learning

**Ways to Differentiate.** Teachers can differentiate this game by presenting the questions in different formats. For example, asking a question using the term *affix* does not give the student a clue about the placement of the affix. However, using the terms *prefix* and *suffix* does let the student know the location of the affix. Also, hints may be given within the question. For example, asking about an affix that means ____ and starts with the letter *c* does not give the student a clue about the placement of the affix but does supply the starting letter of the affix.

## Ology of Morph

The word *morphology* is made up of *morph*, meaning shape, and *ology*, meaning the study of. So *morphology* refers to the study of the internal structure of words, in particular the smallest units of meaning in words: morphemes. Ology of Morph has students analyze words as sequences of morphemes in order to come up with the meaning of the entire word. This game uses bound morphemes, which are prefixes and suffixes that cannot stand alone, such as *geo*, *re*, and *ity*, and unbound morphemes, which are roots within more complex words that can stand alone, such as *popular*. For example, the word *independently* is composed of the morphemes *in*, *depend*, *ent*, and *ly*; *depend* is the root, and the other morphemes are derivational affixes.

Steps to play the game:
1. Put the DVD into your disc drive.
2. Open the file called Ology_of_Morph.
3. Click on the maximize icon to get the full screen.

You will see the following directions: "Welcome to *Ology of Morph*." We will work with the screen shot shown in Figure 12.5 as the process is explained.

This example is associated with the Ancient Egypt unit. The words to be analyzed are in the left-most column, with four columns extending to the right. The object of this game is to type in each of the morphological units. Although there are four columns in which to type, not all words have four morphological units within them. For words with fewer than four morphological units, the last cell is a different color to indicate that it should not be used. In the example, *dehydrate* and *embalmer* are made up of three morphological parts, so the fourth cell, which is needed for *decomposing*, is yellow for those two words.

In general, students will type their response into the corresponding cell and press "enter." A correct answer will turn the cell green, and an incorrect answer will turn the cell red. Participants must be precise, as extra spaces before or after the response will cause the response to be interpreted as being incorrect.

In the example *dehydrate*, the word is broken into three parts, *de*, *hydr*, and *ate*. This game does provide a column that gives the analysis of the word. When the mouse is rolled over the red triangle in the upper right-hand corner of the right-most box, the analysis of the word will show. See *dehydrate*: The removal of water from an object. *Hydra* (Gr) = water and *de* is Latin for "off, down from." *Hydr* is the form before a vowel; *ate* = function.

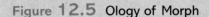

Figure **12.5** Ology of Morph

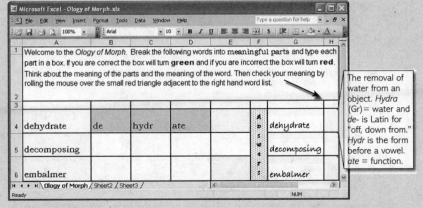

(Margaret McGregor)

This is a presentation of the basic game format and does not include any levels of differentiation that students might need. The possibilities for differentiation are wide and varied and include selection of words, grouping related words, and supporting the student with examples and clues.

## Six Degrees of Connection

In a synthesis of twenty years of vocabulary instruction, Blachowicz and Fisher (2000) make the point of the importance of categorization of vocabulary, which includes semantic gradients. In Six Degrees of Connection, students consider words, their relationship, and their value, before placing them on a prescribed continuum. Words must be what Powell (1986) calls *scalar terms* as there must be gradations between terms to be able to arrange the words in an order. Concepts that work well with scalar terms are degrees of loudness, historical events, mass, volume, processes, sequence of steps, and so on. For example, the words *warm*, *tepid*, *cool*, *hot*, *searing*, and *frigid* if placed in ascending order would be listed in the following order: *frigid*, *cool*, *tepid*, *warm*, *hot*, and *searing*.

Steps to play the game:
1. Put the DVD into your disc drive.
2. Open the file called Six_Degrees_of_Connection.
3. Click on the maximize icon to get the full screen.

You will see the following directions: "Welcome to *Six Degrees of Connection*." We will work with the screen shot shown in Figure 12.6 as the process is explained.

In general, students will type their response into the corresponding cell and press "enter." A correct answer will turn the cell green, and an incorrect answer will

Continued

258

Chapter
Twelve
Activities to
Reinforce
Vocabulary
Learning

**Figure 12.6   Six Degrees of Connection**

Microsoft Excel - Six Degrees of Connection.xls

Welcome to Six Degrees of Connection. You will see a series of words and rules for sorting the words. For example, you might have to put the words in order of size, weight, location, or temperature. Individually type in each word where you think it should go, pressing the return key after each entry. If you are correct the cell will turn **GREEN**. If you are not correct the cell will turn **RED**. Try again!
Be careful with your spelling and your use of spaces. Don't leave a space before or after the word as the computer will recognize this as an incorrect response.

**Put in historical order**

| War of 1812 | Revolutionary War | Spanish American War | World War One | Civil War | Mexican American War |

| Revolutionary War | | | | | |

**Put in ascending order**

| warm | tepid | cool | hot | searing | frigid |

**Put in order from West to East**

| Toronto | Edmonton | Vancouver | Saskatoon | Kelowna | St. John's |

(Margaret McGregor)

turn the cell red. Participants must be precise, as extra spaces before or after the response will cause the response to be interpreted as being incorrect.

In the example, students are asked to place in order the following battles: War of 1812, Revolutionary War, Spanish-American War, World War I, Civil War, and Mexican-American War. Think about the order and then type each battle into the cell. In the example, the first cell is completed: Revolutionary War. Remember, if the answer you type is correct, the cell you type into will turn green; if the answer is incorrect, the cell will turn red. You can always go back and try again.

If you would like to create some original games, go to the file Making_Games on the enclosed DVD. You can then make your own unique games that are aligned and related to your own units of study.

# References

Anderson, R. C., & Nagy, W. E. (1991). Word meanings. In R. Barr, M. L. Kamil, P. B. Mosenthal, & P. D. Pearson (Eds.), *Handbook of reading research* (Vol. 2, pp. 690–724). New York: Longman.

Basurto, I. (2004). Teaching vocabulary creatively. In G. E. Tompkins & C. L. Blanchfield (Eds.), *Teaching vocabulary: 50 creative strategies, grades K–12* (pp. 1–4). Upper Saddle River, NJ: Pearson Education.

Bear, D., Invernizzi, M., Templeton, S., & Johnston, F. (2004). Words their way: Word study for phonics, vocabulary, and spelling instruction. Upper Saddle River, NJ: Prentice Hall.

Beck, I. L., McKeown, M. G., & Omanson, R. C. (1987). The effects and uses of diverse vocabulary instruction techniques. In M. G. McKeown & M. E. Curtis (Eds.), *The nature of vocabulary acquisition* (pp. 147–163). Hillsdale, NJ: Erlbaum.

Blachowicz, C., & Fisher, P. (2000). Vocabulary instruction. In R. L. Kamil, P. B. Mosenthal, P. D. Pearson, & R. Barr (Eds.), *Handbook of reading research* (Vol. 3, pp. 503–523). Mahwah, NJ: Erlbaum.

Blachowicz, C., & Ogle, D. (2008). *Reading comprehension* (2nd ed.). New York: Guilford.

Blachowicz, C. L. Z., & Fisher, P. (2004, March). Vocabulary lessons. *Educational Leadership, 61*(6), 66–69.

Echevarria, J., Vogt, M. E., & Short, D. (2007). *Making content comprehensible for English learners: The SIOP model* (3rd ed.). Boston: Pearson Allyn & Bacon.

Graves, M. F., & Watts-Taffe, S. M. (2002). The place of word consciousness in a research-based vocabulary program. In S. J. Samuels & A. E. Farstrup (Eds.), *What research has to say about reading instruction* (3rd ed., pp. 140–165). Newark, DE: International Reading Association.

Hart, B., & Risley, T. R. (1995). *Meaningful differences in the everyday experience of young American children*. Baltimore: Brookes.

Hiebert, F. (2008, May 4). *Promoting vocabulary development in grades 4 through 12: A comprehensive approach, panel discussion*. International Reading Association 53rd Annual Conference, Atlanta, GA.

Hoyt, L. (1999). *Revisit, reflect, retell: Strategies for improving reading comprehension*. Portsmouth, NH: Heinemann.

Kamil, M. L. (2004). Vocabulary and comprehension instruction: Summary and implications of the National Reading Panel findings. In P. McCardle & V. Chhabra (Eds.), *The voice of evidence in reading research* (pp. 213–234). Baltimore: Brookes.

Lubliner, S., & Grisham, D. L. (2008, May 4). Cognate strategy instruction: Providing powerful literacy tools to Spanish-speaking students. Paper presented at the International Reading Association 53rd annual conference, Atlanta, GA.

260

Chapter
Twelve
Activities to
Reinforce
Vocabulary
Learning

Marzano, R. J. (2004). *Building background knowledge for academic achievement: Research on what works in schools* (pp. 104–114). Alexandria, VA: Association for Supervision and Curriculum Development.

McKeown, M. G. (1991). Learning word meanings from dictionaries. In P. Schwanenflugel (Ed.), *The psychology of word meanings*. Hillsdale, NY: Erlbaum.

McKeown, M. G. (1993). Creating effective definitions for young word learners. *Reading Research Quarterly*, *28*, 16–31.

McKeown, M. G., Beck, I. L., Omanson, R. C., & Pople, M. T. (1985). Some effects of the nature and frequency of vocabulary instruction on the knowledge of use of words. *Reading Research Quarterly*, *20*, 522–535.

Miller, E. (1997). Word web vocabulary. Cummaquid, MA: Sage Education Enterprises.

Miller, G., & Gildea, P. (1985). How to misread a dictionary. AILA Bulletin. Pisa, Italy: International Association for Applied Linguistics.

Montelongo, J. (2004). Concept learning and memory for Spanish–English cognates. Unpublished doctoral dissertation, New Mexico State University, Las Cruces.

Nagy, W., & Scott, J. (2000). Vocabulary processes. In M. L. Kamil, P. B. Mosenthal, P. D. Pearson, & R. Barr (Eds.), *Handbook of reading research* (Vol. 3, pp. 269–284). Mahwah, NJ: Erlbaum.

Pearson, P. D., Hiebert, E. H., & Kamil, M. L. (2007). Vocabulary assessment: What we know and what we need to learn. *Reading Research Quarterly*, *42*, 282–296.

Powell, W. R. (1986). Teaching vocabulary through opposition. *Journal of Reading*, *29*, 617–621.

Rasinski, T. (2008). *Greek and Latin roots: Keys to building vocabulary*. Huntington Beach, CA: Shell Education.

Richek, M. (2005). Words are wonderful: Interactive, time-efficient strategies to teach meaning vocabulary. *The Reading Teacher*, *58*(5), 414–423.

Scott, J., & Nagy, W. (1989, December). *Fourth graders' knowledge of definitions and how they work*. Paper presented at the annual meeting of the National Reading Conference, Austin, TX.

White, T. G., Sowell, V., & Yanagihara, A. (1999). Teaching elementary students to use word-part clues. *The Reading Teacher*, *42*, 302–308.

# Academic Talk: Supporting English Learners

**?** What strategies can I use to provide the most effective scaffolding for ELs?

In this chapter, **Jeannette E. Hamman**, a classroom teacher and a Literacy Coach, addresses the challenge of scaffolding instruction for diverse learners.

Jeannette has worked as a sixth-grade teacher and as a reading specialist and Literacy Coach. In her role as reading specialist and Literacy Coach, Jeannette had the opportunity to help other teachers implement PRC2 in their classrooms.

262

Chapter
Thirteen
Academic Talk:
Supporting
English Learners

"What is the use of a book," thought Alice, "without pictures or conversation?"

—Lewis Carroll (1865)

Although this question may seem simple, it is in fact quite profound, the implication being that the full measure of a book lies in the pleasure gained by sharing it with others.

In recent years, the number of strategies designed to help students share good fiction with one another has increased. Examples of these strategies include Harvey Daniels's Literature Circles (Daniels, 1994) and the Book Club model developed by Susan McMahon and Taffy Rafael. Wider acceptance of these methods has encouraged teachers to expect and to teach students to take a more active role and greater responsibility for their interactions with text. The PRC2 program attempts to promote these same expectations in our students when reading and sharing nonfiction, social studies, and science texts.

Throughout the PRC2 process, there is a scaffolding of cognition and skill development because the strategies used by so-called good readers are embedded within each unit of study. For example, we know that good readers use a multitude of different methods before, during, and after reading in order to construct meaning. Examples include the following:

**Before reading:** Activate what is known, ask questions, preview text, make predictions, and decide the purpose for reading specific text selections.

**During reading:** Check predictions; connect ideas presented in the text; visualize events and characters; ask more questions; and make connections between the text you are reading and other texts, oneself, and the world.

**After reading:** Consolidate text meaning; reflect on themes and ideas that were presented; critically evaluate; and summarize ideas.

Every PRC2 unit has suggestions for these phases of reading as students progress through the designated subject of study.

Until recently, the idea of "what good readers do" has been limited to how students read fiction, with far less effort given to support students' abilities in reading nonfiction. Yet we know that students are required to be able to read nonfiction in order to perform well on high-stakes, standardized state tests.

Ability to read and comprehend nonfiction is one way U.S. students are compared with other young people from around the world.

According to researchers, such as Ralph Fletcher, whom I heard speak at the 2008 Illinois Reading Conference, in Springfield, Illinois, boys much prefer to read (and write) nonfiction (2006). Because there is a dramatic achievement gap in reading between girls and boys in many city schools, it would seem that we need to consider ways to get boys reading. This fact was echoed by Patricia Cunningham at a 2008 seminar in Chicago, who said that one of the reasons girls are outperforming boys in reading is partly because there are so many women teachers. Women teachers tend to read aloud what they personally enjoy and are more likely to recommend fiction for independent reading. Cunningham recounted a visit to a bookstore with her husband. It occurred to her that while they both enjoyed going to the bookstore, they each headed to different areas of the store to browse and shop. Her husband is a nonfiction lover, while she prefers fiction. Perhaps this is a universal truth. I found that the boys in my classroom were as excited about reading as the girls, when they saw the rich array of leveled, nonfiction texts I had available for implementation of PRC2.

The inner-city school at which I work has some good readers, to be sure. However, the school also has a large number of students for whom English is a second language, as well as a significant number of monolingual, struggling readers. For them, it is virtually impossible to read and comprehend our assigned textbooks. Even though it is thought that good textbooks can play a central role in improving content area education for all children, they are often written at a level far too difficult for students to read independently and understand. For many teachers, the textbook and the accompanying manual are the primary sources for curriculum implementation. Sadly, many textbooks used in classrooms are therefore not effective in helping students achieve important content area learning goals. Although teachers try, during grade-level meetings, to find ways to make the text more accessible to students, acquisition of content area knowledge is still a challenge for many children. So, what is different about PRC2, and how is it helping students build content area knowledge?

## Implementation from a Teacher's Perspective

The students that I worked with during my first year in this project were all sixth-grade, inner-city children, attending their local neighborhood public school. Our school population is at 97 percent free and reduced lunch.

264

Chapter
Thirteen
Academic Talk:
Supporting
English Learners

The ethnic mix is approximately 75 percent Latino, 24 percent African American, and 1 percent Other. Of our 810 students, 29 percent are ELs. Our third-grade ISAT scores show a large "opportunity gap" between where we are and where we would like to be with regard to student achievement. However, our scores have increased in both reading and math every year for the past six years.

When I joined Project ALL, I was one of the sixth-grade homeroom teachers and was responsible for teaching language arts to the students in my homeroom and social studies to all of the sixth-grade students. This situation was ideal, as it allowed me to integrate the two curricula for my own class and then share successful content area reading strategies with the children who came to my room for social studies. I found that teaching comprehension strategies within the context of social studies—for example, looking at text structure and features; explicitly learning about using the table of contents, index, and glossary; paying attention to text boxes; and picture captions—helped my students with their reading skills and content knowledge (see Chapter 10).

## Initiation of the Social Interactions

My first experience with the oral-language aspect of PRC2 was to administer Classroom Fluency Snapshots to all the sixth graders. After that, students within each sixth-grade classroom were placed into reading pairs based on oral-reading rate, interpersonal compatibility, and book preferences. Oral reading fluency (ORF) assessment is a powerful tool for teachers, particularly as a precursor to PRC2 and even more so if teachers also take the time to conduct a miscue analysis for each child tested. Although some people may feel that doing an ORF and a miscue analysis for each of their students can be very time consuming, the information it provides is well worth the effort. The same data that help create PRC2 partnerships can also be used to create guided reading groups (Fountas & Pinnell, 1996) and inform teachers as they recommend books for students to choose from for independent reading. The data also let a teacher know how close her or his students are to national reading norms or how far they are from those norms (Hasbrouck & Tindal, 2006). Keep in mind, however, that no single test is definitive. (See Chapters 6 and 7 on assessment.)

I frequently find that working with my students causes me to reflect on my own experiences as a reader, and I am reminded of times when I have been faced with the need to translate from another language into English. On one occasion, I was visiting a museum in Toronto and wanted to read an exhibit card. It had information telling about an exhibit of Native American artifacts that I was extremely interested in knowing more about. Unfortunately, the text was written in French. I was able to translate all but a few words; yet those few words confounded my ability to understand the whole text. It was interesting for me to realize how important a single word can be.

Teachers occasionally find themselves at a loss, confused about why a student may not be able to comprehend a passage of text the teachers unwittingly assume is within the student's capabilities, based on ISAT scores and Classroom Fluency Snapshots. However, it is important to consider that even when those hundred-word passages are administered, miscues checked for, and decoding assessed for fluency, teachers should not assume that a child necessarily understands everything that is written in any given text. It is often only through listening to students discuss what they have read that specific gaps become apparent. The process of PRC2 allows students to think aloud when they need to, in order to determine whether the words they are reading make sense.

As I began implementing the unit on ancient Egypt and introducing the students to the PRC2 process and procedures, I realized I was watching something remarkable unfold. The students began to lose some of their usual air of studied indifference toward schoolwork and began to come alive.

Things moved slowly at first, as some of the students were rather reluctant at times to work with partners whom they probably would not have chosen for themselves. However, over time I noticed that they got used to their reading partners, and in several instances friendships blossomed between pairs of students who did not know each other prior to engaging in this project. I was grateful that one of the pre-assessments in each unit is an interest inventory. I believe the information I gathered about my students with that tool helped me make better choices when creating the dyads. From my observations, it seemed to me that the students were intrigued by what the pre-assessments might lead to. This was rather like the TV commercial for Heinz ketchup, which has Carly Simon singing "Anticipation" in the background. The pre-assessments served to pique interest and create an aura of anticipation among and between the sixth graders as a group.

One tenet of teaching I try to live by is the importance of exploring the prior knowledge held by the students in a classroom. By sharing what they know about a subject and ruling out misconceptions that might be held by members of a group, the entire group benefits exponentially. But what happens when there is no prior knowledge to draw on? As a result of administering the unit pre-assessments and listening carefully during the early conversations around the topic of the ancient world, I realized that my students had virtually

266

Chapter
Thirteen
Academic Talk:
Supporting
English Learners

no background information to build on. I wasn't really sure what to do next, and research is a bit scarce on this point. So, I decided to look for help at our regional library, which has a rich collection of books and a fabulous video collection. I was in luck. The library had several videos depicting Egypt today, as well as showing how things might have been in ancient times. We watched computer-enhanced graphics of how and why the pyramids were built, what daily life might have been like for people, and what the land looks like, especially around the Nile River. Watching and listening to the videos provided the students with a common frame of reference on which to base the discussions that grew up around the sharing of books.

When I first introduced the leveled texts to the students, they were very excited. All the partners were delighted to be looking at books they were able to read and enjoy, while still learning new concepts. The enthusiasm began to build and spread. The pleasure of seeing my students become so engaged increased my own interest in learning more about ancient Egypt and placed me in an authentic role of co-learner in the class. When the students found out that I wanted them to talk to each other about what they were reading, they could hardly believe it.

Discourse in the classroom can mean different things to different people and can take different forms. For many teachers, it simply means the "talk that happens" in a classroom. Unfortunately, the talk that happens is, to a large extent, limited to teacher-initiated questioning as a method of checking for general comprehension. In many classrooms that I have visited, I have noticed that teachers call on children to answer questions designed to show or practice their knowledge. It is rare that students are asked to provide information that the teacher does not know. I have also found that the more a teacher becomes an authentic co-learner in the classroom, the more likely it is that students will begin answering and asking more questions intended to increase what is already known.

Oral language in the classroom is a fundamental instructional tool that strongly enhances teaching and learning because it can be an avenue of expression for students who find difficulty communicating in writing, whether that difficulty is derived from the need to express themselves in a different language from the one they think in and speak or because of other learning issues. Getting kids talking isn't as simple as it seems. In fact it was necessary while designing some of the components of PRC2 to devise a list of conversation prompts for students to use during the beginning stages of the process. These prompts help them know how to keep each other engaged in discourse.

Many inner-city students need to learn how to talk to each other in positive ways that support each other's learning. Students frequently need to be taught that conversation follows a predictable set of rules:

1. Opening up an idea or a theme for discussion
2. Understanding turn taking
3. Recognizing a mutually agreed upon closure

Though these steps seem simple, many of our students benefit from having these speech patterns taught explicitly. One reason for this may be that in the typical classroom the goal is to keep students quiet so that everyone can concentrate on completing the requisite number of workbook pages. Let's face it—seasoned teachers have worked diligently to perfect special ways of glaring at students to quell any infraction of the "no talking" rule, long before students even reach generalized murmuring. If anyone should ask the teacher why no talking is allowed, the response may be one of the following concerns:

- How will I know whether my students are on task if I allow them to talk?
- If I let them start talking, I won't be able to get them to stop.
- Why do they need to talk to each other about their workbook pages?
- How can I record their talk in my grade book?
- How will talking help them learn?

These are all valid concerns and they require some reflection. To create an instructional delivery system to address these issues, it would be beneficial to consider how teachers might be able to develop a more trusting relationship with their students and begin to release some of the responsibility for learning into the hands of the children. One way to do this is to teach them to monitor their own and each other's progress. At the same time, teachers can provide support in that endeavor in the form of PRC2. As students engage in this instructional method, they have the chance to write questions they would like to ask each other, keep a record of interesting vocabulary words, and make notes of the ideas they found most interesting or important in the reading. This, in turn, supports the students as they develop their own ideas and knowledge base of the content associated with the subject matter of any given unit. Discussion around books offers students a way to connect their own lives, cultures, and

268

Chapter
Thirteen
Academic Talk:
Supporting
English Learners

interests to the text they are reading. Iser (1989) tells us, "As readers shuttle back and forth between the text world, and personal experiences and knowledge, the worlds of Literature and the real world become inseparably linked together, and thus inscribe themselves into one another."

Partner Reading and Content, Too, lends itself well to meaningful conversations in the classroom. When a unit is first being introduced to the class, discussion takes the form of sharing background information. This is often best done using a graphic organizer such as a K-W-L chart (Ogle, 1986). Next comes previewing the text. Now students are engaging in exploration and making predictions. Partners have to negotiate with each other to decide how the text will be read, who will read which page, and whether text in captions and text boxes will be read first or saved until after the page text has been read. During the oral-reading stage, students express ideas, clarify meaning, form questions, and create joint construction of concepts. Finally, there is still more verbal expression and sharing of ideas when the whole class debriefs as a group, sharing the most important or interesting information they read that day. The students are really engaged in their own learning.

## Stepping into the Shoes of My Students

For ELs and struggling readers, the oral-language aspect of learning is particularly important. I have experienced this myself firsthand and know how frustrating it can be to try to send or receive a message when basic vocabulary is lacking. I am a monolingual English speaker who recently spent a week in Costa Rica, where the primary language spoken is Spanish. I did my best to get by using the little bit of Spanish I know in order to take care of my most basic needs, such as asking for directions to lodging, finding a grocery store, ordering food in a restaurant, and asking the price of things. Difficult as it was to ask questions, understanding the response added to the challenge. At times, I was plagued by feelings of insecurity regarding my pronunciation, perceived accent, and use of correct grammar. At other times, I would find myself saying a phrase with great pride, knowing that I was beginning to say it more fluently, only to realize I was using it at the wrong time. Well, to use an old saying: Pride comes before a fall.

Navigating that beautiful, but completely unfamiliar, place caused me to reflect, yet again, on the very special needs of our ELs. For one thing, I noticed that I began relying heavily on illustrations and other graphics as visual clues. I found that the few words I recognized were like anchors on which I tried to attach unfamiliar sounds in order to construct meaning. It occurred to me how lucky I am that I already know how to decode words and that doing so could help me attach meaning to sounds and illustrations. This is partly because when decoding the words in Spanish, I was able to take as much time as I needed to sound out the words and check whether the words fit any familiar formats I already had stored. In PRC2, students are able to spend time looking at books that support their language needs, whether the students are ELs or simply lacking in vocabulary.

I think in English, which means that I have to consciously think of every word that goes into any sentence I try to utter in Spanish. Whatever I try to say sounds stilted and is likely to be incorrect, but there is a reasonable chance that the receiver will understand the point I am trying to make. There is no automaticity because I am a novice in Spanish. As a result, I found speaking Spanish harder for me than trying to understand either spoken or written Spanish. Therefore, I felt an odd apprehension about trying to use it. I am not sure why, but I believe it stemmed from a fear of saying something wrong and either accidentally insulting someone or getting laughed at. Fortunately for me, the Costa Rican people were wonderfully friendly and supportive of my efforts. This is not always the case for students in our classrooms. There can be many forces working against the sense of security needed to take risks. Sometimes teachers are not supportive of a student's need to express himself or herself in the native language, and sometimes students are simply afraid of receiving disparaging reactions from their peers. It takes a lot of courage to attempt to make yourself understood when you are not sure if you know the right words or how to pronounce them.

One of the great benefits of PRC2 is the fact that every effort is made to ensure that students have multiple opportunities to express their ideas in their first language as well as in English. This has been accomplished by making sure there are some titles in Spanish among the leveled texts, including some books that are the Spanish edition of texts in English. This allows students to sit together and enjoy sharing the same text in each other's native language by breaking down the communication barriers that are sometimes in evidence. We use language to help us make sense of our world and our place in it. Delpit (2002, p. 47) says, "Since language is one of the most intimate expressions of identity, indeed 'the skin we speak,' then to reject a person's language can only feel as if we are rejecting him."

One object that exists in most of our students' homes is the television set. I noticed how powerful television watching can be as a language learning tool

270

Chapter
Thirteen
Academic Talk:
Supporting
English Learners

because of its heavily oral nature and the fact that it is so repetitive. Normally, I would not consider that to be a plus, but for ELs repetition gives a person the chance to hear a phrase multiple times, and bit by bit the brain is able to decipher more and more of the connected words and eventually even the syllables. Add to that subtitles and you have the double benefit of seeing the written words and hearing the sounds at the same time. According to Blachowicz and Fisher (2000), ELs may need additional opportunities for explicit vocabulary instruction, including immediate repetition, spaced repetition, contextual associations, and talking with others to build word awareness. As a learner myself, I found repetition and multiple exposures to vocabulary important in my ability to retain words I was attempting to acquire.

After a short time in Costa Rica, I found myself mentally playing with interesting linguistic sounds that I had heard enough times for me to be able to isolate them and then reassemble them into some form of context. I have seen and heard ELs do this in the classroom, but I previously did not understand why they were doing it. Now I can see that it is a mechanism they use to help acquire language skills at their own pace.

One example that comes to mind when I think of my students using interesting linguistic sounds happened one day when our *Weekly Reader* magazine was delivered. On the front cover was a picture of King Tutankhamen's mask and the words "King of Bling." By this time, my students had been reading about Egypt for nearly a month and felt a certain confidence in their developing knowledge. Because the title of the magazine article on King Tutankhamen's wealth was written in adolescent slang, the students were even more keen to read it. However, there was another part to this story. I brought a copy of the magazine to share with my colleagues in Project ALL. *Bling* was not a term they were familiar with, and so it turned out that some university professors, doctoral students, and others learned some vocabulary words that our students were already familiar with. In this way, the oral-language aspect of learning has again shown itself to be instrumental in the transference of information, the evolution of the English language, and the reinforcement of the idea that true learning must be a two-way street. America is sometimes referred to as a "melting pot"; at other times, it is described as a "tossed salad." Regardless of its epithet, we know that a large number of dialects are alive and well in every language. It is therefore important to remember that the bilingual students in your classroom are likely to speak different dialects, depending on their linguistic heritage. My students enjoyed keeping a written log of occasions when they discovered that they had different words for things. This only adds to their language enrichment.

By combining the use of video pieces with the PRC2 process, the students have the extra benefit of hearing the oral commentary and the opportunity to discuss how the video and audio media fit with the information they are reading in their chosen text. Another way this can work is to allow the students to audiotape themselves and then listen to that conversation or to share it with other sets of partners.

When our students are reading to each other, listening to each other, and discussing ideas, they have the luxury of time and space to engage in the type of repetition needed to help them develop these language and reading skills. I have heard students read and reread certain sections of text in order to make sure they are able to read it aloud fluently. The fluency comes from determining the sense that the words are intended to convey. Without grasping that meaning, the reading sounds choppy and disconnected. Sometimes students have difficulty knowing exactly why they are unable to comprehend the meaning of the text, but because they have a partner when engaging in PRC2, they are able to ask each other for help and to guide each other toward a deeper sense of the message embedded in the text. Over time, students develop confidence and begin to take more risks with reading, questioning, and expressing themselves. Nevertheless, reading dyads are also a form of self-check; students learn how to ask someone else for clarification when comprehension eludes them. If both students are having trouble with a word or concept, they know it is time to get another opinion. The oral-language aspect of PRC2 encourages students to ask other sets of partners for help in determining meaning of text. Though there is no hard-and-fast rule for knowing when it is time to ask the teacher for help, the students seem to wait until three or four dyads have been included in the conversation without satisfactory resolution of the problem as an indicator of when to seek further help. Thus oral language creates a freer flow of ideas, more confidence in personal knowledge base, and a self-created "norming" of knowing when to get an adult's perspective. This happens as students are driven to find things out for themselves while simultaneously maintaining a willingness to speak up when they need help.

Through observation of several groups of students, I have noticed that children working individually are less likely than children working in pairs to ask the teacher for help when it is needed. Instead, they keep their heads down, hoping not to be noticed or, worse, called upon for an answer. Or, they may become some of your disruptive students, covering confusion with hostility or satire. Either way, the energy required to maintain high states of internal stress can be redirected if students find something to feel motivated about.

272

Chapter
Thirteen
Academic Talk:
Supporting
English Learners

The students I have worked with in this process have surprised all of us in ways that could not be foreseen. For example, one day some very important guests visited my school to see how PRC2 works in real life with real kids. In talking to the classroom teachers of the rooms that were going to be visited ahead of time, I found out what each of their deepest concerns were. One teacher (Ms. L) was worried that some of her guests might misunderstand her students with special needs if they were unable to fully maintain their social skills. The day of the visit we decided to just let things be as normal as possible and trust our visitors to understand that behavior issues go with the territory sometimes. The two teachers began PRC2 time and the visitors moved freely throughout the classroom, being greeted by the students, listening to them, and participating in their conversations. The visitors sat down with different groups of students and asked them about what they were doing and what they were learning from the books they were sharing. The students were happy and proud to have people visiting them because they were proficient at something. As I was walking back to my classroom with the guests, our conversation revolved around certain pairs of students who had really stood out to us. One of the visitors was truly taken aback to find out that he had been chatting with two of the lower performing students, as determined by standardized tests. One of the students in particular suffers so strongly from an emotional disorder that he normally has to sit in a space more or less to himself. Although his teacher keeps him well surrounded by classmates, his desk is situated so that he doesn't actually sit next to anyone, except when he is specifically working in a small group or during PRC2. Our visitor was so impressed by the eloquence of this young man and his partner (who were reading a vibrant graphic novel about Geronimo) that he thought the students had been "planted" in order for the guests to notice them. He was genuinely surprised but happy to realize what a difference partner reading is making in the lives of our students.

The sense of relief that the partners feel can be seen on their faces and heard in their voices when they begin to recognize their own ability to use what they have learned as a way to navigate less familiar settings and texts. It is fascinating to watch a pair of students who are deeply engrossed in the PRC2 process attempting to communicate their understandings based on their pre-existing schema and the incorporation of new information gleaned from a recent reading. It becomes much more than simply reading a book together. It is almost as if the students are building something precious together. The sense of purpose that exists between student pairs increases their willingness to use multiple forms of language to make certain the message they are trying to express has been received. At times they show great animation as they increase the use of body language to help convey the oral message.

When ELs feel a strong enough urge to share their learning in a supportive environment, it is interesting to listen to the ways students gradually arrive at an understanding with each other. At first, the words used may be very general. For example, when some classmates were informally attempting to discuss the building of the pyramids, I noticed that they were using terms such as *triangle building* and *dead place*. Later the same students were able to share ideas about that same concept using the words *pyramid* and *tomb*. Gradually the students were using more of the unit vocabulary in their discussions with each other.

There appears to be a strong correlation between the effort to communicate verbally and the acquisition of language skills. This in turn increases the ability to construct meaning and deepen comprehension. It is basically a developmental cycle of learning based on the use of oral language. See Figure 13.1 for a visual diagram of the relationships. The connection between language acquisition and new knowledge can be scaffolded for students by the teaching of cognates and by focusing on the morphology of words while working on word study (see Chapter 11). One interesting thing about cognates is that they not only provide a method for students to create meaning but also sometimes guide ELs to use second-tier words in conversation and therefore have the potential to enrich the

Figure **13.1** **The Language/
Communication Cycle**

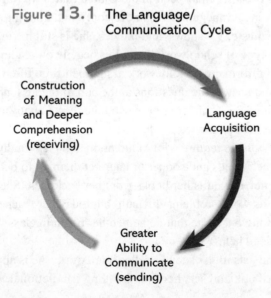

274

Chapter
Thirteen
Academic Talk:
Supporting
English Learners

vocabulary of native English speakers in the classroom. Two students I listened to had the following interaction as they read a poem together:

*Luis:* What do you think *amiable* means?

*Marcus:* I think it means that they're friendly.

*Luis:* How come you think that?

*Marcus:* Because in Spanish *amigable* means "friendly."

*Luis:* That's not the same, but they do look kind of the same.

*Marcus:* Well in Spanish, *amiable* means sort of like "nice."

*Luis:* Okay, if you try to fit it in the sentence when you read it, it makes sense, so I believe you.

Clearly not all ELs have the same academic background nor do they have the same language abilities or needs, which is why PRC2 can be such a useful supplemental learning tool in any classroom. It is sound instructional practice, as it addresses differences in reading-readiness levels, learning styles, life experience, interests, and cultural backgrounds in all students. It provides a simple avenue for true differentiation.

The PRC2 process works quite differently from the traditional method of transmitting content area knowledge and can mean the difference between success and failure to a struggling student. Take, for example, a young lady I will call Yessenia. Yessenia is a bright student, but she is struggling with her social studies class. She has been in the United States for only ten months, and, although she has begun to feel more confident talking to her friends about games, music, TV shows, and movies, she is still having a very difficult time with the type of schoolwork that relies heavily on reading a textbook in order to learn information. Homework assignments too often consist of "Read these pages and answer the questions at the end of the lesson."

After school, Yessenia goes home and then has to babysit her younger siblings while her parents work. She often has to cook dinner and clean up. The younger siblings require a lot of attention and play loudly. It is her job to take care of their needs and sooner or later get them all to bed. Eventually, when all is quiet, she pulls her books from her backpack. She begins with math. She finds word problems difficult, but today her teacher has asked her to finish working out some that he helped her begin in class. Yessenia is grateful for this added help.

When she gets to her social studies homework, she is apprehensive. She opens the textbook and sets her Spanish–English dictionary beside her on the kitchen table. The words in the textbook make almost no sense, and the dictionary provides little or no support. The concepts associated with ancient Egypt are complex and difficult to grasp. This is especially true for someone who has no prior knowledge of the subject. Looking at the pictures, Yessenia notices that the pyramids look a little like some of the ancient ruins she remembers near her home in Mexico. This makes her feel sad and homesick. The illustrations are interesting to her, but the homework assignment is beyond her language abilities. Now she must make a very difficult decision: Her teacher has told her that getting her homework done is of great importance. Failure to do so will result in a detention for her. She cannot afford a detention as her parents count on her being home from school as quickly as possible each day because of the hours they work. Yessenia's teacher said she must call a classmate for homework help when she is unable to complete assignments. Unfortunately, there is no phone in her house. She wants to be a good student and comply with her teacher's directions, but she cannot and she is too proud to let her classmates know about the difficulties she faces in her life. This student is badly in need of a different way to learn. The textbook and dictionary she is using are not providing her with information she can use. The input is not comprehensible for her in this format.

The next day Yessenia is in trouble with her monolingual (English only) social studies teacher, Ms. B. Ms. B does not fully understand her student's living situation. The enrollment papers were short on details and her previous school records were unavailable when the family registered their children in the fall. Ms. B. had sent home a request for emergency information, but when the paper was returned it had no phone number on it. Ms. B. is frustrated by her inability to communicate with the family and makes a note of some topics she will want to discuss when parent-teacher conferences come around.

The day of report card pick-up Yessenia's father is working and unable to attend the parent-teacher conference. This is unfortunate because, of her two parents, it is her father who speaks more English. Her mother goes to the school to talk to the teachers. Yessenia's homeroom teacher is bilingual and is able to talk about Yessenia's progress in math and language arts. The academic talk that occurs between this mother and the teacher, Ms. A, informs her that Yessenia shows promise because she is intelligent, but there is great concern that she will perform poorly on the high-stakes testing later in the school year because she is coming from what is perceived to be an educational deficit. Yessenia's mother feels a mixture of sorrow, confusion, and embarrassment. These feelings are far stronger after she meets with the teachers who provide

276

Chapter
Thirteen
Academic Talk:
Supporting
English Learners

Yessenia with instruction in social studies and science. Because of the departmental program, Yessenia spends part of each day with teachers who do not speak Spanish. Through the aid of an interpreter, the social studies teacher explains that Yessenia has been doing very poorly and might fail the class if she does not complete more of her assignments.

The science teacher told a different story in her classroom. The sixth-grade science curriculum is much more hands-on than the social studies class. Students work in collaborative, small groups to experiment, record data, analyze results, summarize, and reflect on personal learning. The most important part of all this is that most of the members in Yessenia's small group are bilingual. This gives Yessenia the opportunity to think and speak in her own language in order to discuss the concepts related to the science lesson, while still hearing and sharing those same ideas expressed in English by the teacher and with other non-Spanish-speaking classmates. There is a great deal of discussion before, during, and after experiments. Students are encouraged to help each other ask and answer questions about the text they read. Discourse also occurs while students collect, analyze, and report results on data.

Yessenia's entries in her science journal take a variety of formats; they include numeric data, notes in Spanish (to help her remember directions), diagrams, labels, unfamiliar vocabulary words, and reflections on her learning, which her teacher has asked her to try to write in English. These reflections have increased significantly over the first quarter of the school year. In September, Yessenia was only able to write two or three simple sentences in English. By the tenth week, she is writing one or two paragraphs. The opportunity to discuss ideas before writing and the hands-on nature of the class make the learning situation friendlier toward Yessenia's needs. The academic input is more comprehensible. Yessenia's mother has received conflicting information regarding her daughter's abilities, so she returns to the homeroom teacher and shares her concerns. Ms. A. listens and understands the difficulties that Yessenia is facing. Ms. A. promises to raise the issues and concerns to the sixth-grade team at the next grade-level meeting.

# Extending Thinking and Learning

Scenarios such as this play out regularly in our schools and can be ameliorated to a great extent through the use of the PRC2 process, which fits equally well with science and social studies, and it includes oral-language support for vocabulary, fluency, prosody, comprehension, questioning, negotiation, and so on. By comparing the student-centered, instructional delivery method used by the science teacher with the methods used by the social studies teacher, it can be seen that the importance of oral language in the classroom cannot be overstated. The oral support and accessible text that go with each PRC2 unit scaffold students toward attainment of new knowledge and skills.

As a teacher who has implemented PRC2 in my classroom, I can tell you that it is a dynamic teaching method. It allows students to make learning their own. Evidence of this has occurred in multiple forms. For example, the first time I introduced the Ancient Egypt unit, I thought it would be beneficial to our bilingual students to provide as much visual information as I could. I hung posters of Egypt around the classroom: the people, the land, the pyramids—anything I could find. I also made a display of all the books we had on the subject. One early morning I walked into the classroom and noticed that the number of books on display seemed to be increasing. Upon further investigation, I realized that the students had been visiting the local library and bringing books to share with their friends. Students were devouring everything they could find about ancient Egypt so that they could talk to one another about the amazing things they had learned. Even more interesting was to find out that the students were extending the learning environment into their homes. Parents were stopping me in hallways, chatting after meetings, bringing books with them to parent-teacher conferences—talking to me and to one another about different books about Egypt that were being shared with the families at home. Further development of this showed itself in the form of the Conversation Board. A student had saved a trifold board from the previous year's science fair. He put a new backing on it and some pictures about Egypt he had found in a magazine. My students and I added items of interest as the unit progressed, and the board was used frequently as a conversation starter when guests visited our classroom and between the students themselves. The students could not resist going to see if there was anything new since the last time they had looked. The unit seemed to be taking on a life of its own, which was perfect because that was evidence, from my perspective, that the students were grasping the responsibility for their own learning even faster than I could release it to them.

The leveled texts and the learning unit created a solid base on which I could attach complicated learning concepts. It allowed me to model the use of academic terms and key vocabulary I thought the students needed to be familiar with to develop ideas around general domains, such as government, culture, and daily life. But the hunger with which the students attacked the subject inspired me to go to further lengths to feed their interest.

As a Chicago teacher, I am lucky in the fact that we have excellent resources available to help extend student learning outside the classroom. One

278

Chapter
Thirteen
Academic Talk:
Supporting
English Learners

way this has happened is by incorporating class trips to the Chicago Field Museum and to the Oriental Institute of Chicago, both of which have fascinating collections of Egyptian artifacts. During such trips, students are able to see original artifacts for themselves. It is wonderful to hear the excitement in the children's voices as they almost tumble over one another, trying to get to the exhibits' mummies, urns, models, statues, and, of course, hieroglyphics. Visits such as these add to the authenticity and depth of conversation that later occur as students continue sharing their supplemental PRC2 texts. It is not possible for all teachers to take their students on field trips. However, if they are Chicago teachers, they can still share authentic artifacts with their students through the use of "discovery boxes" that teachers may borrow from many of Chicago's museums. Use of these boxes greatly increases the social aspect of learning and provides students with a more hands-on opportunity to explore core knowledge in both social studies and science.

This year, working as a literacy coach, I have seen oral language develop in more than one classroom. I have had the pleasure of supporting two fifth-grade teachers as they implemented PRC2 units in their classrooms. One classroom was bilingual, the other monolingual. The first of the units was Social Studies and focused on Native Americans; the second unit was Science and focused on simple machines. It was interesting for me to see that these students responded in a similar way to the PRC2 process as the sixth-grade students I had introduced it to the year before.

As the unit on Native Americans was introduced, the students immediately began verbally sharing background knowledge they had learned together the year before. Many of these students have been together since at least third grade. The initial conversations were extremely interesting to me as an observer because I was able to watch students share their enthusiasm for learning together. Learning about Native American life was apparently something they had really enjoyed, and the sense of excitement in the room was palpable. I asked the students why they enjoyed this subject so much and was told that it was because their previous teacher had "made it cool." Probing further, I found out that the fourth-grade teacher had encouraged the students to work together in groups to come up with questions they wanted answered about how the native people lived, about the many different nations, and about where the native people had lived. Because the students had worked together, they knew what their classmates should already be aware of and who the "experts" were on different topics. As the students discussed this prior knowledge they deliberately helped one another try to remember facts and events. Naturally, this information was collected on a K-W-L chart for future reference with a large space left open for a column in which information would be added that either supported or negated this collective background knowledge.

Encouraging students to work and talk together as they are learning has an important effect on the physical structure of the brain. Neuroscience is beginning to provide evidence for many principles of learning that have emerged from laboratory research. It has shown how learning changes the physical structure of the brain and the functional organization of the brain. Greenough (1976; Greenough, Juraska, & Volkmar, 1979) conducted an interesting study using rats and found that the combination of learning and socializing adds synapses to the brain. Physical evidence shows that learning experiences alter brain structure. The brains of animals raised in complex environments have more blood vessels per nerve cell and become denser than those of animals raised in regular lab cages. The significance of this is that the more active any type of cell is, the more fuel it needs. The rats' brains were shown to increase in density if they were kept in a stimulating environment *and* were allowed to socialize with others. They also performed better on problem-solving tests. Interestingly, their brains did not show any physiological change in brain density if they were kept in a stimulating environment but alone or if they were kept in a social setting but were not allowed to explore or learn. This brain research, in addition to supporting theories of social learning such as Vygotsky's statement that "human learning presupposes a specific social nature and a process by which children grow into the intellectual life of those around them" (Vygotsky, 1978, p. 88), sheds light on the importance of the implementation of PRC2 at my school.

Another piece of research that has a bearing on the activities engaged in during PRC2 is the landmark publication *Becoming a Nation of Readers* (Anderson, Hiebert, Scott, & Wilkinson, 1985). This report makes a very strong statement in support of reading aloud: "The single most important activity for building the knowledge required for eventual success in reading, is reading aloud to children" (p. 23). The report states that reading aloud is essential not only in the home with young children but also at school with older readers (p. 51). I find this important because there are times during social studies and science classes when it is necessary for the teacher to read information aloud to students. One thing that makes PRC2 so powerful is that the students themselves take turns reading information aloud to one another. It is time we begin contemplating ways we can encourage our students' brains to develop synapses that associate pleasure with reading and sharing opinions and ideas.

280

Chapter
Thirteen
Academic Talk:
Supporting
English Learners

In the following brief conversation, two eighth graders discuss their opinions of verbally sharing ideas with each other:

**Question:** Does talking about what you are learning help you?

**Karla:** Sharing ideas is a way of getting better understanding. You think of something, and once you start talking, you get a better understanding of what your thoughts are.

**James:** It gives you more confidence in your reaction to people. Hearing yourself speak is a good thing. Sometimes you hear the confidence in your own voice.

**Question:** How does hearing other people's ideas help you?

**Karla:** Hearing other people's ideas that are similar to your own can help you open up and see where the ideas will take you.

This conversation, though short, is evidence that elementary/middle school students are capable of metacognitive processes. These students are aware that it is through the exchange of ideas that they can grow and develop further themselves. Teachers can learn a great deal from listening to their students as they work together to create meaning from print with which they are interacting and from observing the ways students are able to connect that meaning to real-life situations or to other media they have seen, heard, or read.

One of the best ways for teachers to monitor these types of student discussions is through the use of the PRC2 observation notes form (see Appendix 3.1). Although teachers are listening to their students read and discuss books, they are able to write down a great deal about the students' methods of communication. Keep in mind that there is so much more to sending and receiving messages than simple verbal expression. Facial expressions, body language, tone of voice, rising and falling pitch, hand gestures, and eye contact can all add volumes to what a person "says." This is important for any pair of students attempting to discuss a passage they have read but even more so for students who are in the process of developing vocabulary. If native English speakers are struggling with vocabulary, it may be evidence that they do not have the necessary background knowledge to help them comprehend the words they are trying to use as building blocks to create their underlying schema of concepts. Lack of vocabulary acquisition often leads to knowledge gaps in the mesh of the concept web the students attempt to create as they read. The PRC2 process provides students multiple opportunities to engage in word work. This takes many forms, and virtually all of them require some sort of verbal activity. One example of this is the incorporation of games such as Jeopardy (see Chapters 9 and 12) in the process.

Teachers can learn a lot about their students if they take the time to engage in this important PRC2 step. It can inform them about specific difficulties or strengths students may have. Observations of student behaviors, while reading, can provide insight into student interests, self-concepts, motivation, and whether the book they are reading is a good match for the student pair. It is the opportunity for the teacher to hear how the students think things through, to see students holistically, and to develop a much closer bond between teacher and students. This takes some of the guesswork out of teaching as it is firsthand data collection, which may be used for comparison later with other types of assessments, both formative and summative. During the process of observing students read to each other, teachers are also on hand to step in when a teachable moment arises. Sometimes it becomes apparent through listening to partners read that students may be mispronouncing words, especially if they are unfamiliar words. As students work through their language development, there may be times when hearing correct pronunciation can help students understand a word they have seen written and developed a "mental sound" for that is not actually the generally accepted way of saying the word. By hearing students' pronunciations while reading, the teacher can offer immediate feedback and support.

Through regular observation and note-taking, teachers can learn a lot about the academic and social needs of their students. It allows them to notice trends regarding individuals, pairs, and the class as a group. This knowledge can be key to unlocking the question "What strategies can I use to provide the most effective scaffolding for my students?" Is it to help them link new learning to prior knowledge, master new vocabulary, or perhaps make sense of unfamiliar text styles?

Though there has been progress in recent years to make textbooks more representative of a wider view of American ethnicity, biases are still evident. By encouraging students not only to read the textbook but also to read and discuss the supplemental leveled texts in the PRC2 unit, students are given the opportunity to link prior knowledge, life experiences, classmates' comments, family folklore, and text. The use of questioning as part of that dialogue can be a significant support mechanism in the connecting process. To some extent, students need to be guided in their ability to ask questions. This is something that can be modeled not only by the teacher but also by proficient partners.

282

Chapter
Thirteen
Academic Talk:
Supporting
English Learners

Questioning is not limited only to asking each other about items of interest in the text, but it involves also questioning the author. By offering students access to supplemental leveled texts, the opportunity to encounter different perspectives arises. Teachers who model this strategy for their students are empowering them to think more deeply about what is written and why it is written. Monitoring and scaffolding these thought processes are another example of why it is important for teachers to be vigilant in their use of observation time in PRC2. While concentrating on student conversations, teachers have a window into each student's own reality. For example, a student from England who has only been taught British history will very likely have a different view of the Revolutionary War than a student who was born and raised in the United States. In the same way, students who have lived in different parts of the United States may bring different knowledge about geography, lifestyles, folkways, art, music, Native American culture, and so on than young people who have lived all their lives in the same neighborhood may. Sharing opinions and worldviews strengthens students' abilities to recognize their own knowledge and opinions and to open their minds to accept more information thus growing cognitively.

As a literacy coach, I am aware that teachers wrestle with issues of assessing students. I have been asked by teachers how formative assessment such as reading-behavior observations and anecdotal records of oral-language use by students can translate into something that can go into a grade book. My response is that the pre-tests and post-tests; Classroom Fluency Snapshots; interest inventories; and student maintenance of a journal containing vocabulary, questions, and reflections on the books they have read, along with the teacher's anecdotal records, are all supporting information, enabling a teacher to focus on areas of weakness or concern. This is the type of data most useful when planning lessons.

## Reality Check from Teaching in the Real World

One unforeseen way in which PRC2 has helped strengthen our literacy program occurred in our seventh- and eighth-grade departmental program. Every day the seventh- and eighth-grade students rotate between teachers. Because of the number of teachers available, there was a small discrepancy in time distribution and scheduling: each of the four core subjects is taught to these students in equal blocks of time. This seems logical, but it does not comply with the

State of Illinois guidelines regarding how many minutes each subject should be taught each day. The students were receiving too little language arts time and extra minutes in science, social studies, and math. This has been a cause of stress for the language arts teacher, who has been working hard to ensure her students get her undivided attention while they are in her room. The unforeseen advantage of PRC2 is that by conducting partner reading during social studies class and science class, as part of the instructional time, the amount of time spent reading the leveled texts increased the number of minutes our students were developing reading skills and complying with state guidelines (see Chapter 8 on guided reading). Clearly PRC2 is a process that fits with our regular curriculum like a hand in a glove.

## References

Anderson, R. C., Hiebert, E. H., Scott, J. A., & Wilkinson, I. A. G. (1985). *Becoming a nation of readers: The report of the commission on reading.* Washington, DC: National Institute of Education.

Blachowicz, C., & Fisher, P. (2000). Vocabulary instruction. In M. L. Kamil, P. B. Mosenthal, P. D. Pearson, & R. Barr (Eds.), *Handbook of reading research.* (Vol. 3, pp. 503–525). Mahwah, NJ: Erlbaum.

Carroll, L. (1865). *Alice's adventures in Wonderland.* London: McMillan.

Daniels, H. (1994). Literature circles: Voice and choice in the student-centered classroom. York, ME: Stenhouse.

Delpit, L. (2002). No Kinda Sense. In L. Delpit & J. K. Dowly (Eds.), *The skin that we speak: Thoughts on language and culture in the classroom.* New York: New Press.

Fletcher, R. (2006). Boy writers: Reclaiming their voices. Portland, ME: Stenhouse.

Fountas, I. C., & Pinnell, G. S. (1996). Guided reading: Good first teaching for all children. Portsmouth, NH: Heinemann.

Greenough, W. T. (1976). Enduring brain effects of differential experience and training. In M. R. Rosenzweig & E. L. Bennett (Eds.), *Neural mechanisms of learning and memory* (pp. 255–278). Cambridge, MA: MIT Press.

Greenough, W. T., Juraska, J. M., & Volkmar, F. R. (1979). Maze training effects on dendritic branching in occipital cortex of adult rats. *Behavioral and Neural Biology, 26,* 287–297.

Hasbrouck, J., & Tindal, G. A. (2006). Oral reading fluency norms: A valuable assessment tool for reading teachers. *The Reading Teacher, 59*(7), 636–644.

284

Chapter
Thirteen
Academic Talk:
Supporting
English Learners

Iser, W. (1989). *Prospecting: From reader response to literary anthropology.* Baltimore, MD: Johns Hopkins University Press.

Ogle, D. (1986). K-W-L; A teaching model that develops active reading of expository text. *The Reading Teacher, 40,* 564–570.

Vygotsky, L. (1978). Mind in society: The development of higher psychological processes. Cambridge, MA: Harvard University Press.

# Index